CW01338755

WALLY CASSIDY
The Other Half Lives

PHOTOGRAPHS 1989–1993

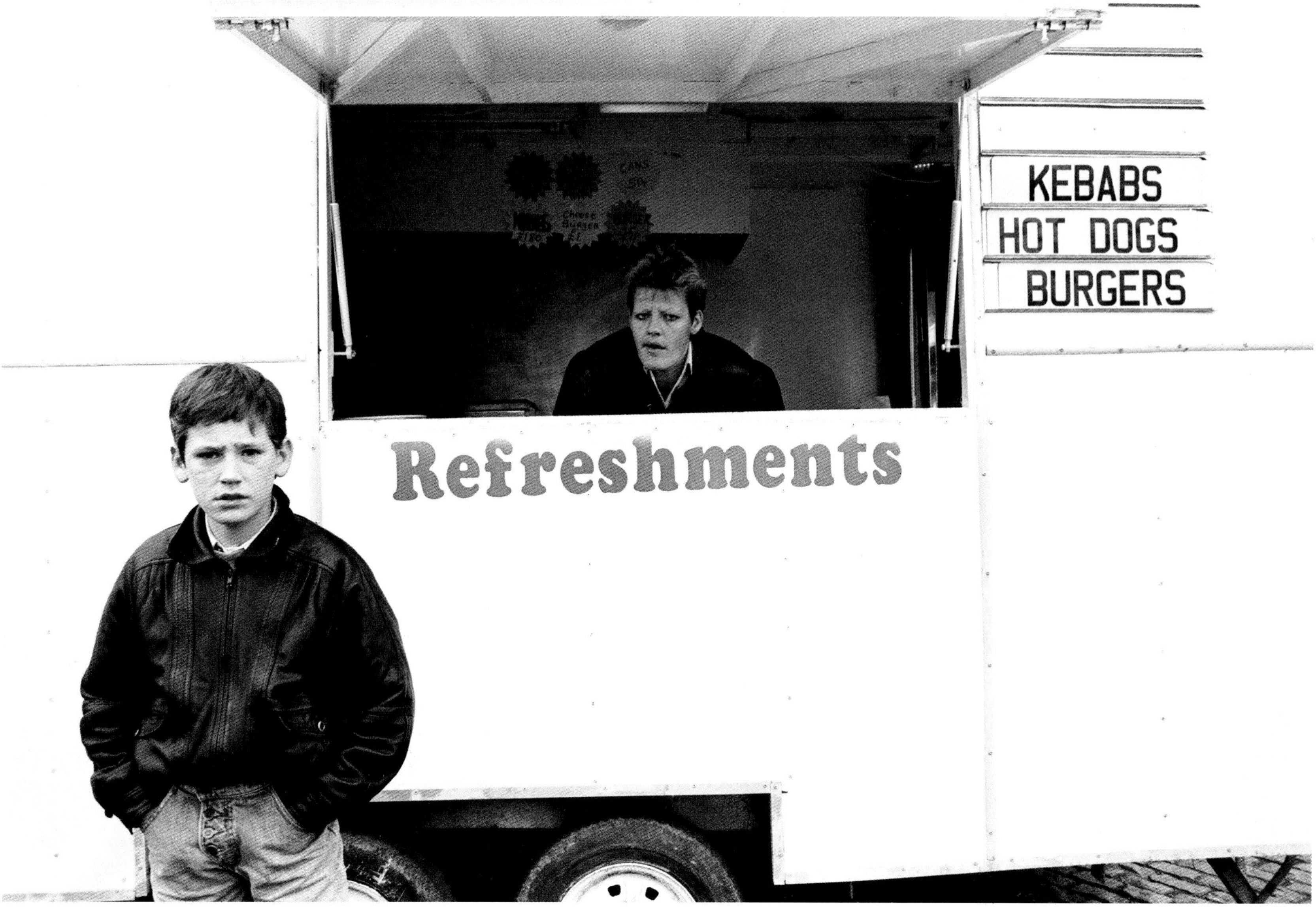
KEBABS
HOT DOGS
BURGERS
Refreshments

WALLY CASSIDY *The Other Half Lives*

PHOTOGRAPHS 1989–1993 | *Foreword by* TONY MURRAY | *Introduction by* GAVIN CORBETT

First published 2014 by

HI TONE BOOKS

Dublin 7, Ireland

Photographs copyright © 2014 Walter Cassidy

Introduction text copyright © 2014 Gavin Corbett

Foreword text copyright © 2014 Tony Murray

ISBN: 978-0-9569493-2-5

All rights reserved. No part of this publication may be reproduced
in any form or by any means without the prior permission of the publisher.
A CIP record is available from the British Library.

3 5 7 9 10 8 6 4 2 1

DESIGN: Niall McCormack
TYPEFACES: Futura, Trade Gothic, Filmotype Giant, Bauer Bodoni

Printed and bound in China by 1010 Printing

CONTENTS

FOREWORD *by Tony Murray* — 7

INTRODUCTION *by Gavin Corbett* — 8

STREET — 12

PROTEST — 52

SMITHFIELD — 82

PUNKS — 104

Notes on Photographs — 142

ACKNOWLEDGEMENTS

For my daughter Mia

I would like to thank the following people for their help in making this book possible. To my dad for instilling the idea of recording history, Podge O'Farrell for the introduction to street photography, John Kelly for walking the streets together, Tony O'Shea for *Dubliners*, Garry O'Neill for putting an ad in a record shop, Niall McCormack for creating this book, Gavin Corbett for writing the introduction and Tony Murray for the foreword, Orla Fitzpatrick for proof-reading, Laura James for help with negatives, Deko and P.A. of Paranoid Visions for access to gigs, my brother Stephen for the website and David Monahan for the test prints. Thanks also to *Rabble* and Come Here To Me; to all the punks and skins who let me kip on their sofas and floors and Facebook friends for likes and comments.

Wally Cassidy

wallycassidy.com

FOREWORD

THIS IS NOT JUST ANOTHER PHOTOGRAPHIC BOOK ON IRELAND.

It is much more than that. Cassidy's work is both a mirror and a window on an Ireland that is both historical and contemporary. The images neither romanticise nor sentimentalise the subjects. These are not the photographs of a self-conscious artist who cleverly juxtaposes subjects against backgrounds nor the self-referencing constructed exploration of 'self'. The photographer does not explicitly appear in the work. Yet the 'self' speaks and leaps from the pages of this book. Clearly, Cassidy was both an active participant and visual essayist of the times and events that marked this period of our history.

It is not surprising that much of this work has not been published before, as it illuminates dark corners and uncomfortable vignettes of Irish society. This work does not sell in galleries; appear on walls of corporate Ireland or of the political elite. This is not the Ireland of the stereotypical old man drinking stout in a 'back lit' pub, the doe-eyed freckle faced child or the rural rusting gate that has dominated Irish photographic culture. This is photography 'from' the street not 'of' the street. However, while appearing to be 'grab' shots, there is evidence of careful attention to the classic social documentary photographic concerns and conventions.

These images were taken in a pre-digital age when the craft of photography was cumbersome and required time and commitment. This was an age before 'everyone was a photographer'. Photographers saw themselves as playing an active role as both social commentator and observer. This work is not about the photographer or his ego, but focuses on the intellectual demanding discipline of constructing narratives, which challenged the prevailing and conventional images of the time. Cassidy's photographs remind us of the power of a well-constructed and crafted image and the pivotal role photography plays in defining who we are.

TONY MURRAY

INTRODUCTION

IN THOSE DAYS, THE BUS LEFT YOU AT THE TOP OF GRAFTON STREET.

The frilly skirt of a building on the corner was a new shopping centre. It was always empty. Your teacher had said it would soon shut down. Someone had opened a Batman shop inside because of all the hype over the *Batman* film. That was typical of the whole place – a doomed enterprise. Before the shopping centre there was a gap in the street where punks sold clothes and jewellery. The punks were still about, but now they were spread out along Grafton Street. They'd scare you. They'd be sitting on bins and seemed to laugh at passers by. You'd be looking at the flowers at Chatham Street and they'd startle you with "Dellllightful arrangement!" They'd be propping up the corner at West's, leaning with their full weight on the glass. You were conditioned to be scared of them. Your dad pointed them out in Dun Laoghaire or Blackrock Market and said, "There's some gougers." Some of them seemed to have snotty noses. Your dad said that wasn't snot, that was glue. But the pope approved, he said. He said the pope had said, "Young people of Ireland, I love Uhu."

You meet a friend outside McDonald's. You have to go searching for him in the crowd of two hundred people your own age. There's a titter from the girls as the Dice Man rears up behind a pack of Cureheads and freezes. Everyone agrees that he's gay. You move on with your friend down the bit of Grafton Street that doesn't seem like Grafton Street to College Green. It's busy and exciting here. You feel like you're in the big city. The Bank of Ireland is covered in a layer of soot. So is the front of Trinity, but the carvings of garlands that don't so much get the soot make it look like there's a frosting on it too. Between the dirty great buildings the buses roar around the curve. They really do roar, like those tanks at the Spring Show. They're mainly green although some of them are still the colour of a Fig Roll or that bit around the filter of a cigarette.

You head into the Virgin Megastore. Upstairs you clack through the posters. Your friend steals a poster of Metallica from the middle pages of a book of guitar chords for *And Justice For All*. He tells you that this was the place that a man once rode a horse into. "Rode a horse into?" you say. "Yeah," says your friend. "He was called the Master of the Universe." You leave, slightly skipping at the doorway because of the poster in your friend's bag. On O'Connell Bridge you stop to look at bootleg tapes. They're all packed together in a case like something from Russia. There's Tina Turner, Elvis Costello, and a band called Paranoid Visions.

On O'Connell Street you're fighting for space. The footpaths are so narrow. You keep thinking: "Hillsborough, Hillsborough." Up ahead you can hear banging and shouting. In the centre of O'Connell Street the warty old trees are shedding their leaves. Ahead now you can see the protestors. You look at their placards but the words don't go in because everyone's always protesting about something these days. At the GPO too – it's a bottleneck here, and if you don't keep to the inside of the pillars you get pushed on to the road. Then the crowd suddenly parts. Mad Mary comes through with her big cross and her chunky rosary beads.

All day you've been hearing distant explosions that remind you of one of the pieces of business at hand. You swing left at Henry Street. You don't have to search for long; a man who looks like Steve Nicol asks if you want fireworks. You buy a couple of packs of bangers and a roman candle each. You continue on up Henry Street and into Mary Street where all the ex-army shops are. You've been thinking of buying a Rambo knife for a long time. You look at the display under glass in Army Bargains. Your friend is looking at bomber jackets. You already have one; yours is wine. Your friend tries on a black one with a fur-edged hood, then buys a plain green one. You tell him he's going to look like some kind of Brit hooligan or something. He has long hair, Hi-Tec runners, and he can't make up his mind what he wants to look like.

Outside Army Bargains your friend says he knows a shorter way to Parnell Street. "Ah, here," you say as he leads you up a place called Mary's Abbey. This is right at the edge of the part of town you'd never go into. You stop at a corner and stare across at the spooky fruit markets and think of Jack the Ripper. Up yonder somewhere is Benburb Street where the prostitutes are and North King Street where a man got taken out in a pub. Bleak is the word, you say to yourself.

You double back to Capel Street where all the hardware shops are and you find your way anyhow to Parnell Street. It's not much of a street. It's a road with a lot of car parks on it. At the back of the Ilac Centre the lady makes you sit up on a stool and try on the size 8½ nine-holes for comfort. You'd buy the 21-holes only your dad would have a spasm. Your friend has a pair of ox-bloods at home. You go for black. The lady asks you where you've come from. You tell her you've come all the way up from Stephen's Green. "But sure, you could have bought them round the back of the new shopping centre," she says. "There's still some stalls left." She's missing the point, you think. Then you wouldn't have had your day out in town: the long walk, the buzz, the people who crossed your path, stepped in from the side – all the drama.

WALLY CASSIDY'S DUBLIN IS FULL OF DRAMA.

In these pages, on these streets (they begin to feel like one and the same thing), you'll find heated protests, burning dummies, punks pissing on post-apocalyptic waste grounds, falling horsemen, dogs ready to pounce, and the odd famous face. You can practically hear the clang of metal barriers being rushed and the rattle of knuckles on placards. Even the scenes where not a lot appears to be going on have a charge through them; small moments, seized in the blink of an aperture, given a force and a beauty because of the shapes that they form. As an amateur photographer myself (in both the literal and loose sense of the term), I marvel at Wally's ability to find arresting scenes in the random confluences and partings of everyday life, and at his nerve in getting so close to his subjects. There are many reasons to linger over each and every one of these pictures.

Nostalgia, surely, will be one of those reasons. I delighted in seeing again Roches Stores shopping bags, long and dour overcoats on rank-and-file gardaí, and Smithfield in the days when it was a scrap merchant's back yard. Every photo here comes with a beautifully dated patina of the early 1990s. I felt happy and sad to be reminded of a time when I, like Wally Cassidy, was young (although I was a little too young to be having the fun that Wally seemed to be having). I wanted to get in a time machine and go back. Nostalgia is a trickster, of course; it's a softener and a great editor. But Wally is a great editor too (and what's a street photographer if not an editor?). You're only the next picture away from being reminded that these were pungent and pretty terrible times.

To be alive then meant to live through the last stages of a great era of conscientious agitation, whether you were aware of it or not (and I certainly wasn't). In Ireland, brave outriders lit a trail in the dim post-war decades, but the intransigencies of Irish society meant there was a sudden, late rush: in the early 1990s we were still fighting what seemed, even at the time, like archaic battles over gay and women's rights.

It seems only right – artistically, and in every way – that the photographs here are in black and white. Dublin in the early 1990s really does seem a long time ago, of a piece with the 1950s rather than with the Dublin of now. It was the last time in our recent history when things looked so different. From the mid-1990s we've been running the post-modern treadmill, only most of us with no irony. It's almost as if culture took its cue from Francis Fukuyama's declaration that we were seeing "the end of history", even if history itself remained oblivious.

In Wally's Dublin (and Thurles; mustn't forget there are photos of Thurles at the time of Bacchus – I mean Féile – here too), fashion and music and everything else that makes up the pop-cultural landscape were following a more-or-less straight continuum before it took that nauseating loop-the-loop. Poverty, and analogue technologies, kept things simple too. It's tempting to call it all a time of innocence. We were poor then, as now, but we hadn't just come through a boom that showed us what we could have again. The boom was just ahead, but we didn't know it; you could argue till the cows come home about how that boom changed us, but it's not going out on a limb to say that it certainly changed Dublin.

The architectural historian Niall McCullough has a lovely way to describe the materially damaged Dublin before the construction boom: like a dried-up honeycomb, whose ugly, empty lots at least permitted the imagination to fill them, to wonder what sort of city Dublin physically could become. Dublin, in the absence of much else, was a playground for the imagination. We filled it from within rather than without; with our colour and noise and activity. But if we stopped to think about them at all, we thought of those empty lots as a blight, a consequence of politicians' wilful misunderstanding of how a city should function. Wally's photo of the punk peeing in a brownfield wasteland evokes in one brilliantly economical prospect this Dublin of teetering ruins and DIY diversions. No matter how many times I study that picture I just cannot locate the scene. You could be on the moon, or you could be in the tundra.

This was the charnel city my parents sped me through as a boy, and that I was happy to loiter in as a young teen. I didn't care that it wasn't a beautiful place. I was scared and overwhelmed a lot of the time, but I found the edginess exciting. It was a place where you'd given up hope that anything could be possible, and so you made things possible. You made arrangements by home phone or payphone, and weekends were planned around the information on an inky flyer. You still had the sense that youth cults had emerged from cracks in the ground and not, as today, been created by a consultant. You were a seagull or a pigeon, a flagstone or a coalhole, or you were just happy to bob and weave through it all. The streets heaved with the energy of bedlam; people came at you left and right making you do a double-take or look away. Always there was the sense of manifold movement, of out-of-sight commotion, undercurrents and secret signs. A theme running through the collection here are Wally's beloved punks. They are like a subterranean river, one of a number flowing through the city.

In these photographs, he has distilled the life in those times. Enjoy them for the quality of their composition, enjoy them for all that they document, and be carried along.

GAVIN CORBETT

STREET

FOR SALE
TO LET
WAREHOUSE
Druker Fanning
& Partners
6797007
THE OFFICE OF
PUBLIC WORKS
-caring for our heritage
Royal Canal
Restoration
BINN'S BRIDGE TO JONES'S ROAD
AUTUMN '92
SPECIAL
12 PAGE
SUPPLEMENT
ON THE
ALL-IRELAND
FOOTBALL FINAL
IRISH
Press
BIG
MATCH
ANALYSIS
Herald
TOMORROW!

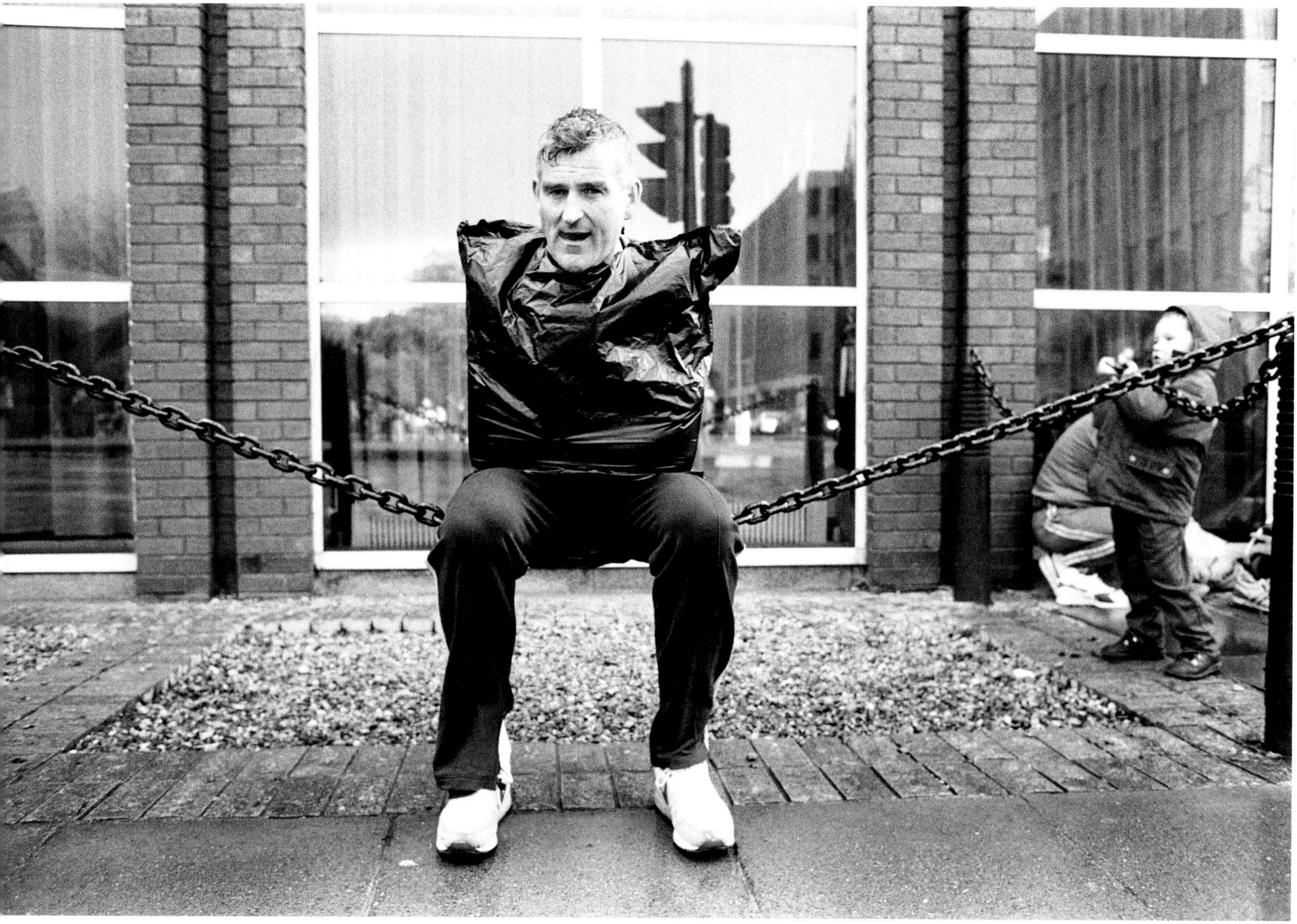

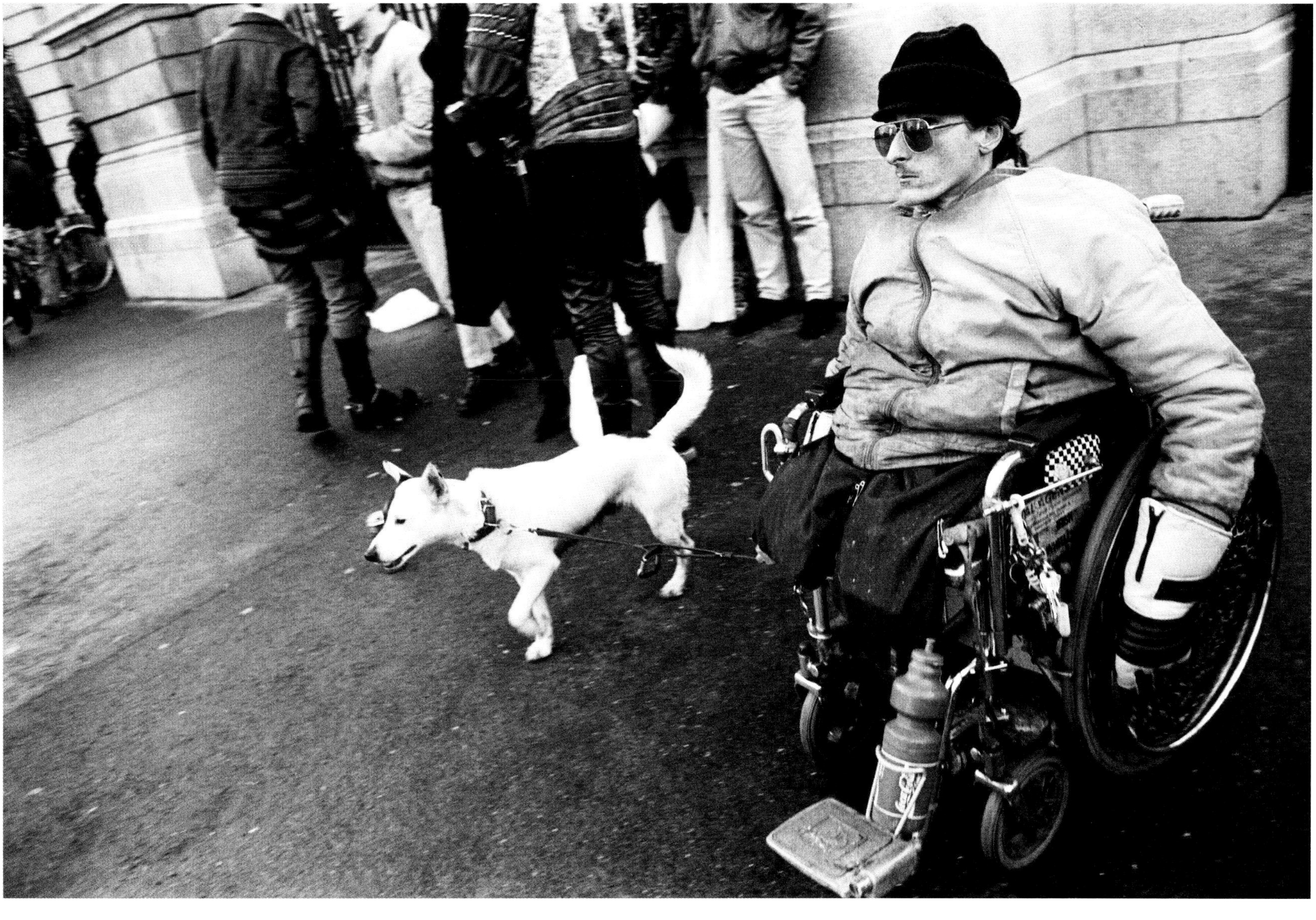

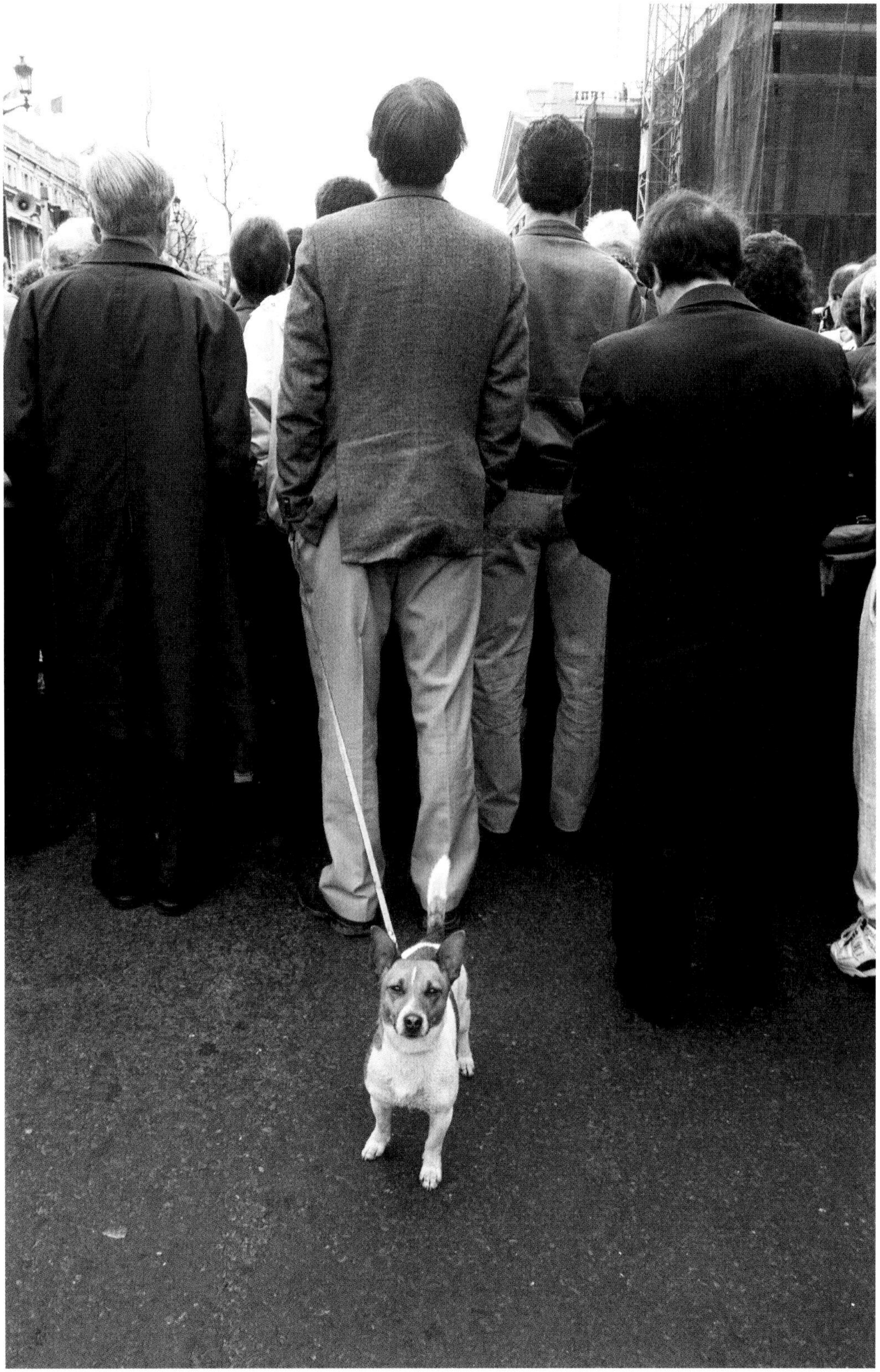

17

THE PROPHET MOHAMED
WAS A
PIGS ARSE
THE WEAKENING OF THE LEFT-WING
INTERNATIONALLY, IS INTERNATIONAL
EXTREME DANGER. EDUCATION & OR-
GANISATION OF GENUINE SOCIALIST/
HUMANITARIAN MOVEMENTS, IS
NECCESSARY + URGENT
DARNDALE
Rule
ELAINE
SANDY
24-9-90
24.9.90
INTERESTS OF COURSE
IS MILITARILY PROVOCATIVE
THAT THE USA + ISRAEL
COUNTRIES + AS A PRETEXT FOR
INTERNATIONAL WAR-CRIMES.
THAT.
24.9.90 DELAYED
EUROPEAN AGRICULTURAL UNIONS UNITE
16.9.90 WRITTEN HERE 24.9.90
TO IRAQ
FOOD + MEDICINE TO IRAQ
ALL FOREIGN MILITARY OUT! OF ARAB REGIONS
26.9.90
THE ARAB QUESTIONS SHLD BE SOLVED BY THE AR

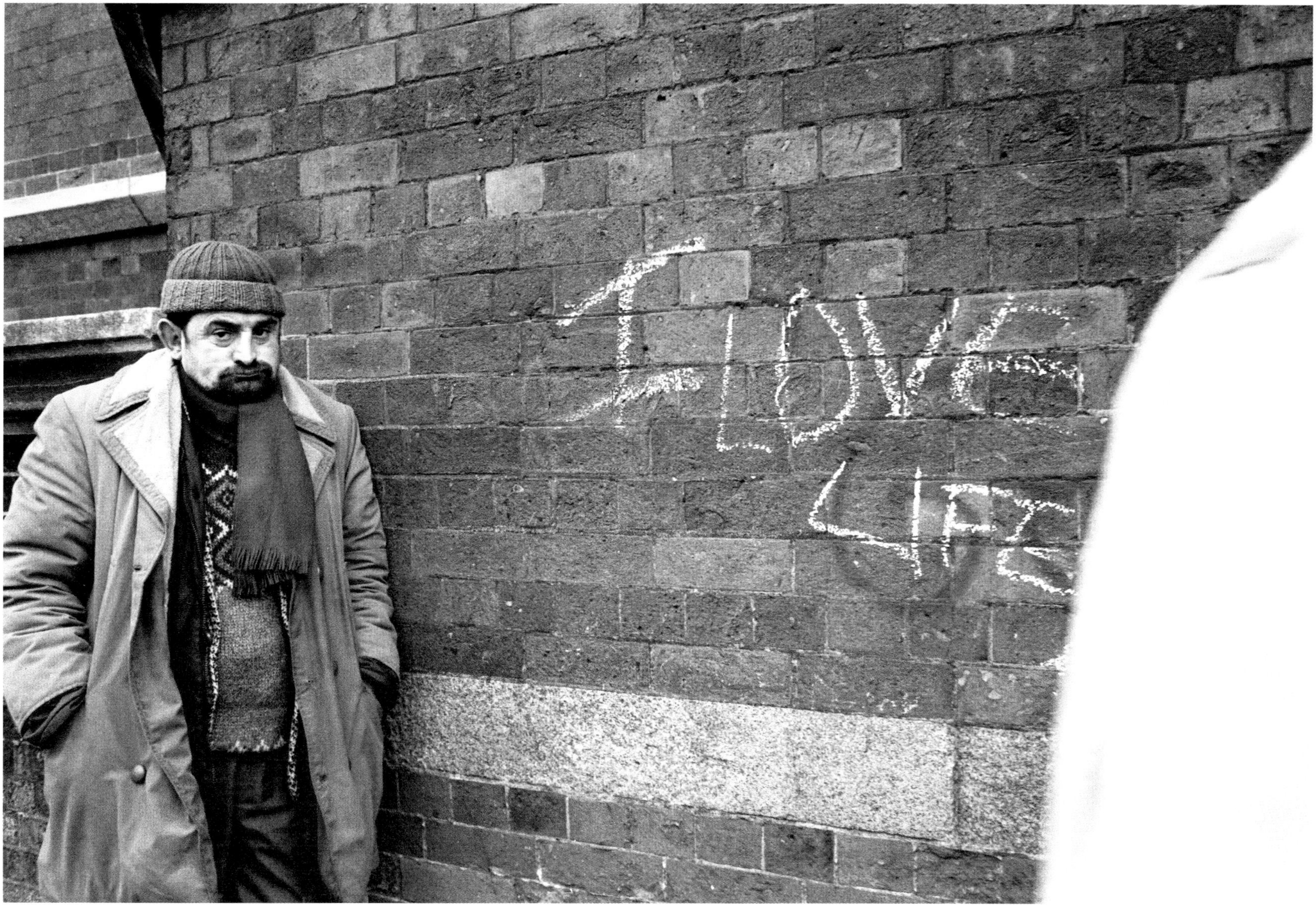

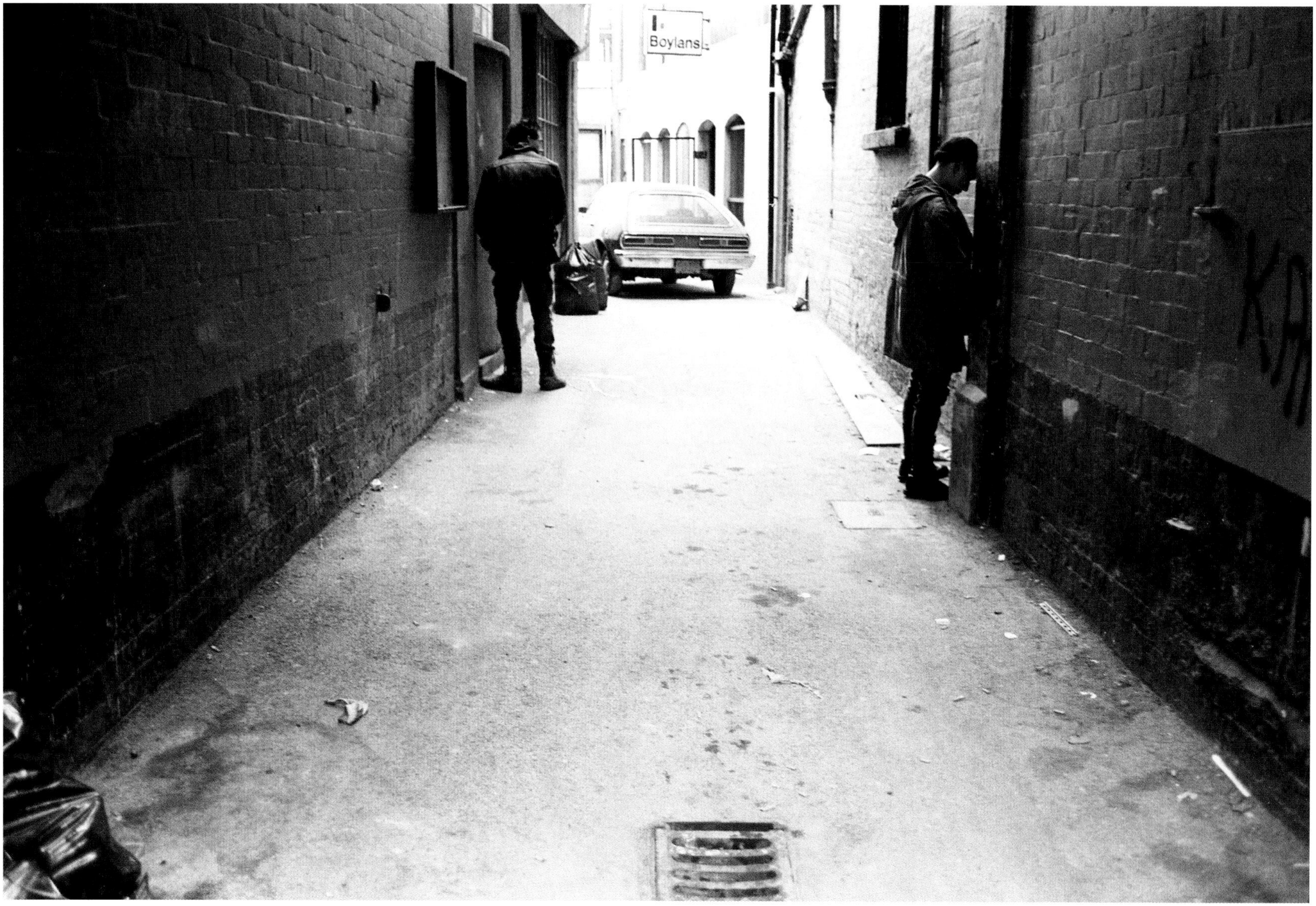
Boylans

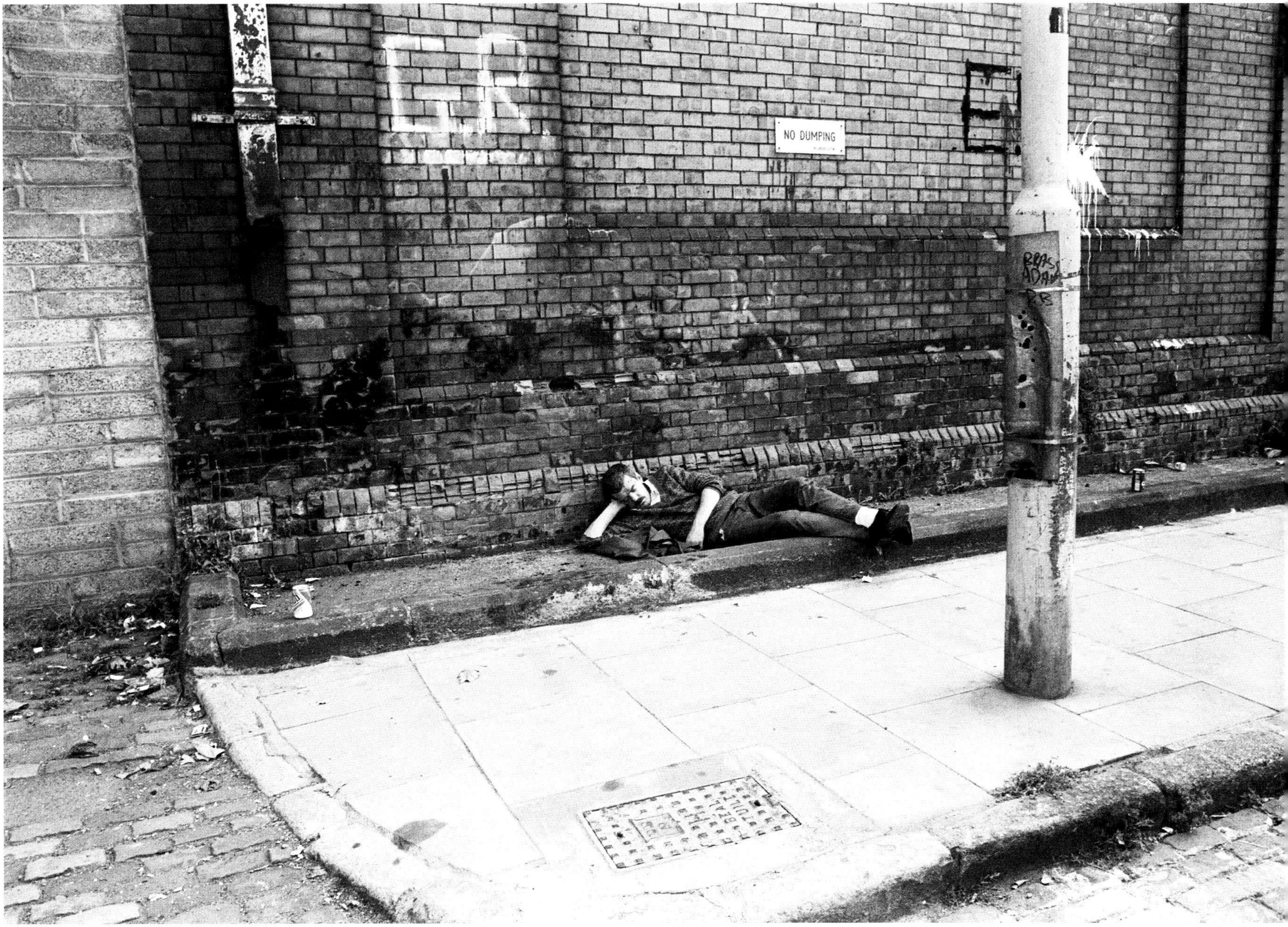
NO DUMPING

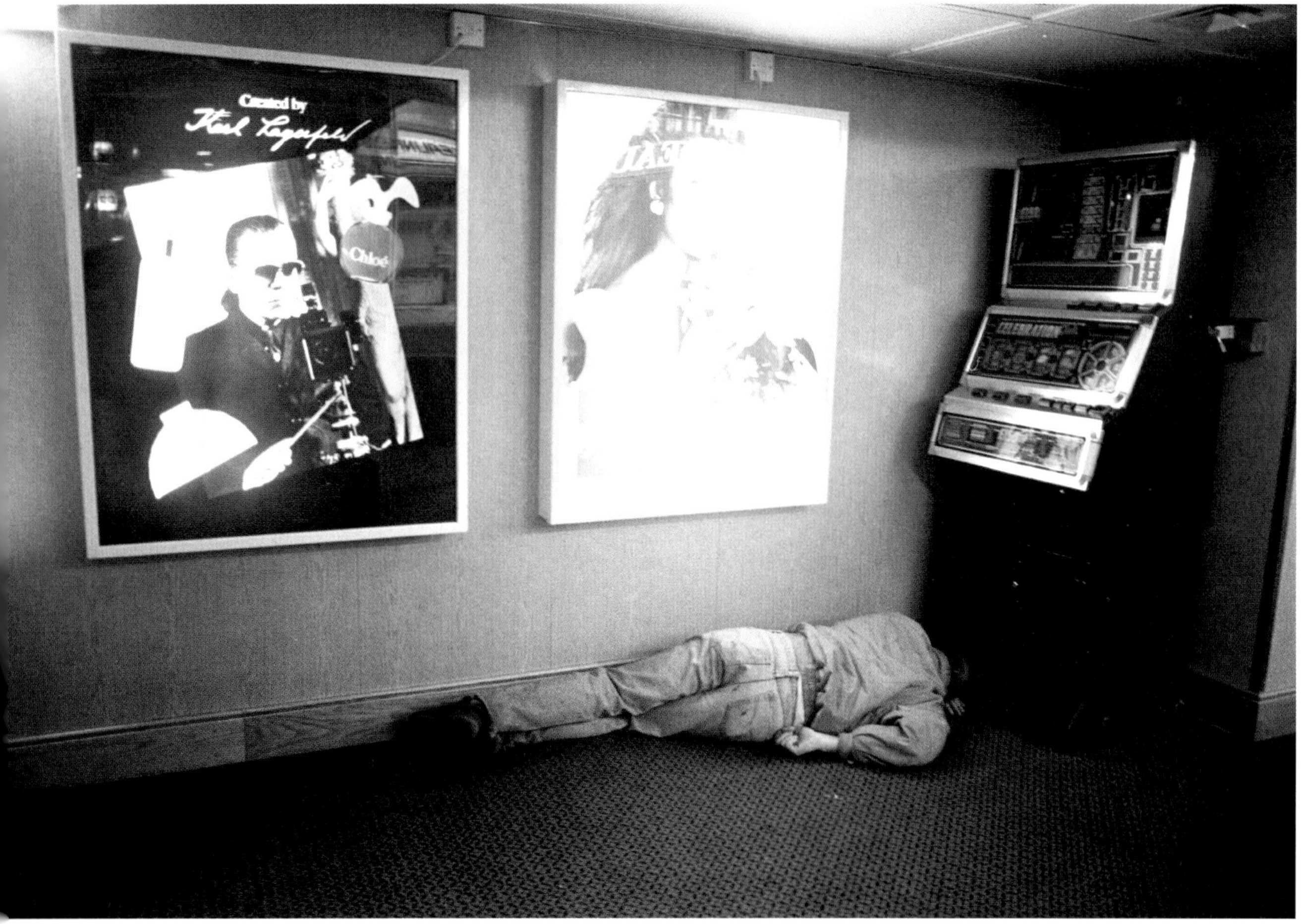
Created by
Karl Lagerfeld
Chloé

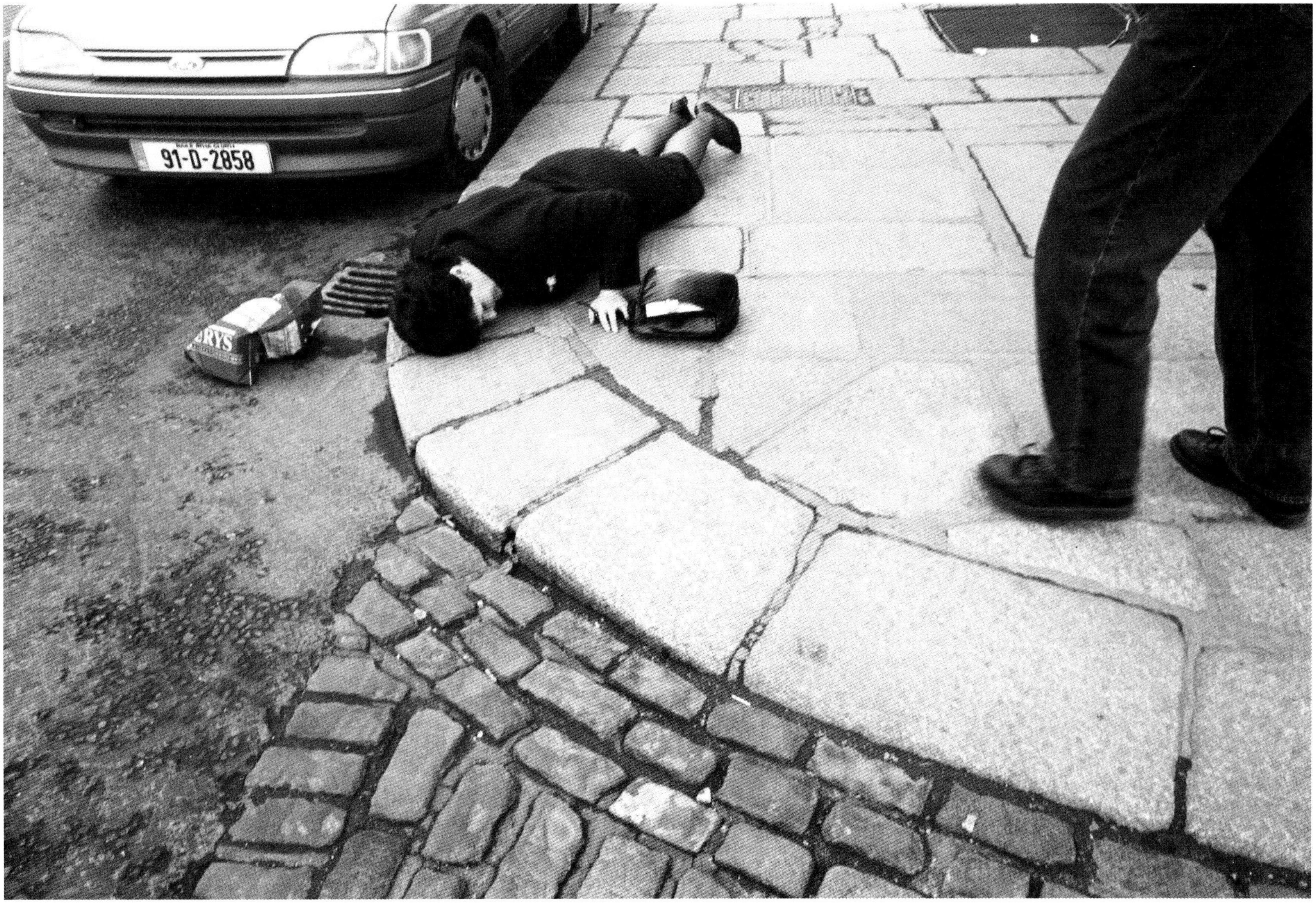
91-D-2858

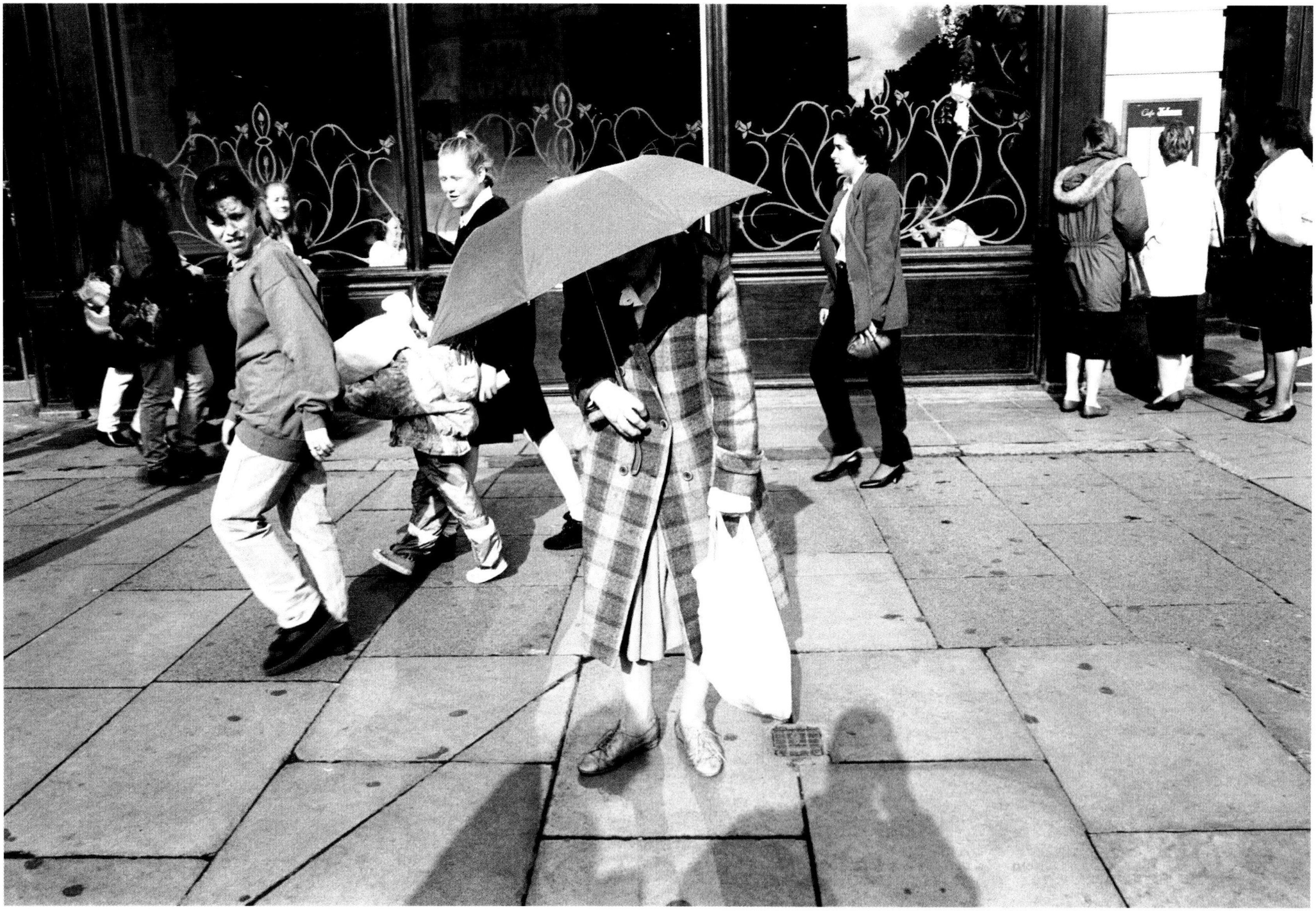

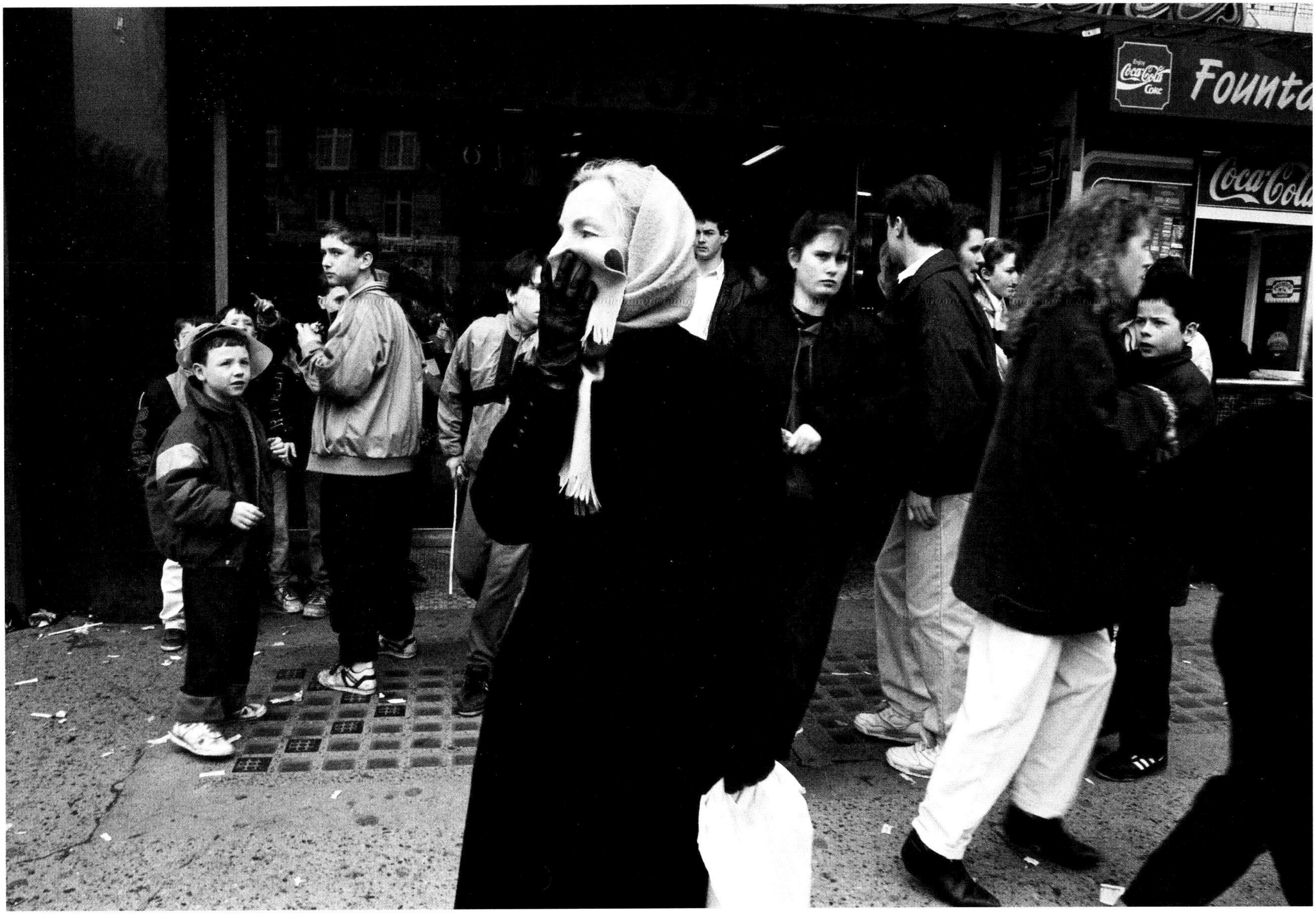
Coca-Cola
Coke
Founta
Coca-Cola

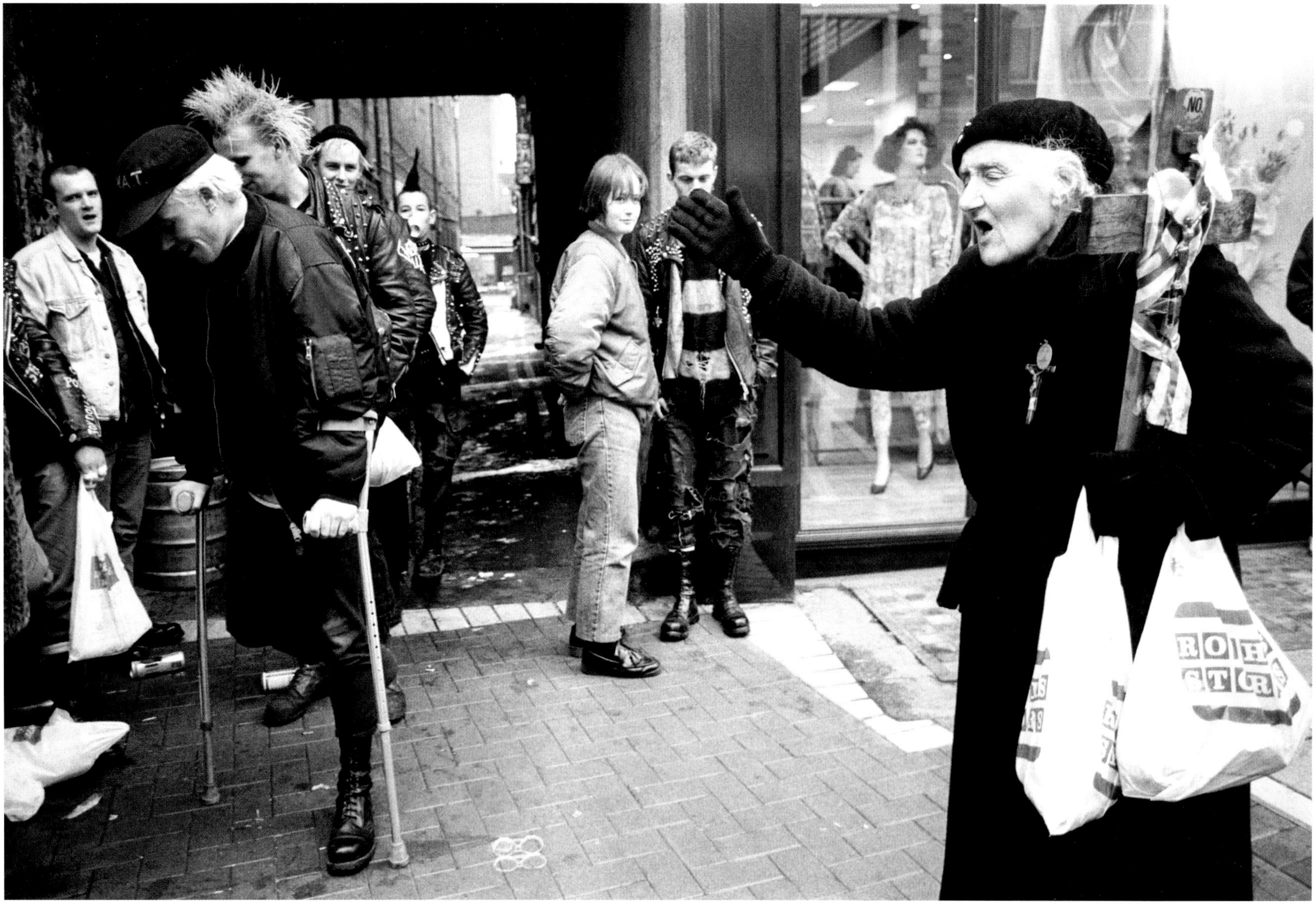
NO

27

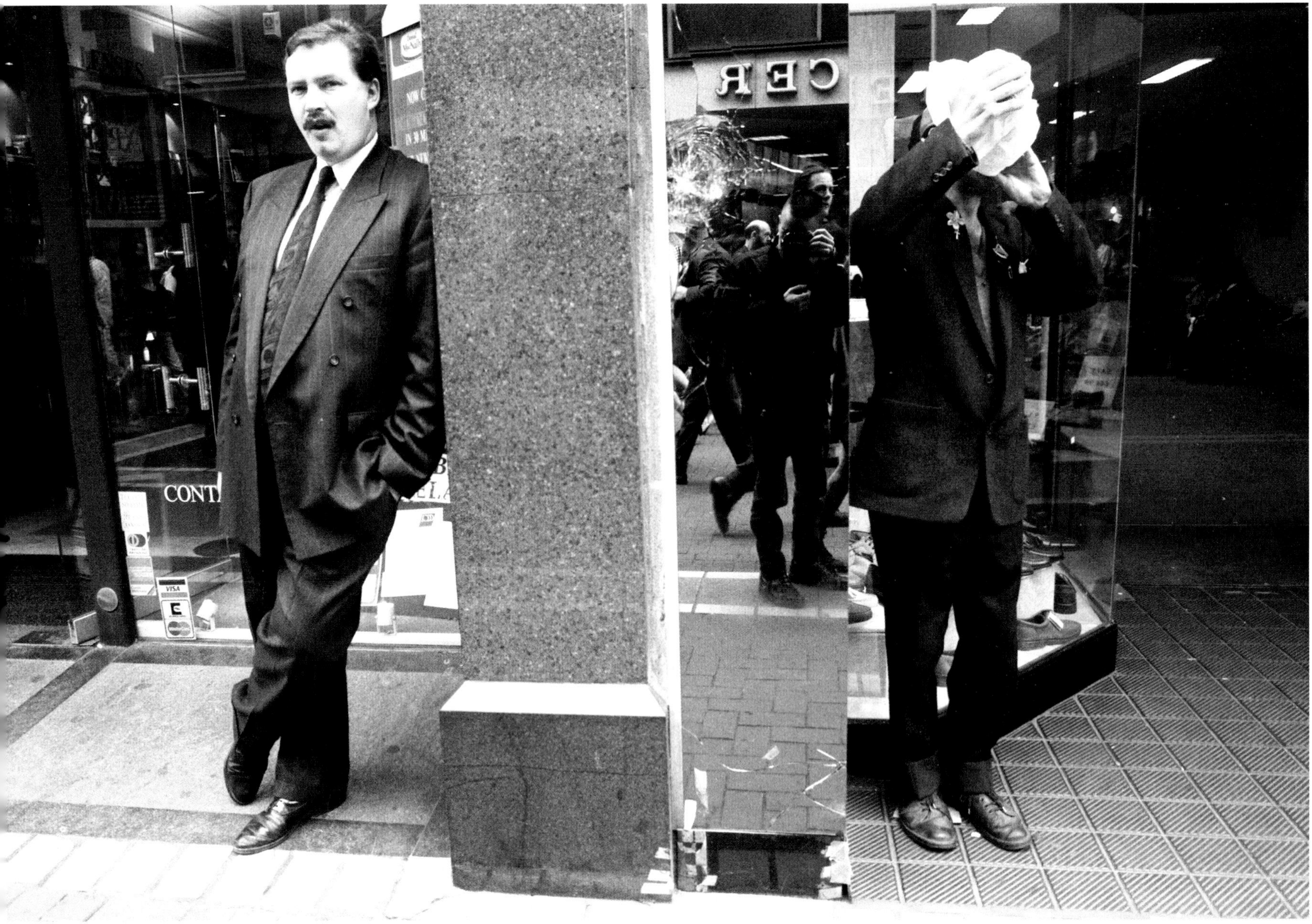

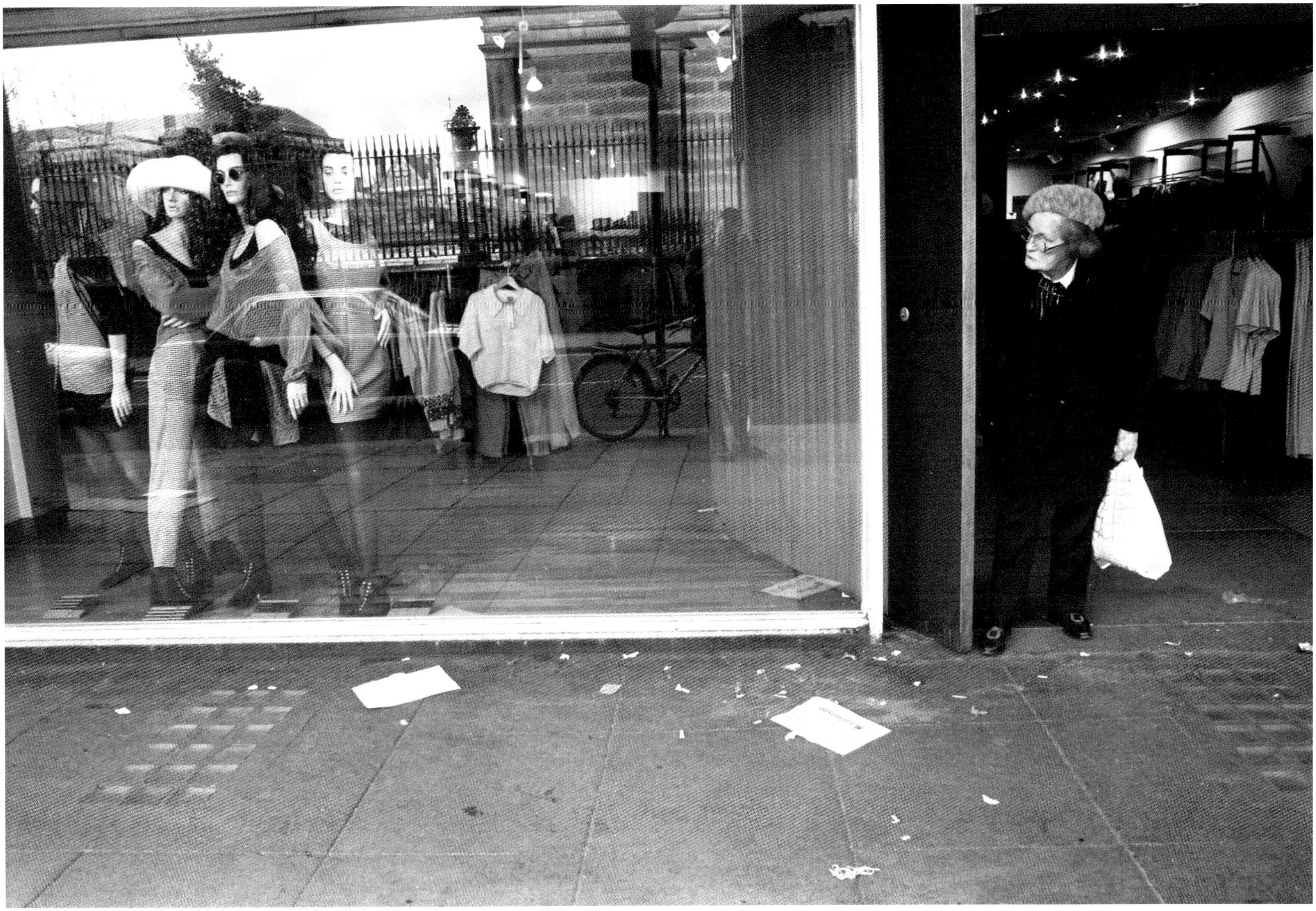

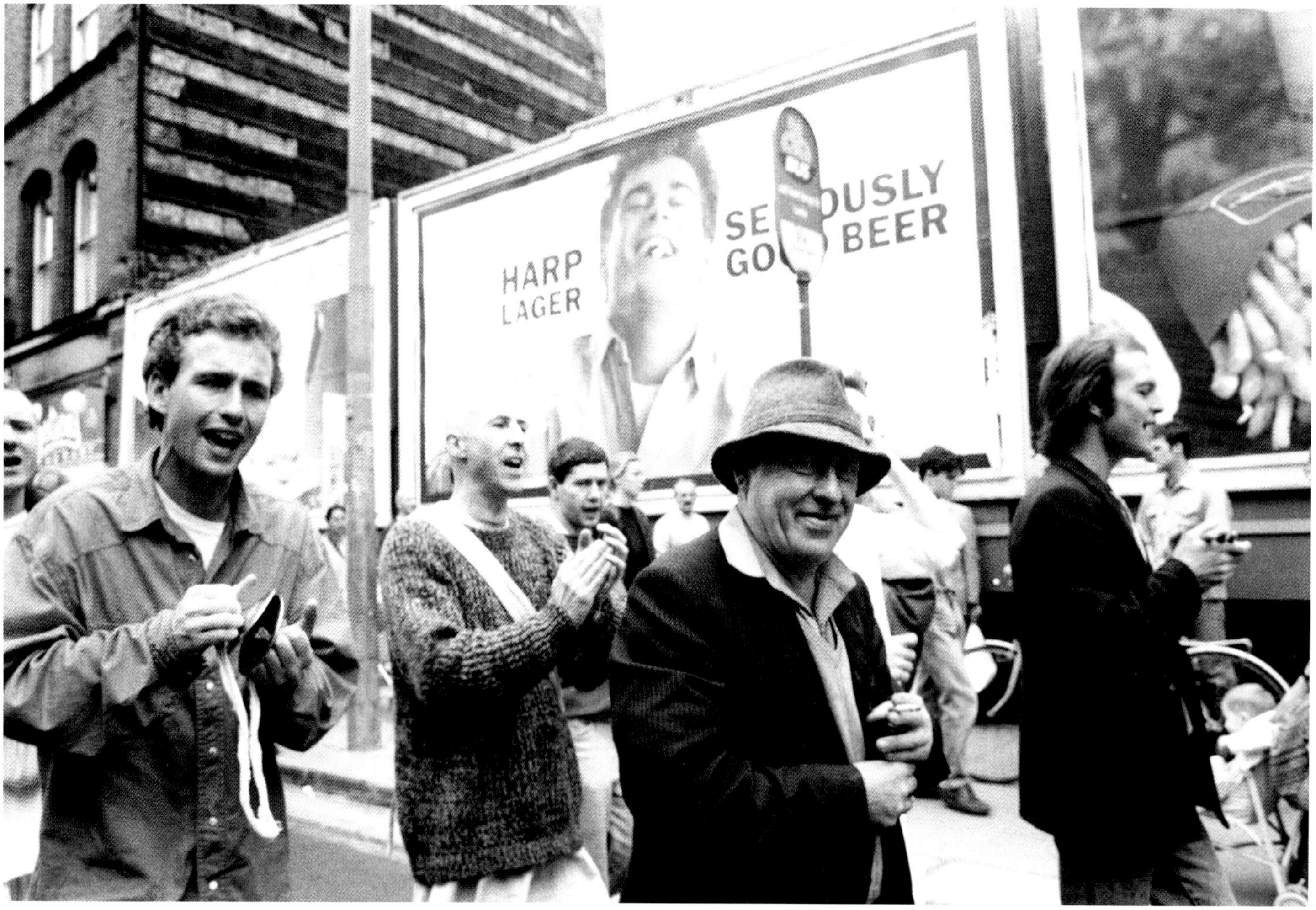
HARP
LAGER
SE OUSLY
GO BEER

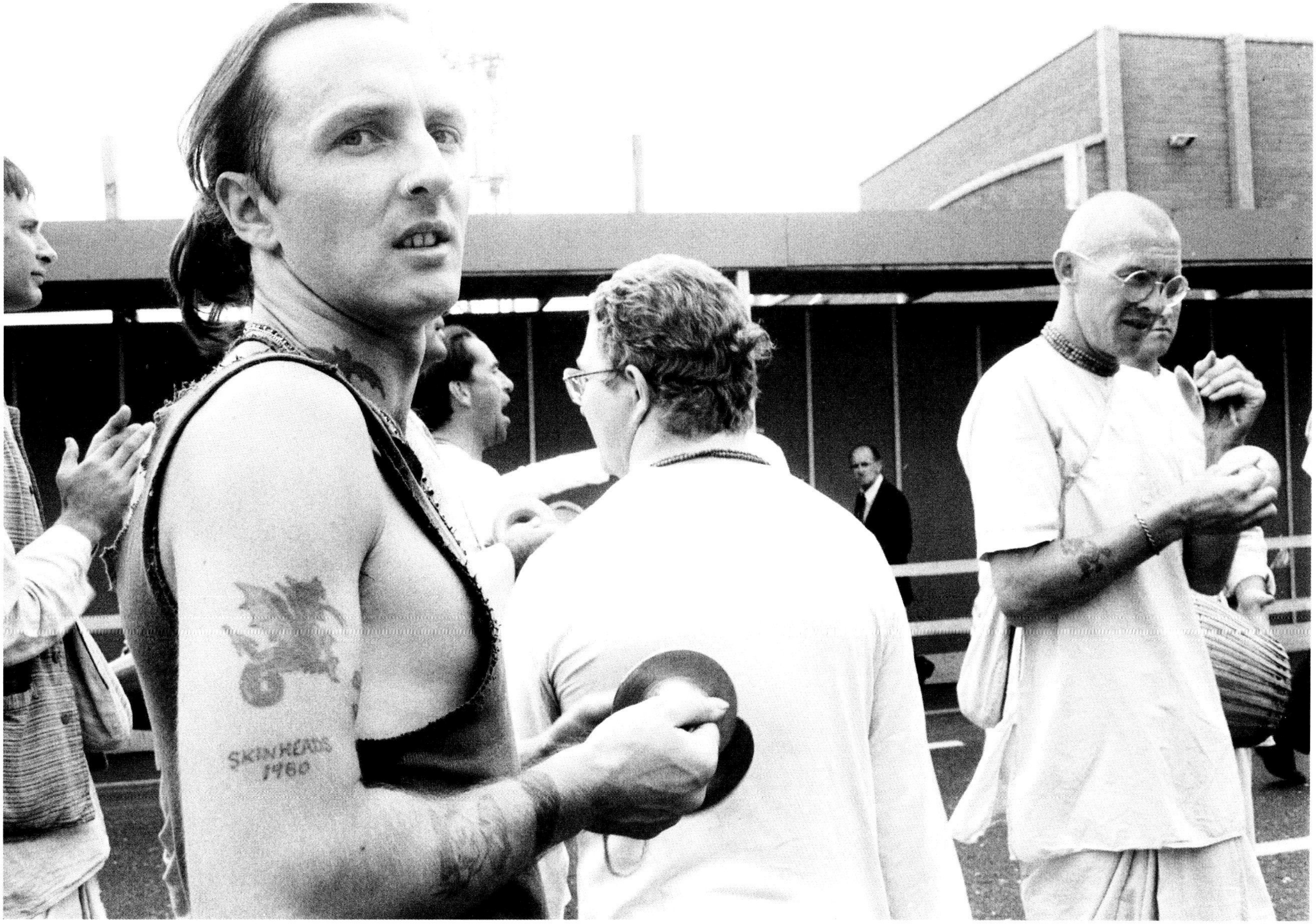
SKINHEADS
1960

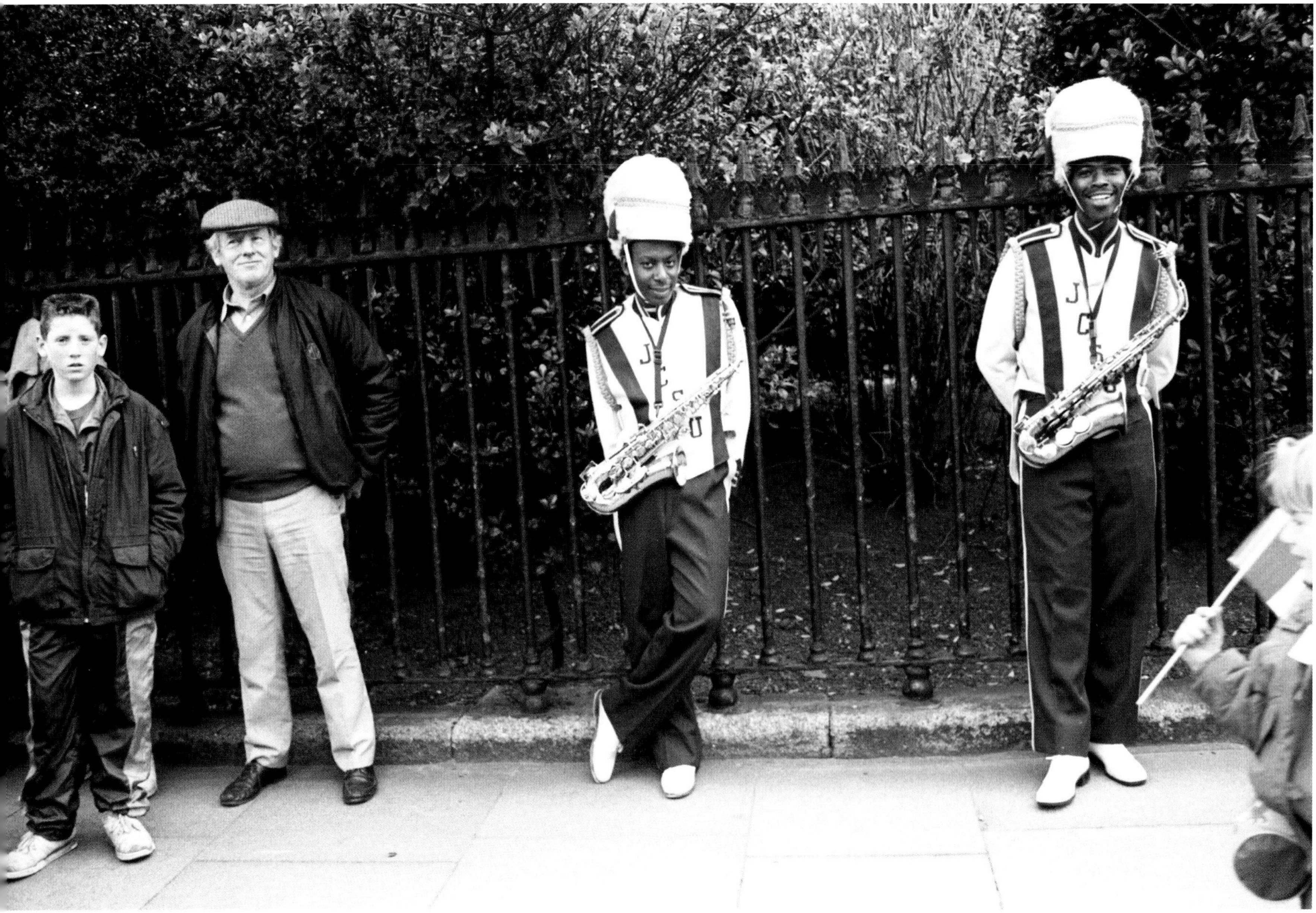

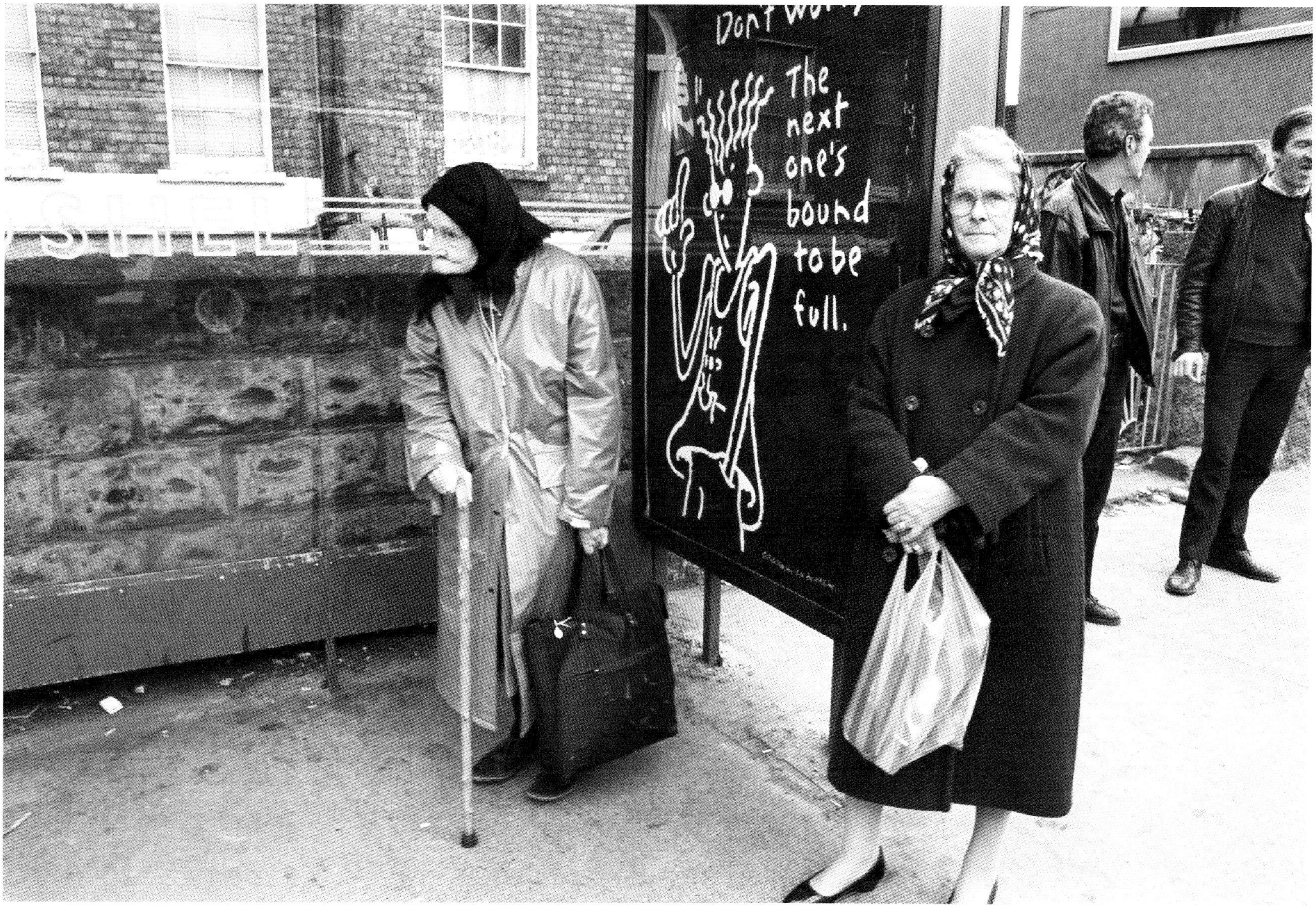
The next one's bound to be full.

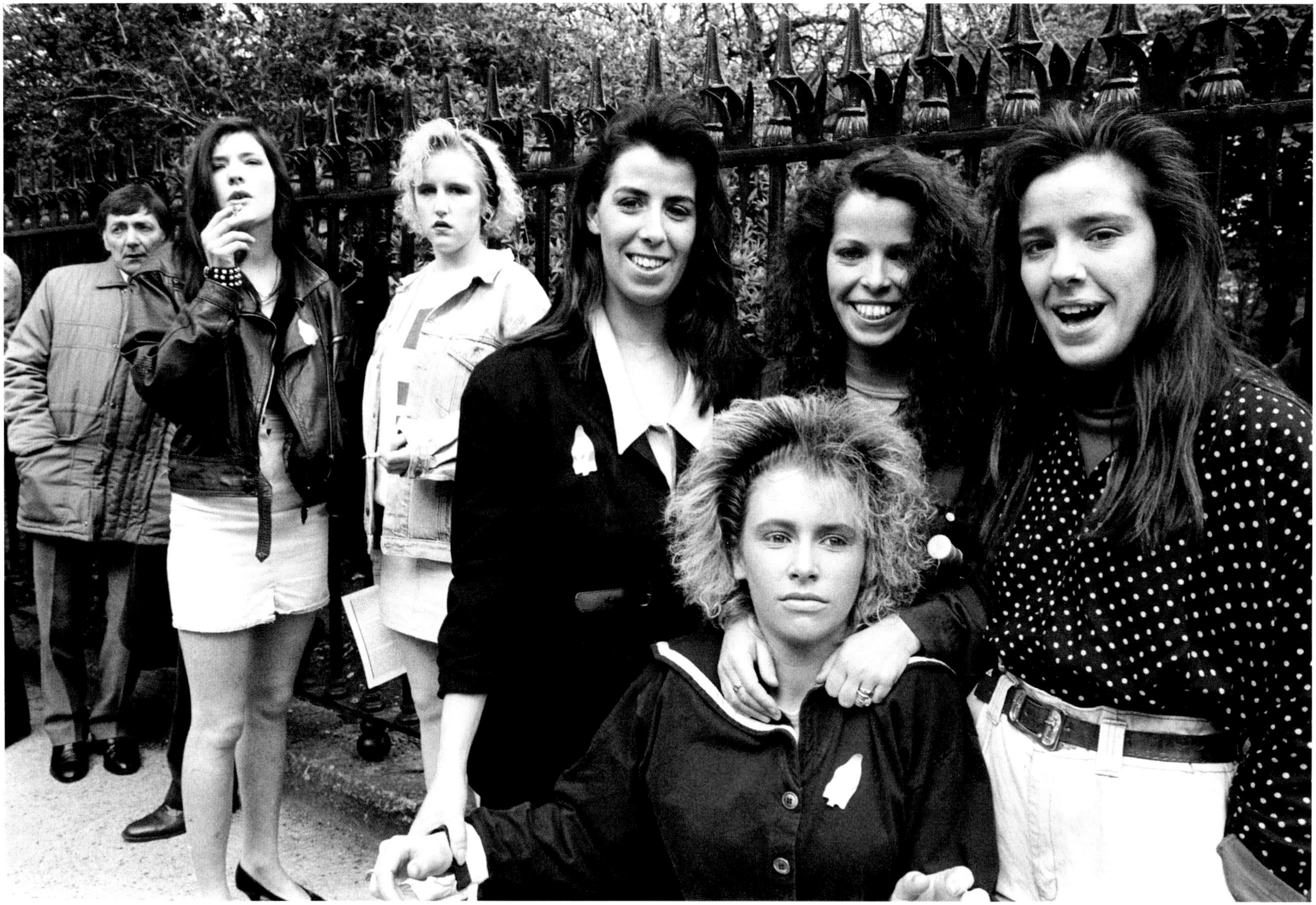

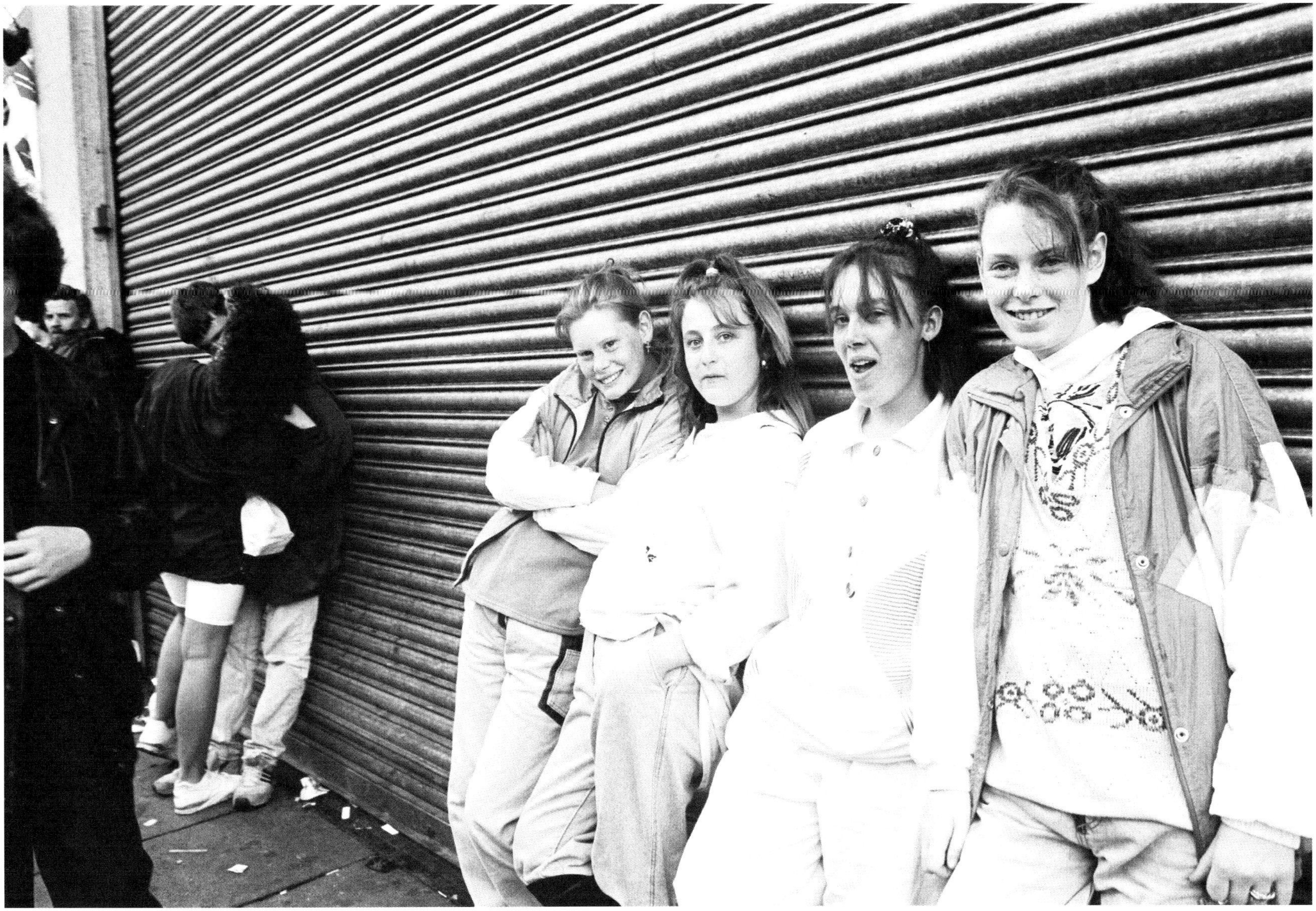

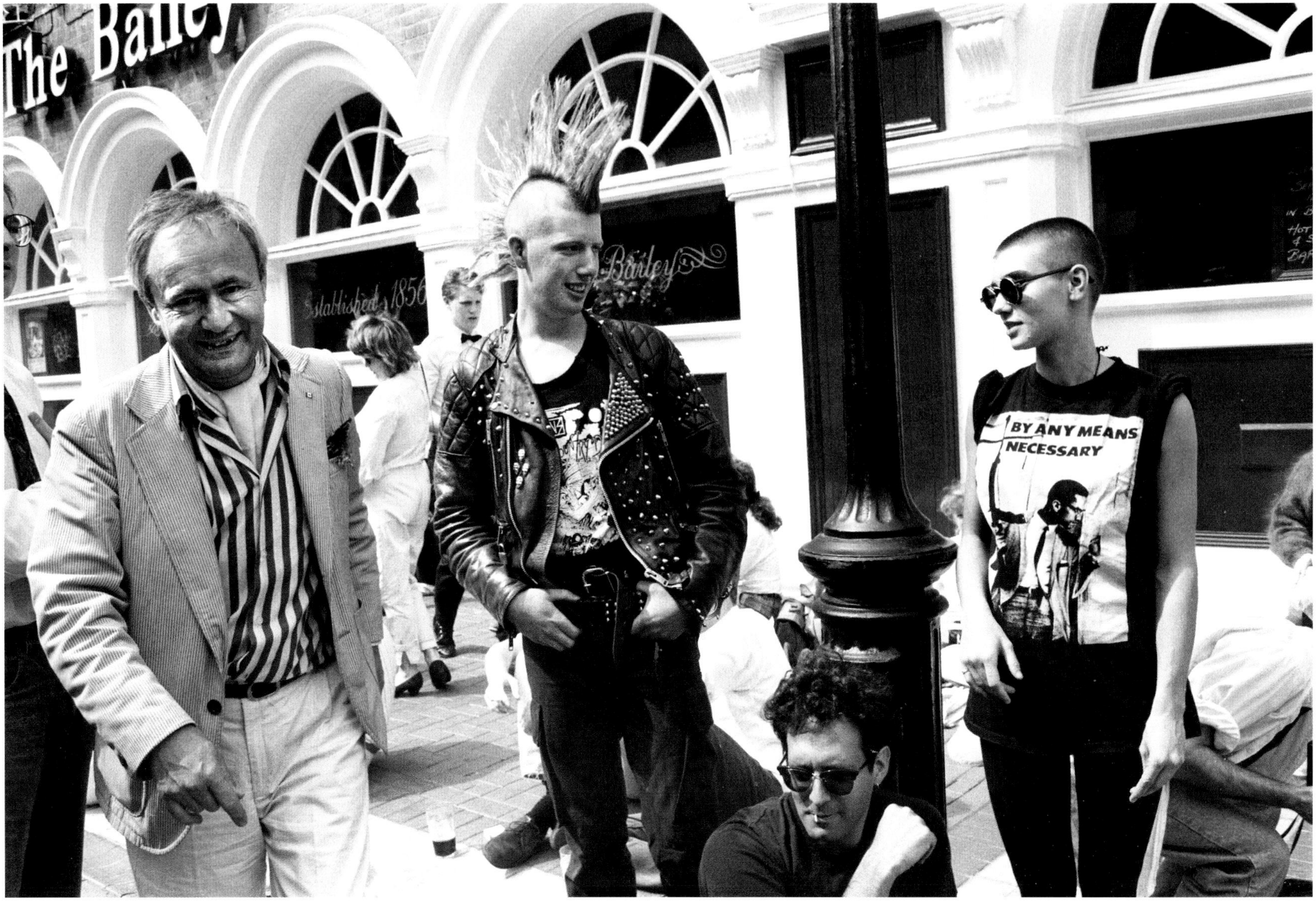
The Bailey
Established 1856
Bailey
BY ANY MEANS
NECESSARY

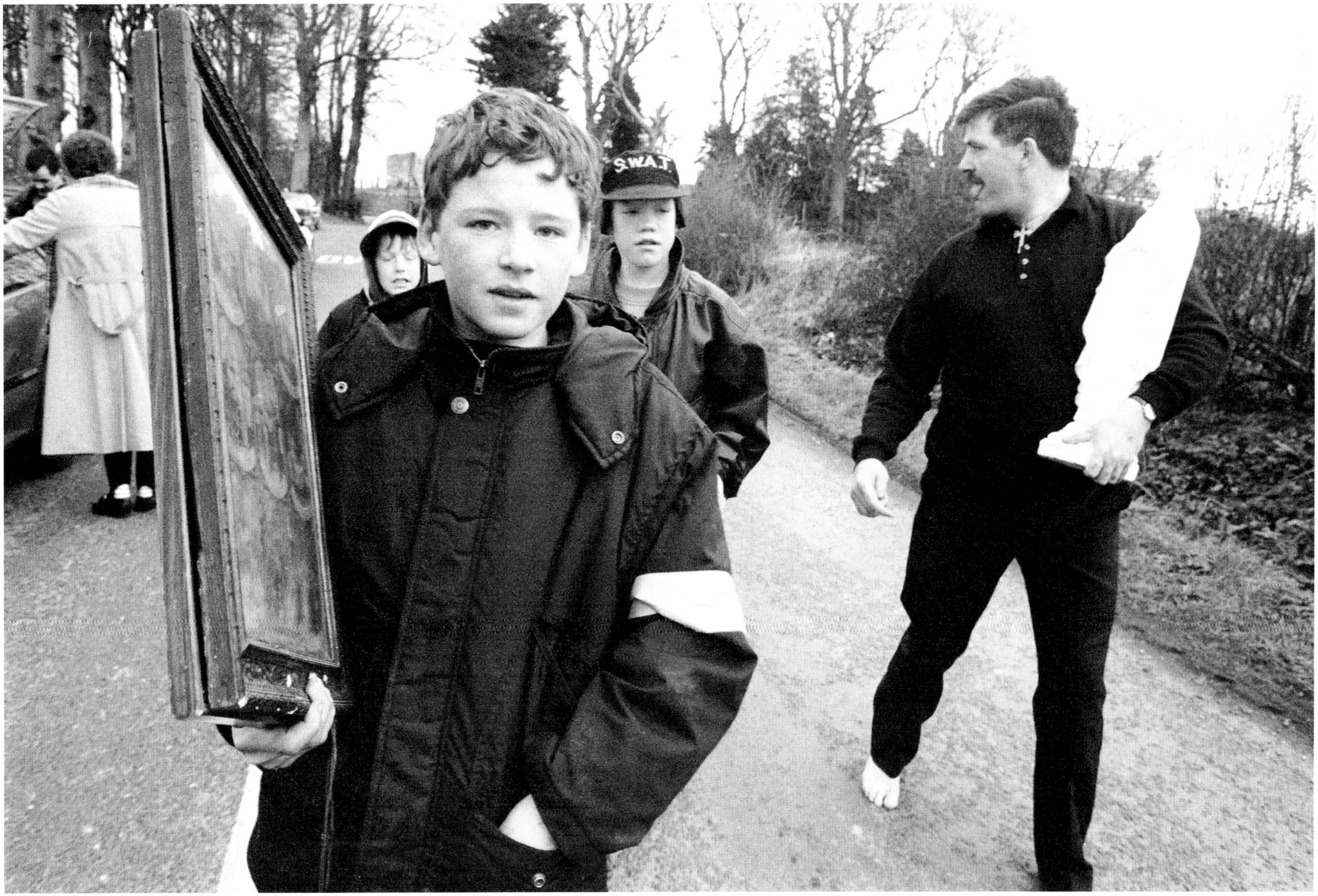
S.W.A.T

COMING SOON TO THE S.F.X
DON'T DREAM IT- BE THERE
RICHARD O'BRIEN'S
ROCKY HORROR SHOW
ALIVE ON STAGE
AIB
Centre
Bank
100 Grafton Street
CENSORED!

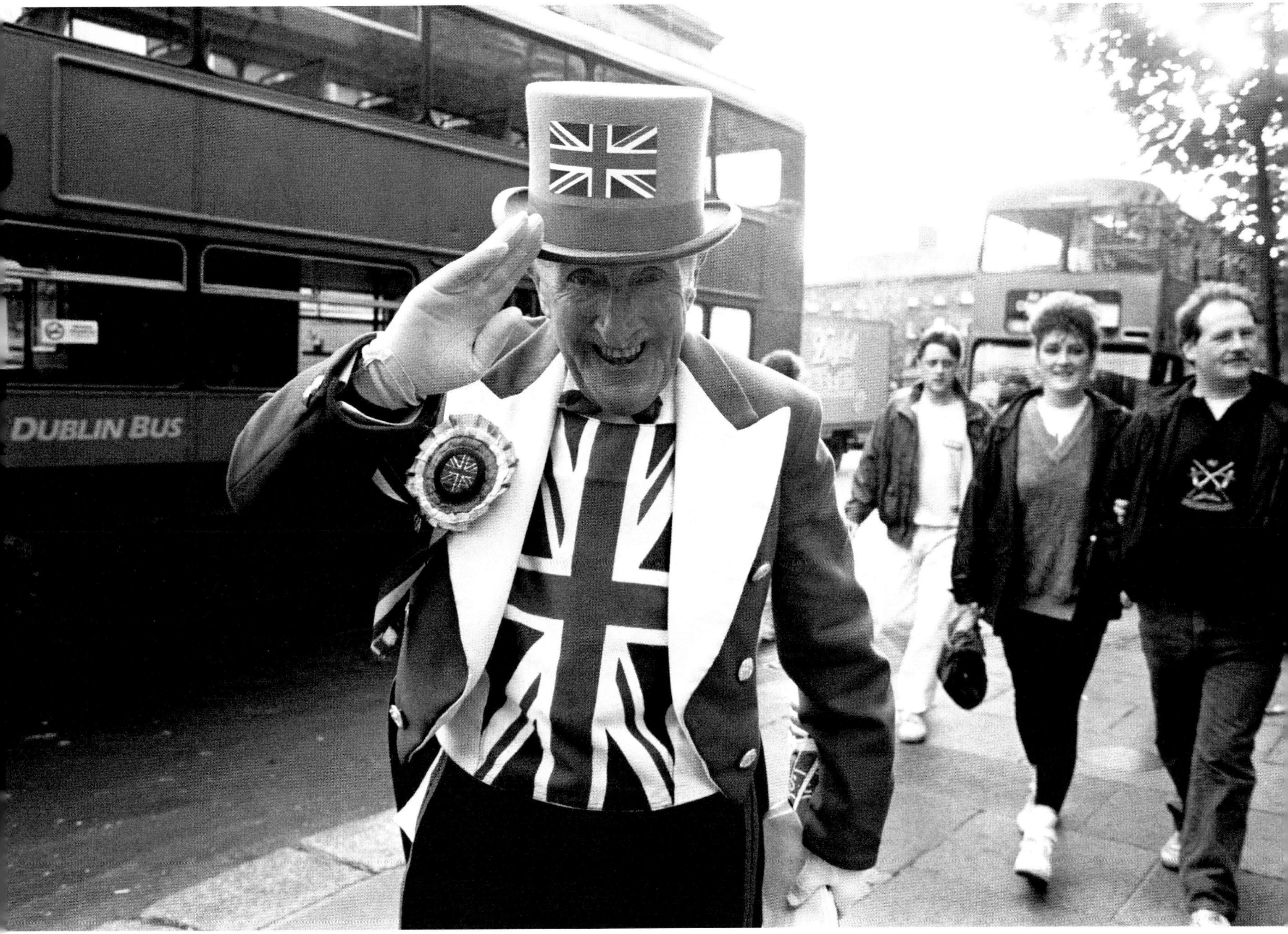
DUBLIN BUS

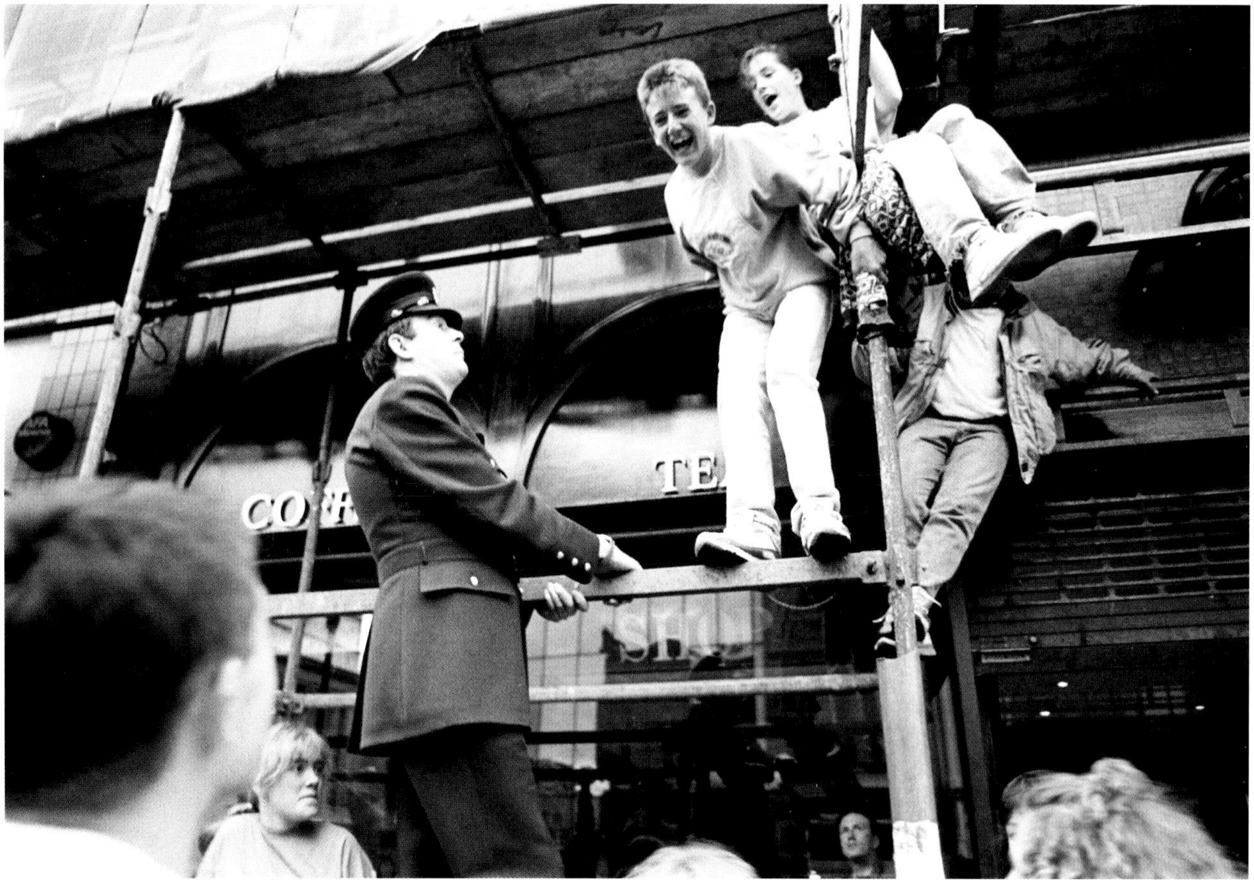

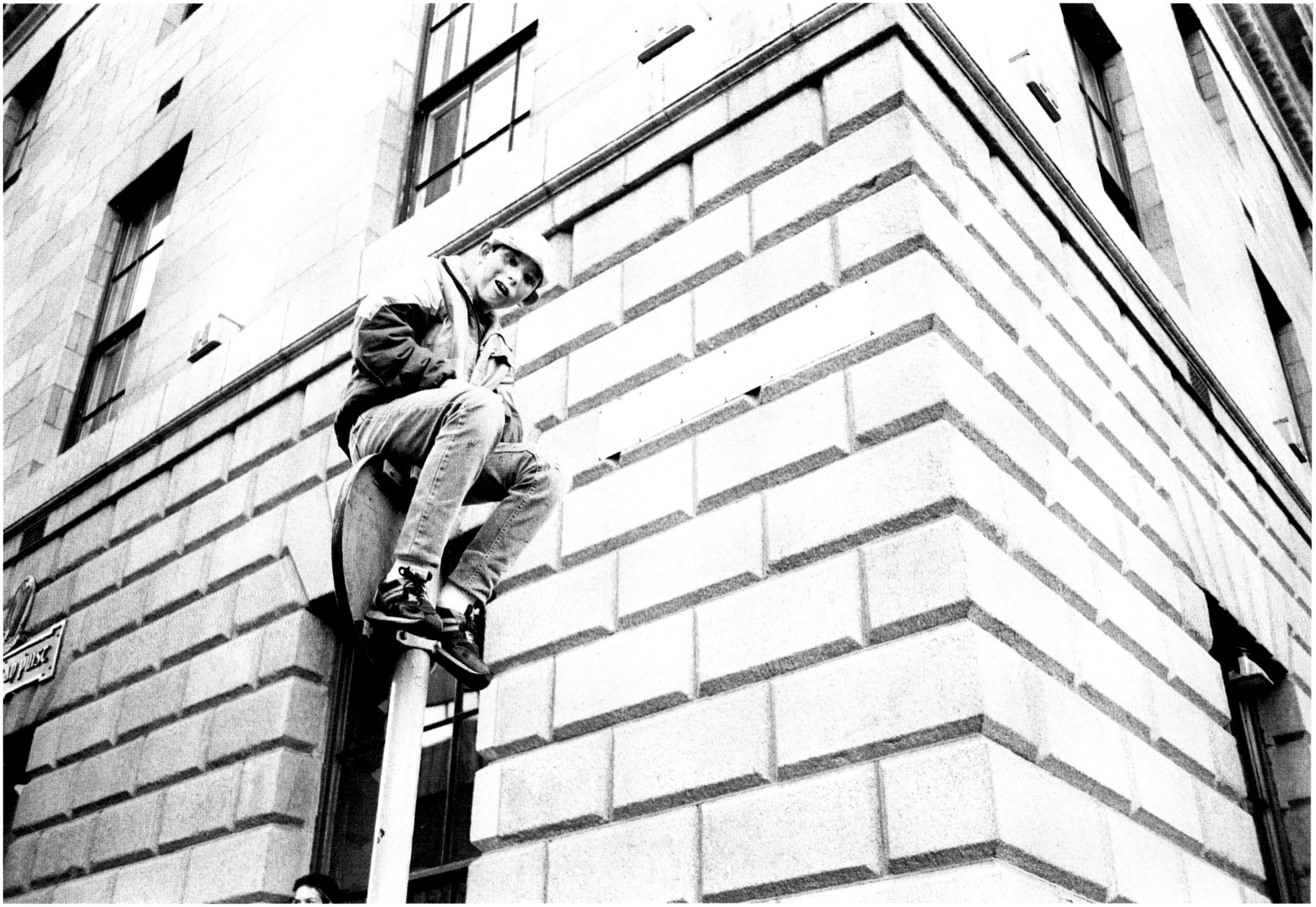

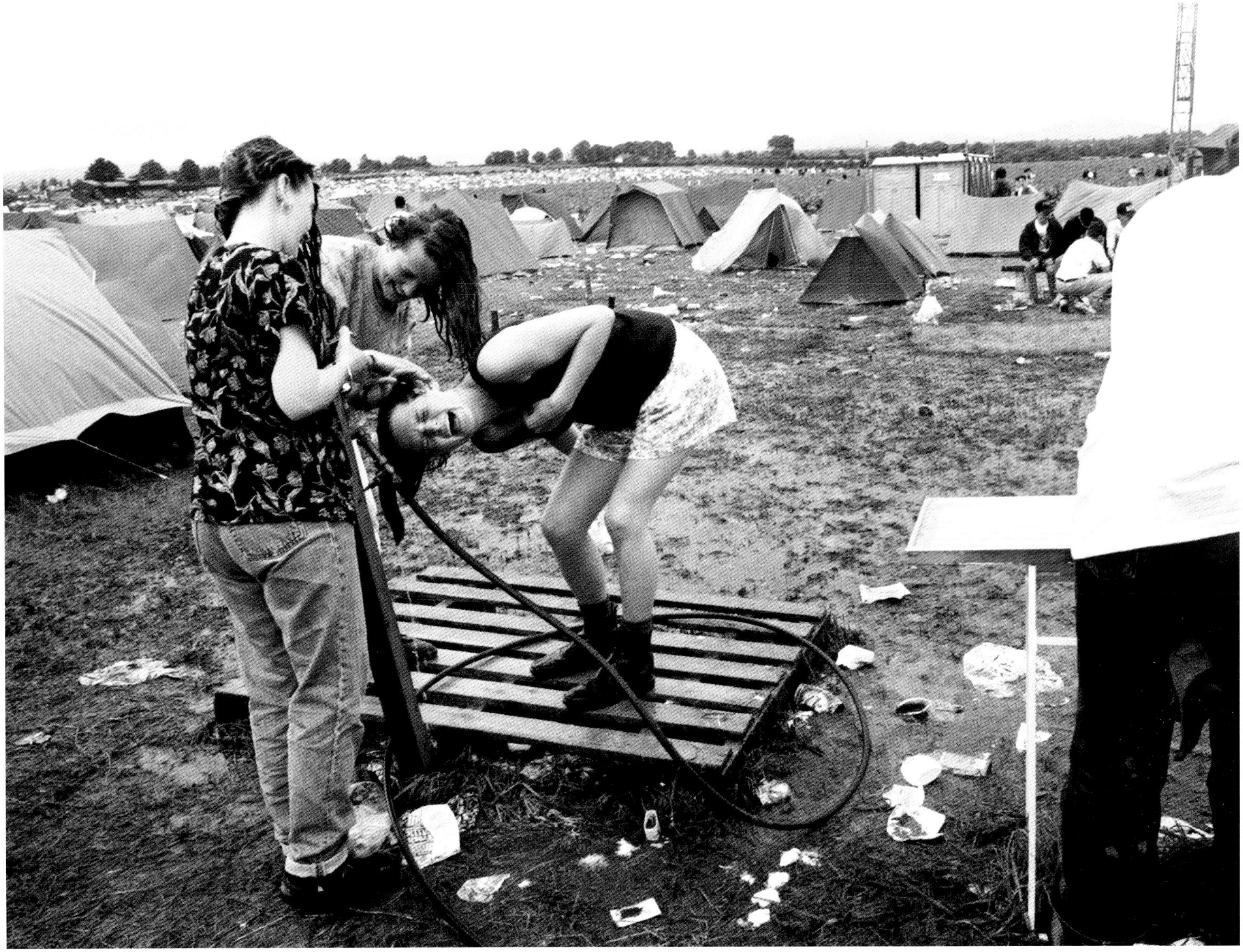

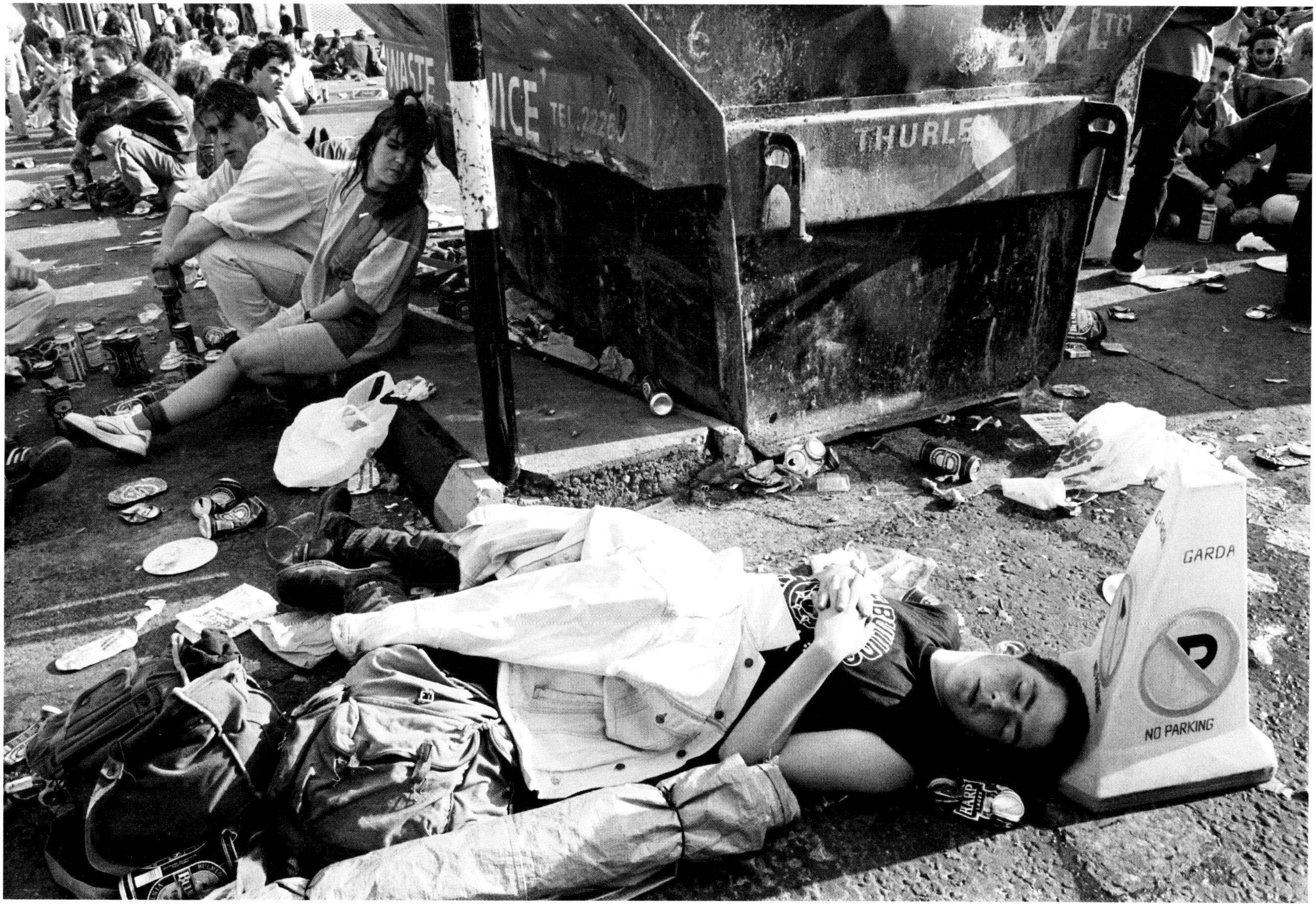
GARDA
NO PARKING

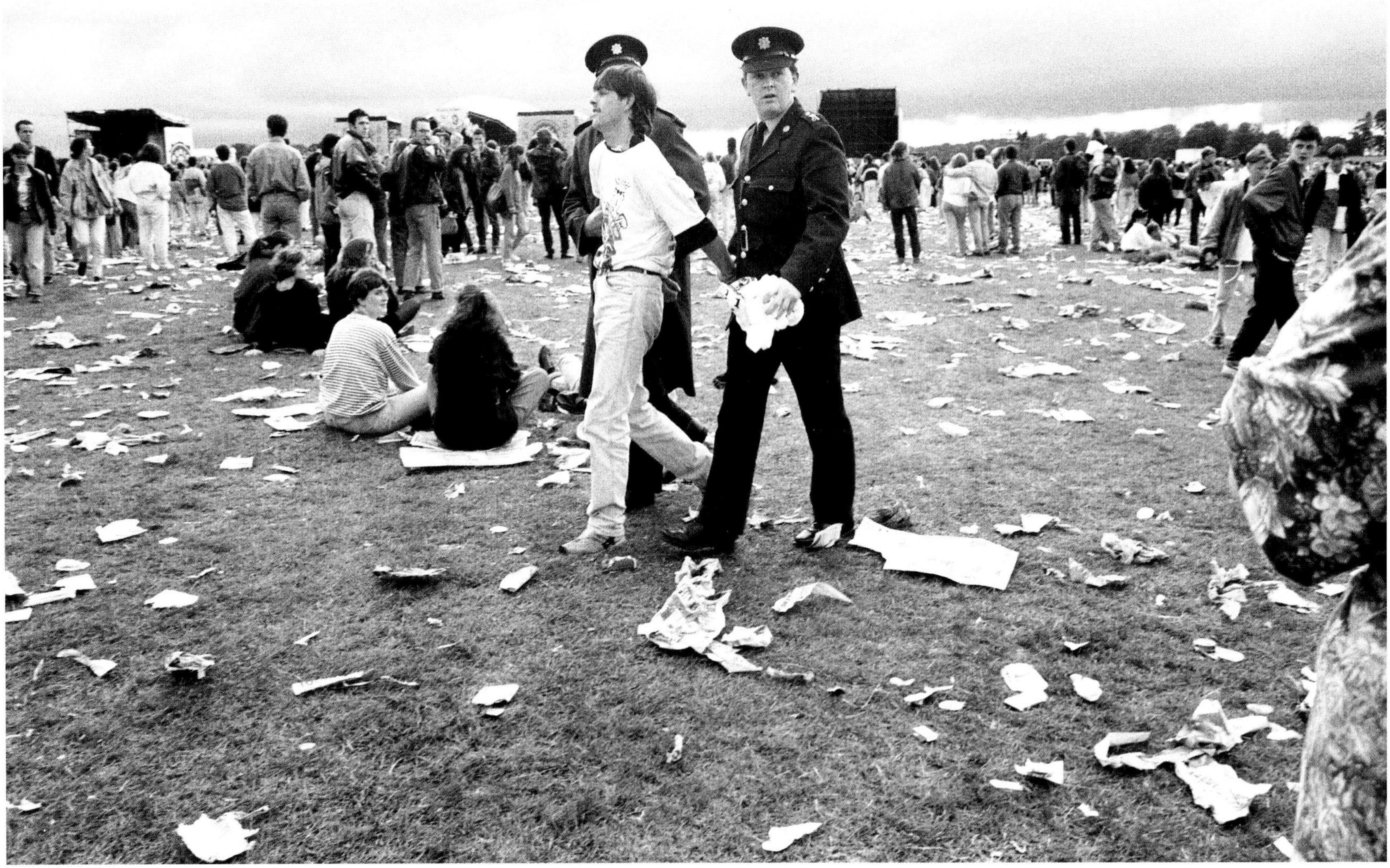

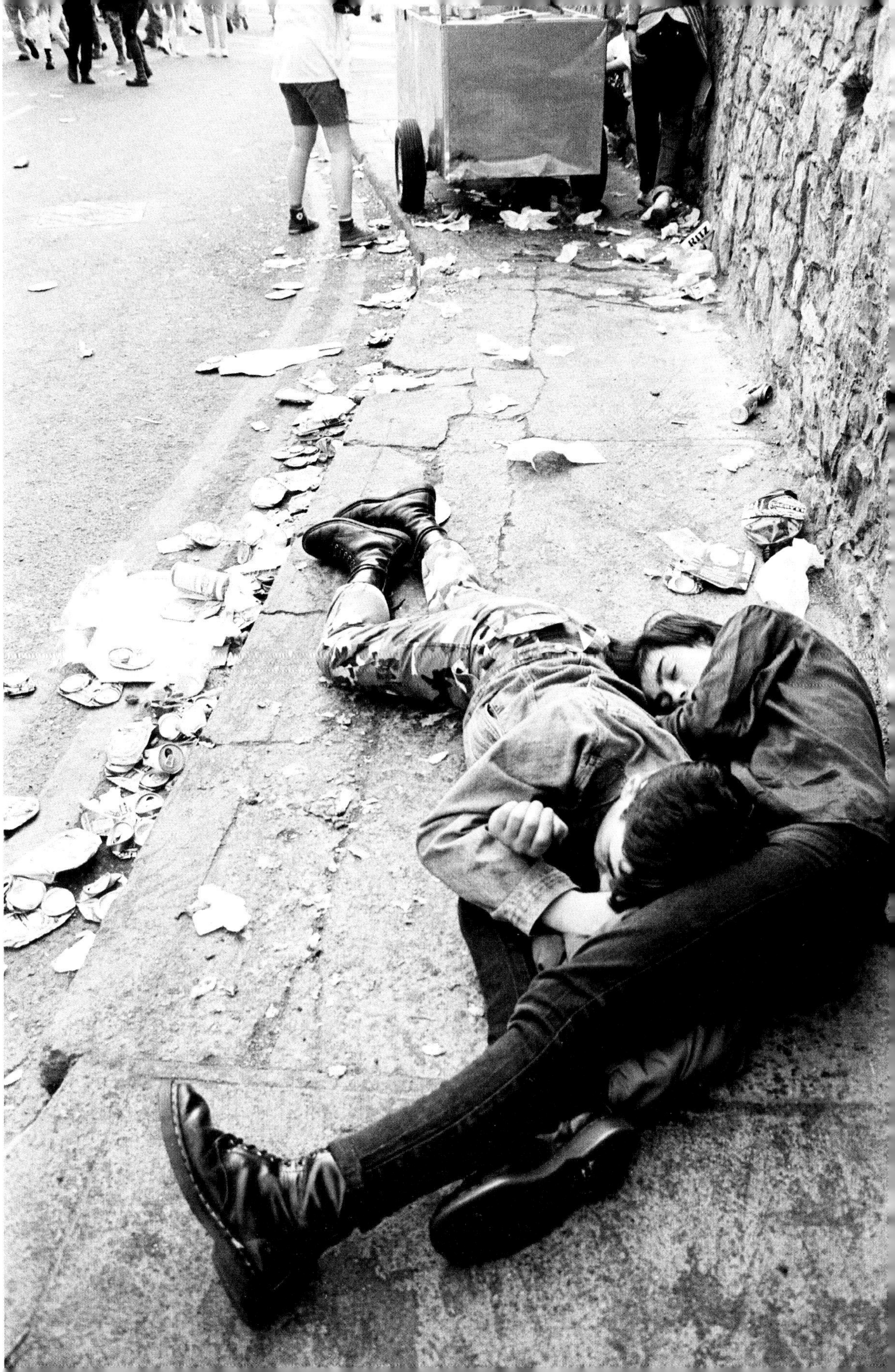

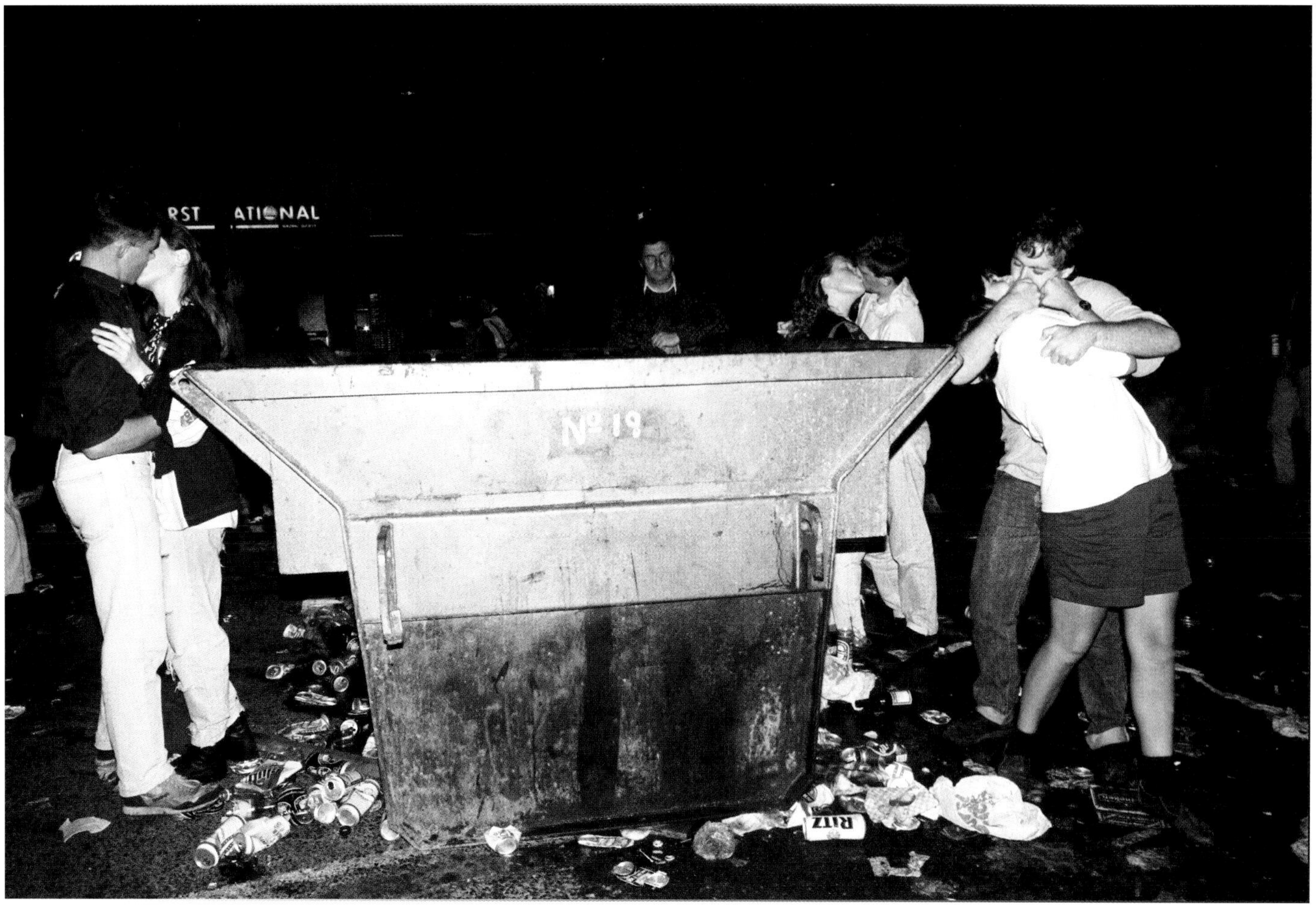
RST ATIONAL
Nº 19
RITZ

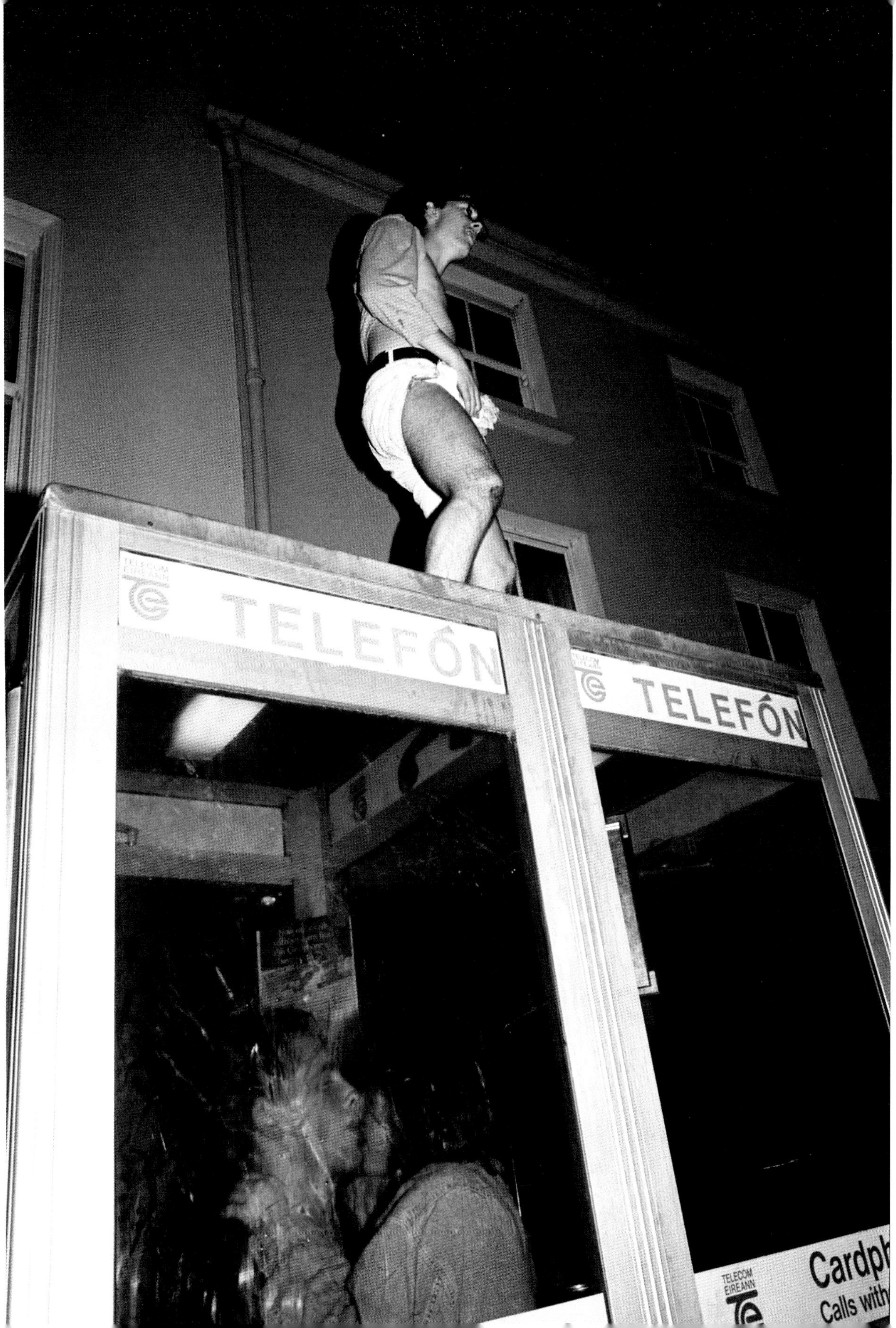
TELECOM EIREANN
TELEFÓN
TELEFÓN
TELECOM EIREANN

EALU · EMERGENCY EXIT TO OPEN
EYE SPY
SECURITY CAMERA ON BOARD THIS BUS

49

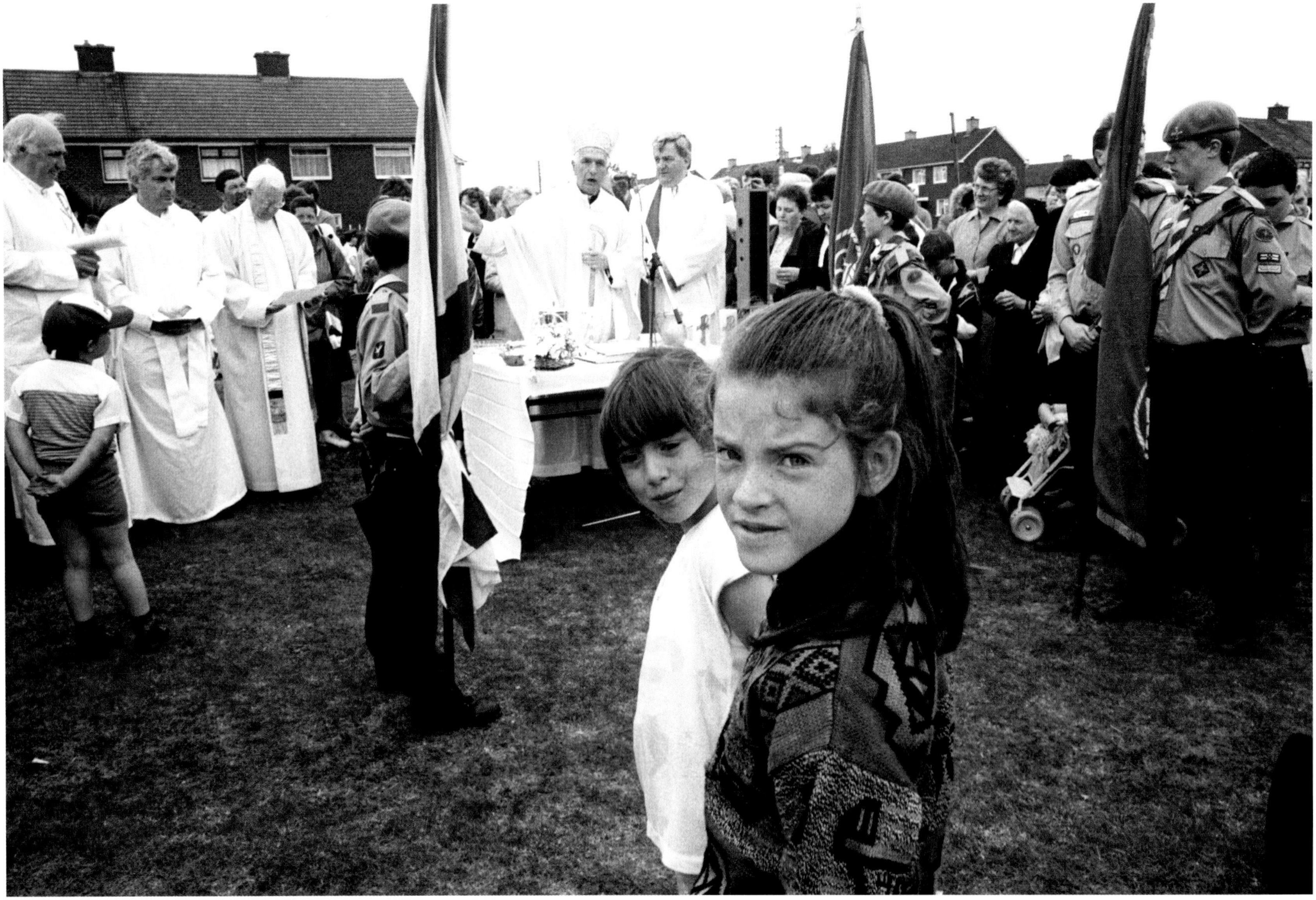

DREAMED
AND ARE DEAD

1867   1882   1916

PROTEST

British Injustice.
Santa Claws came early for the Birmingham Six.
The fight goes on.

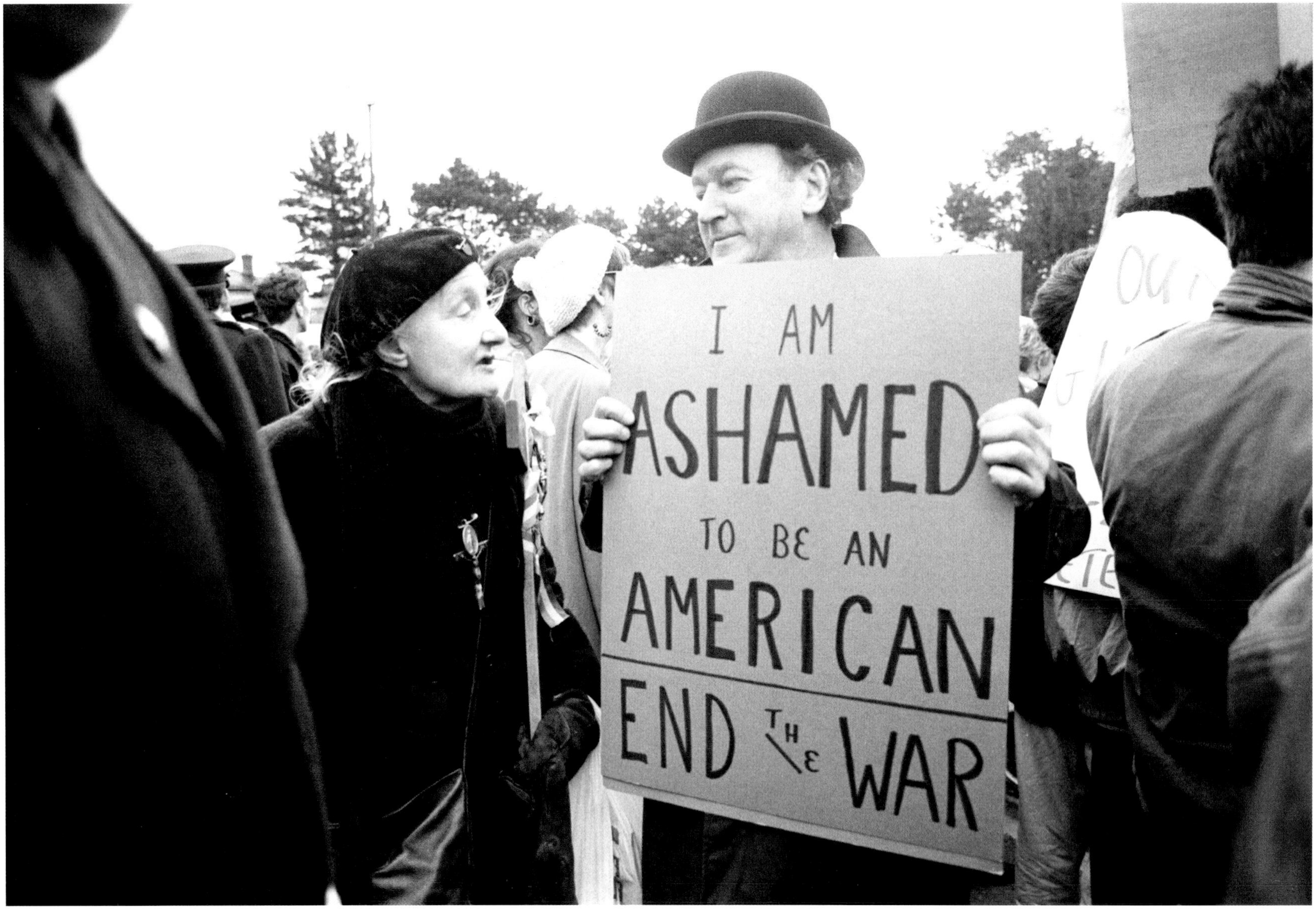
I AM
ASHAMED
TO BE AN
AMERICAN
END THE WAR

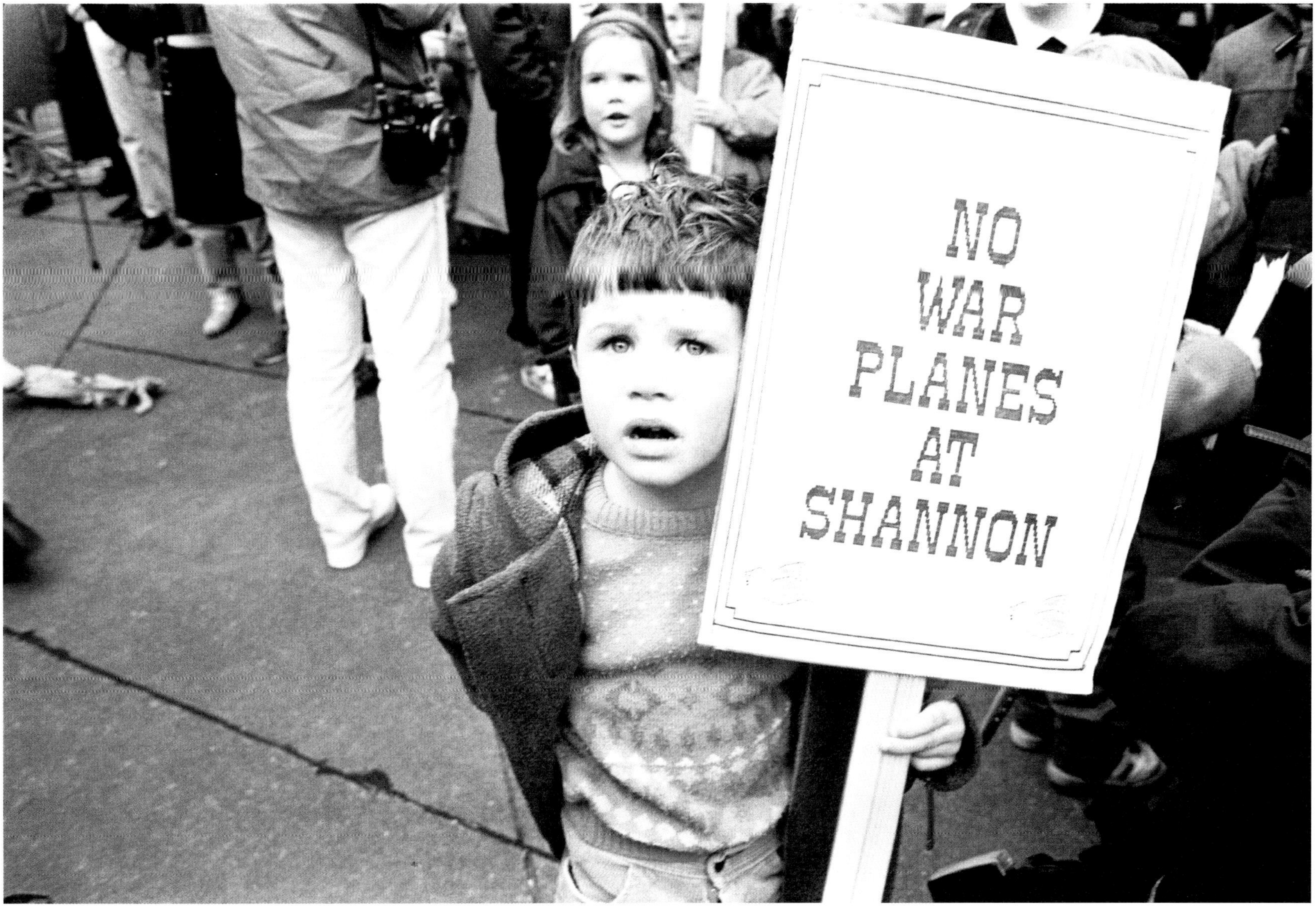
NO
WAR
PLANES
AT
SHANNON

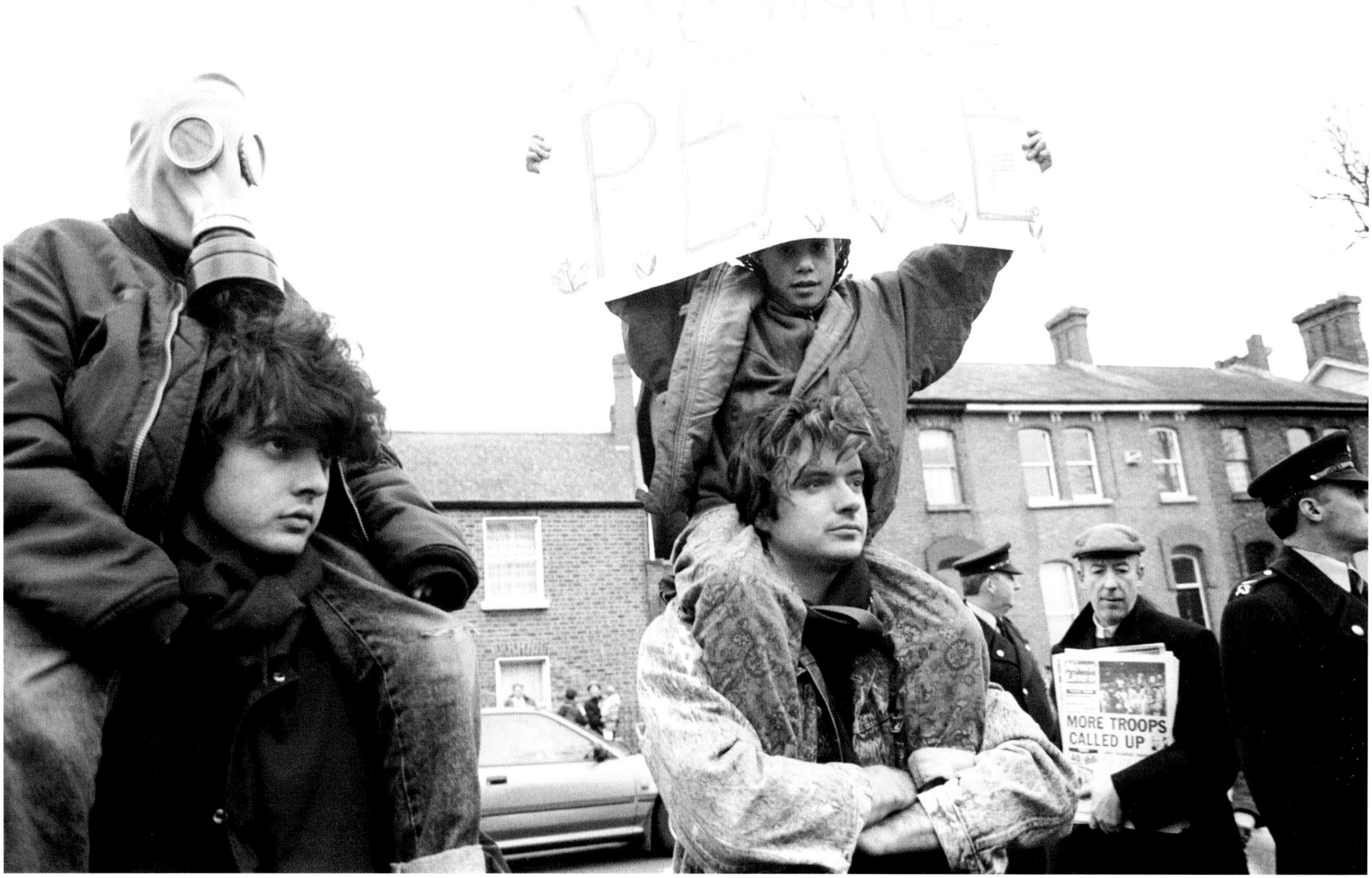
PEACE
MORE TROOPS
CALLED UP

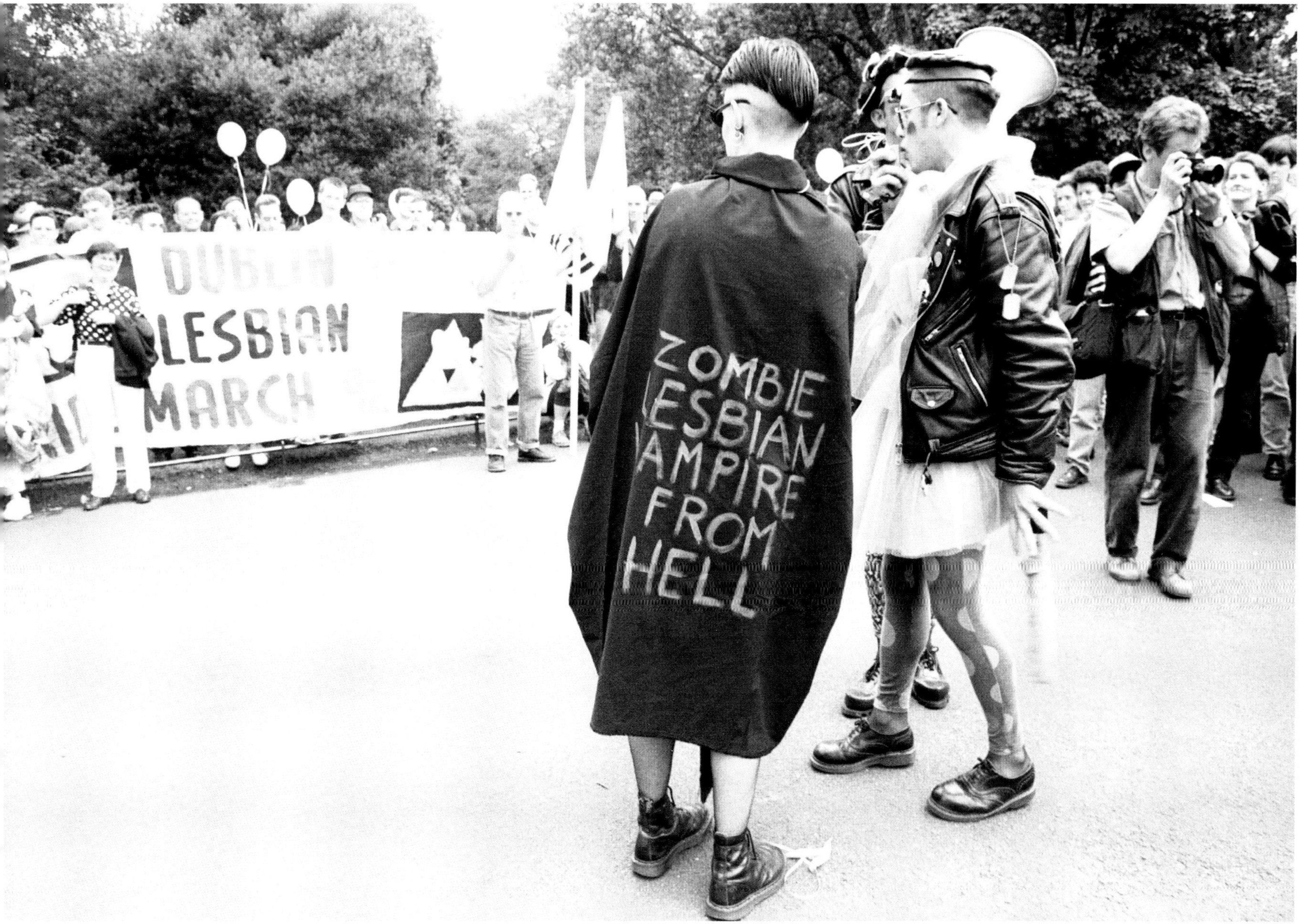
DUBLIN
LESBIAN
MARCH
ZOMBIE
LESBIAN
VAMPIRE
FROM
HELL

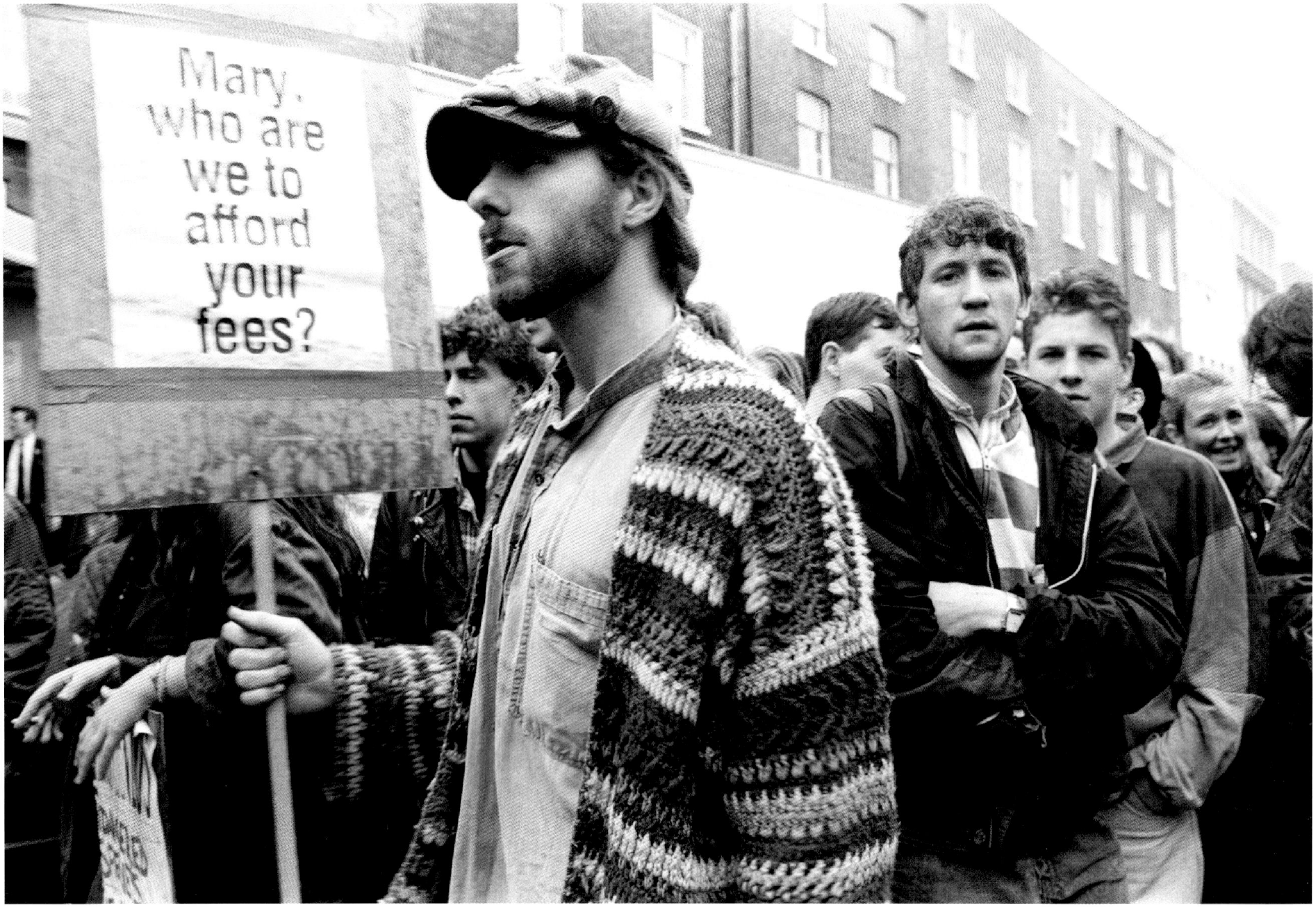
Mary.
who are
we to
afford
your
fees?

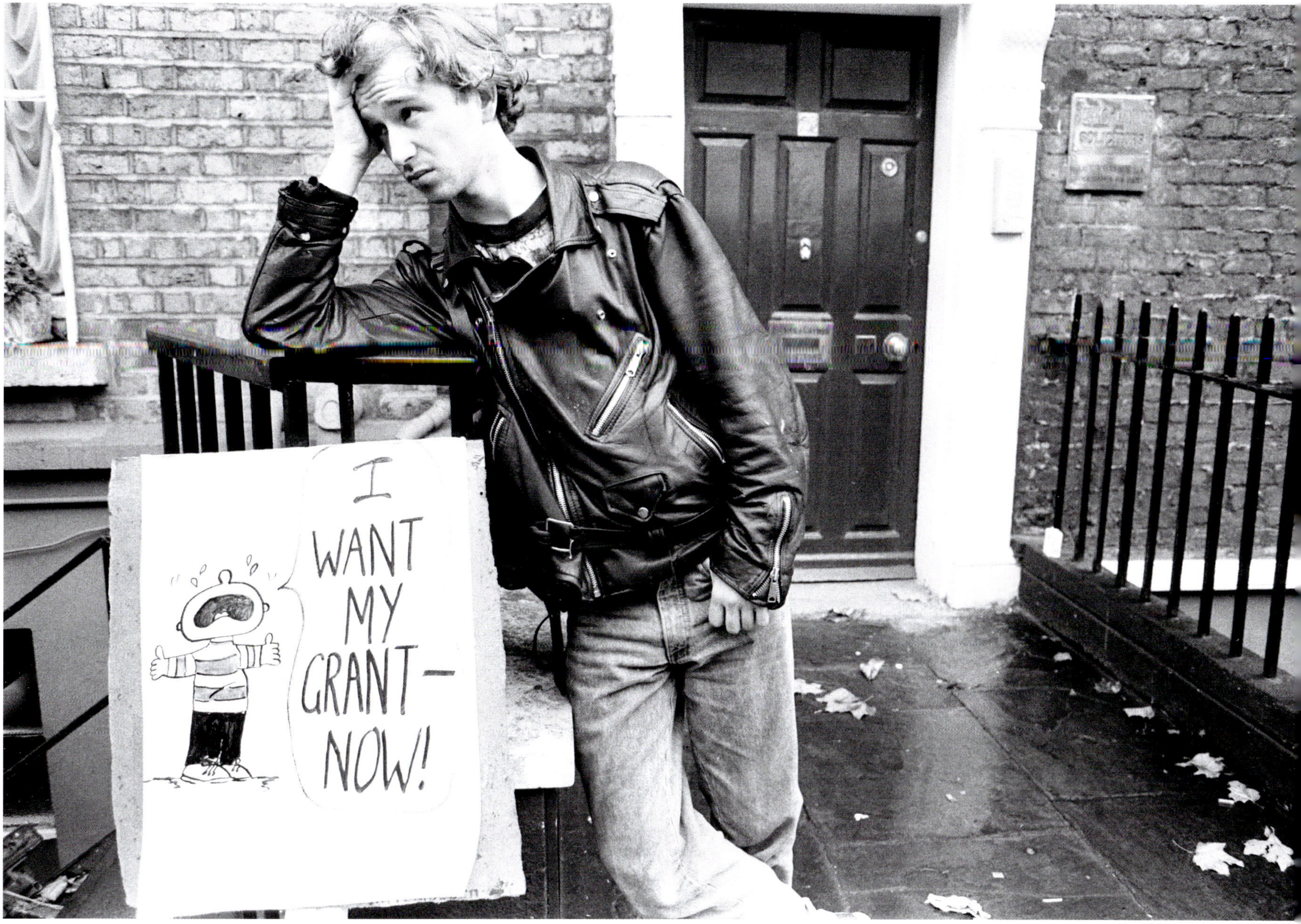
I WANT MY GRANT– NOW!

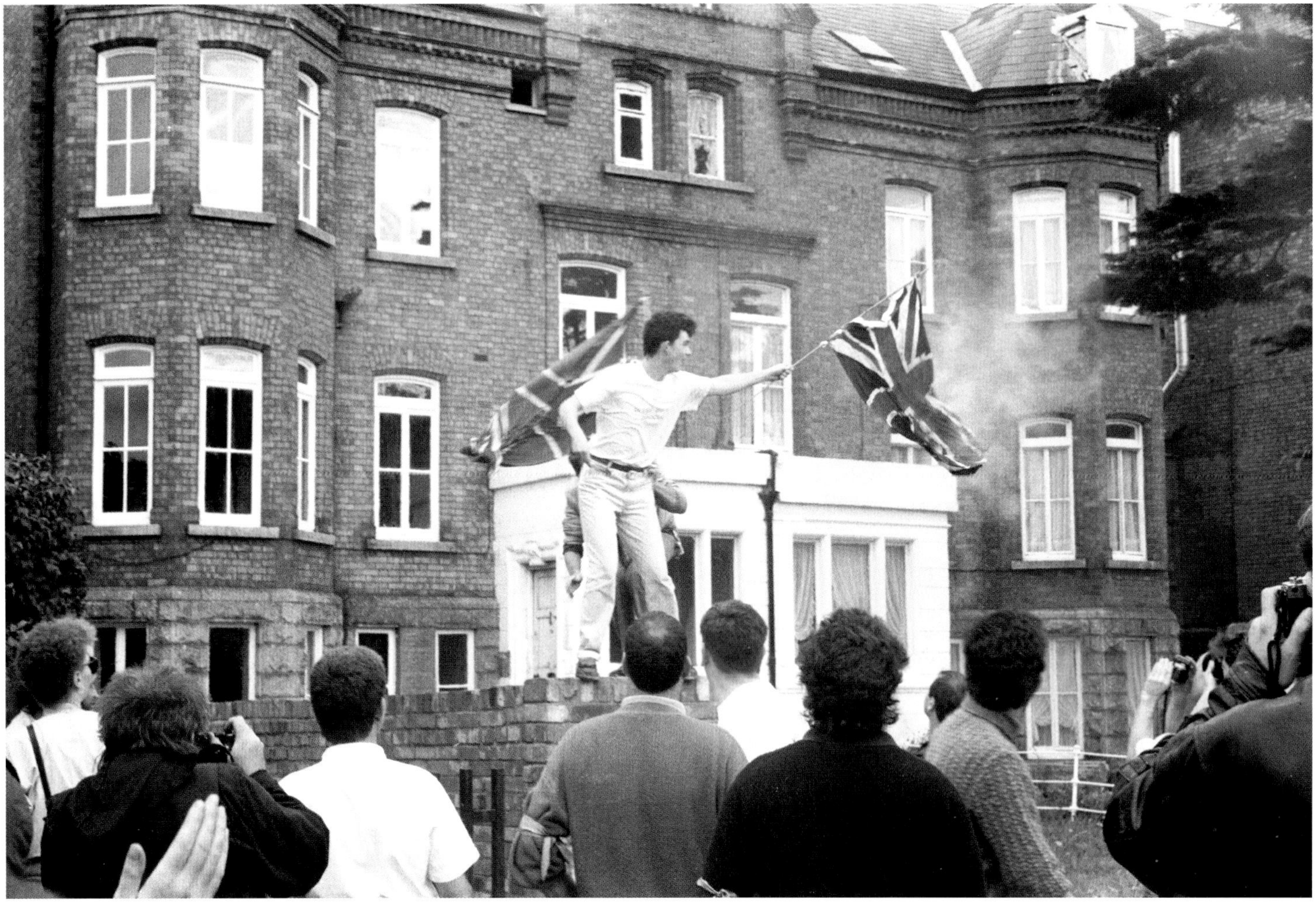

61

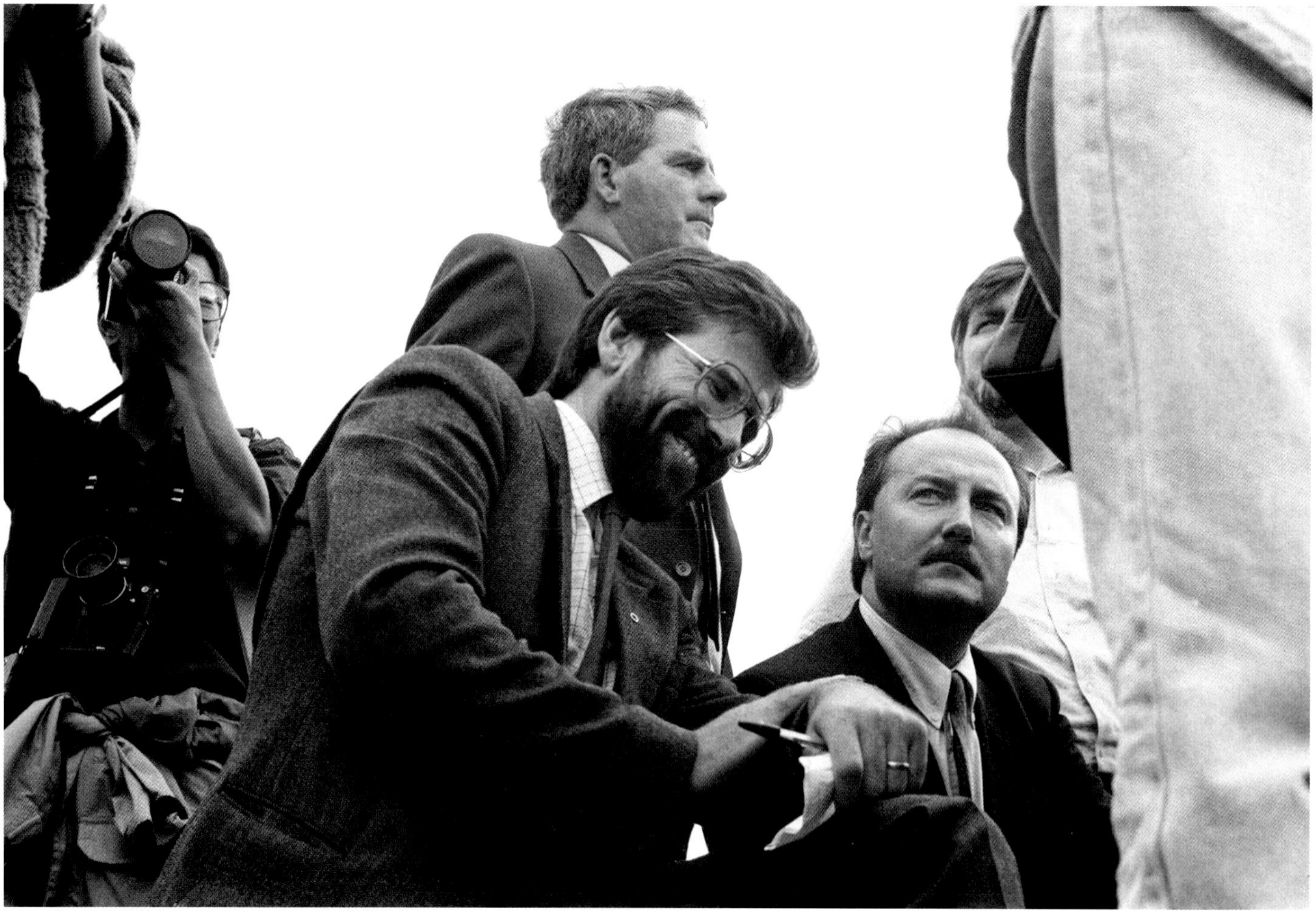

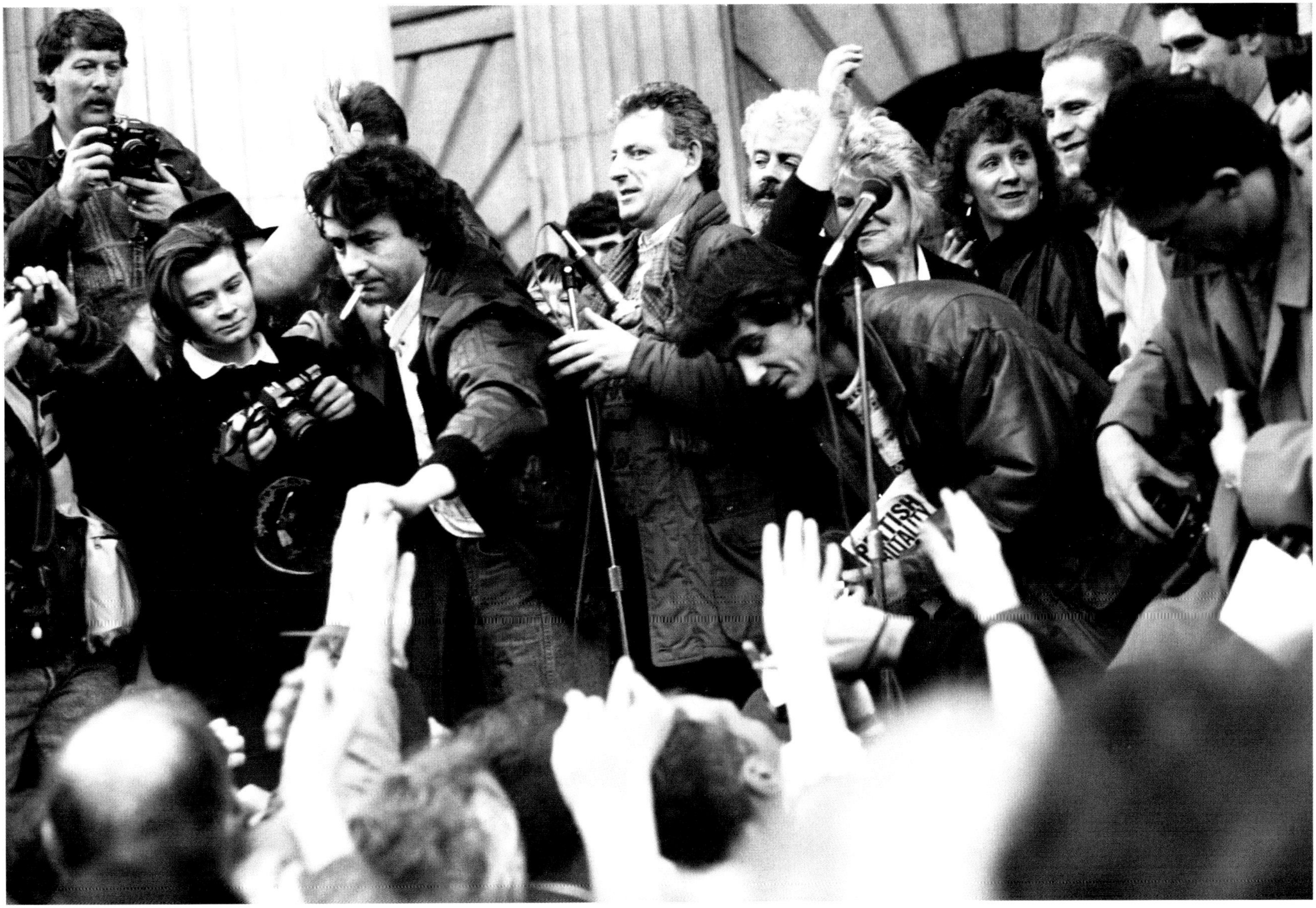

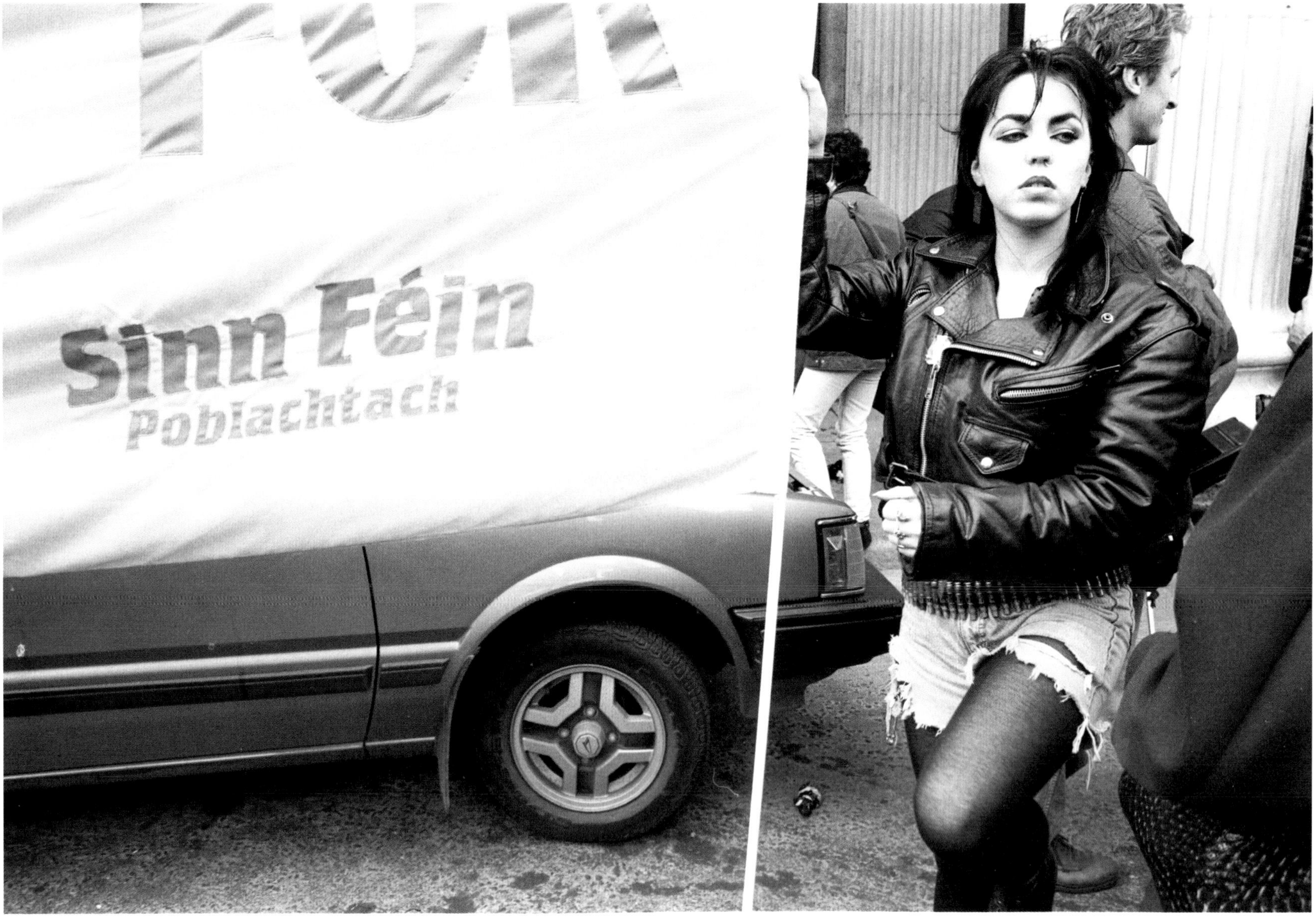
Sinn Féin
Poblachtach

65

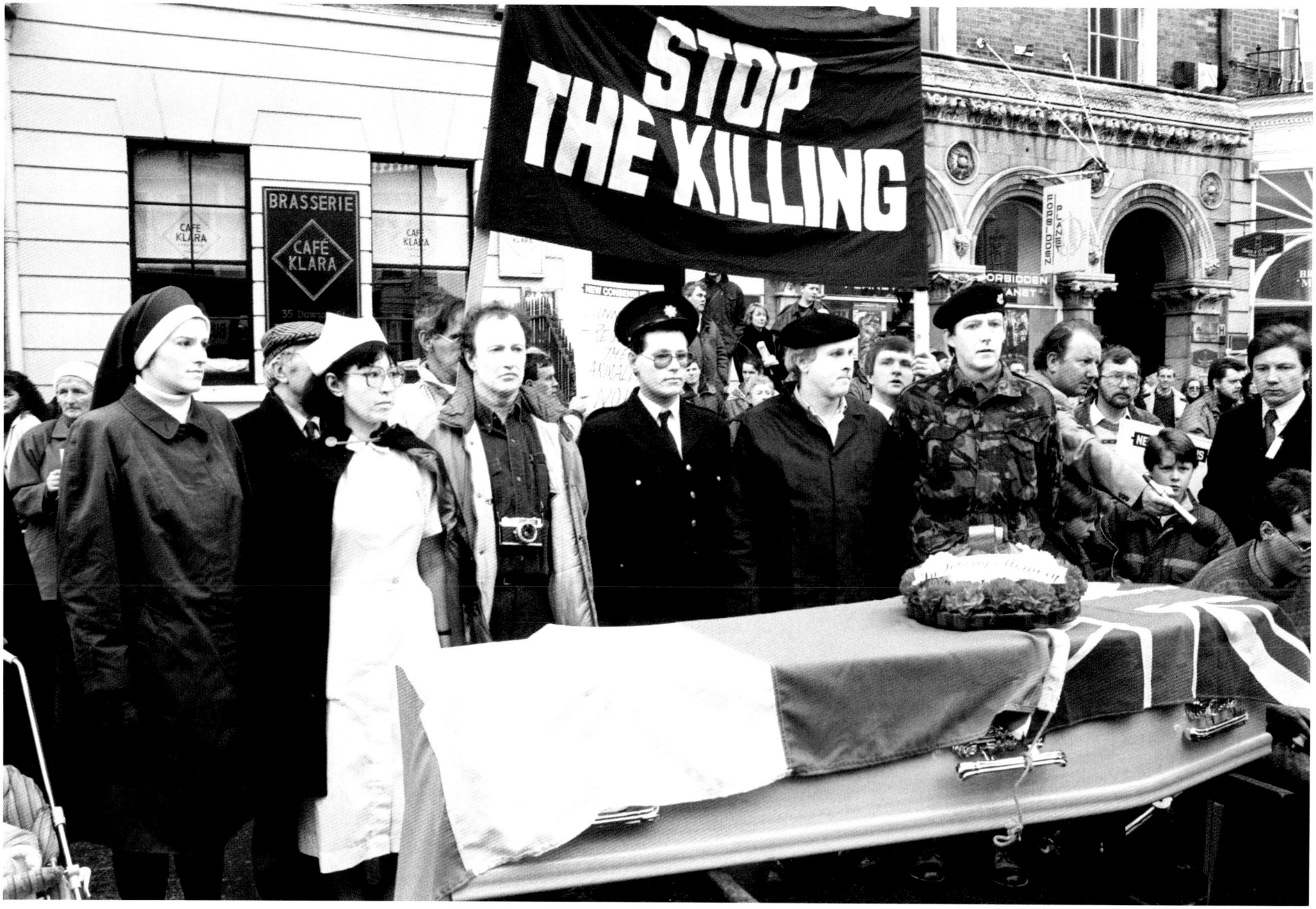
STOP
THE XILLING
BRASSERIE
CAFÉ
KLARA
FORBIDDEN
PLANET

IF THE POPE COULD GET PREGNANT..
PREMIER
FOR LIFE FOR CHOICE
I'M SUICIDAL WHY DON'T U BELIEVE ME?
YOUTH FOR CHOICE
FOR LIFE FOR CHOICE
I'M X AND I NEED AN ABORTION
YOUTH FOR CHOICE
IF YOU CANT TRUST ME WITH A CHOICE HOW CAN YOU TRUST ME WITH A CHILD?
FOR LIFE FOR CHOICE
I WAS RAPED. I'M 15. I NEED COMPASSION AND CHOICE
YOUTH FOR CHOICE
RELATIONSHIP I DON'T WANT ANOTHER BABY
I'M PREGNANT AND I'M HAPPY
MY MOTHER HAD A CHOICE

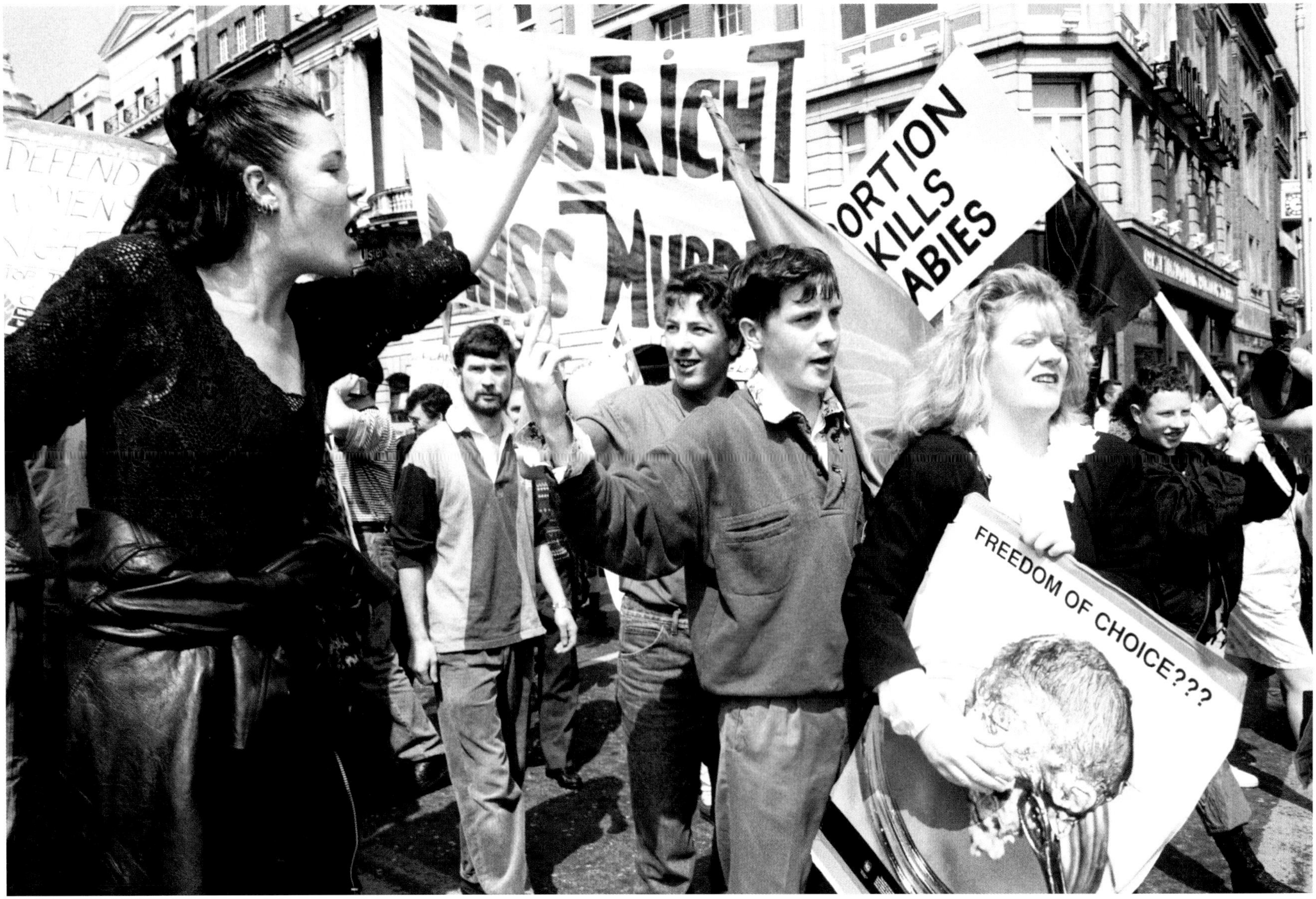
ORTION
KILLS
ABIES
FREEDOM OF CHOICE???

69

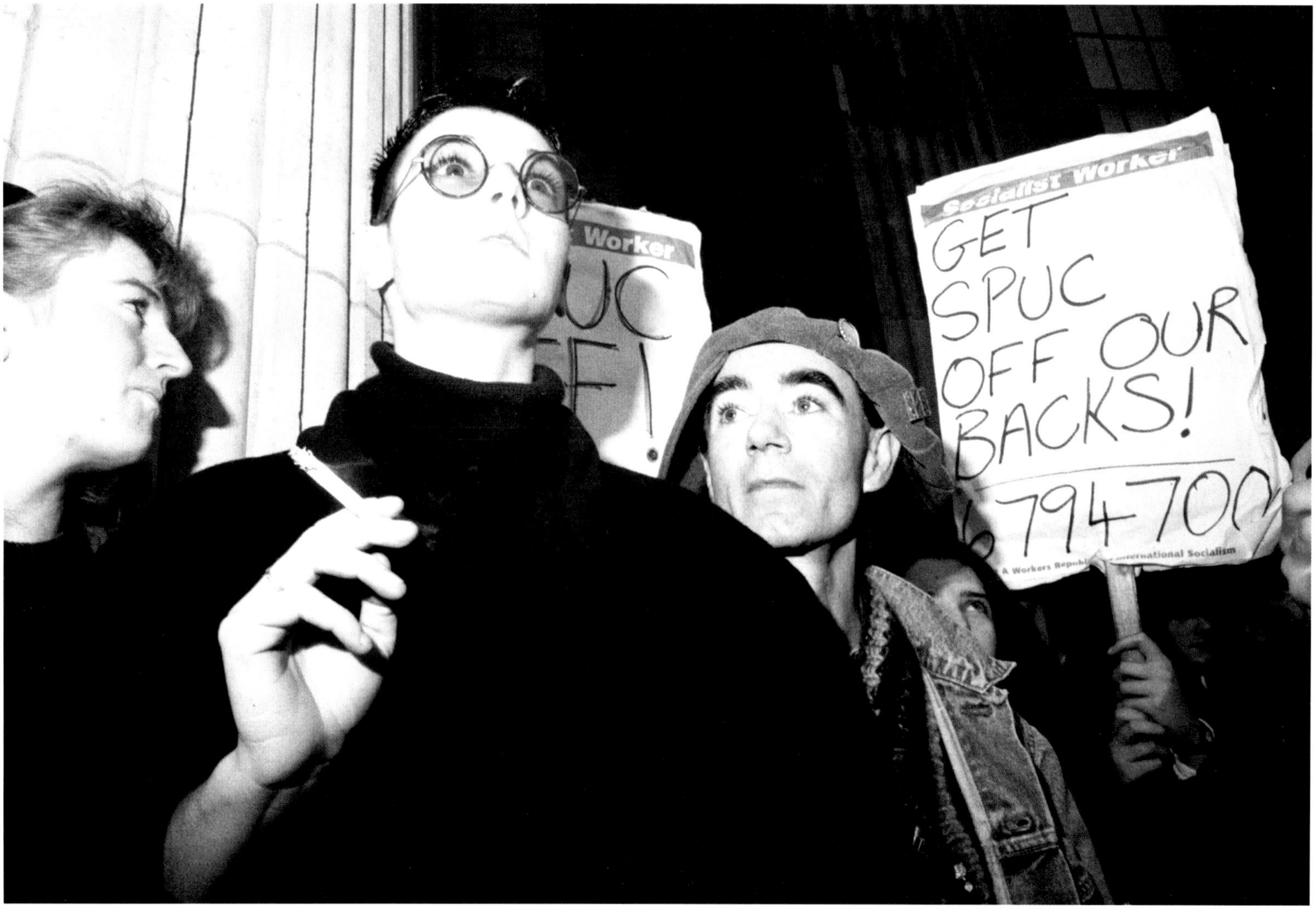
Worker
Socialist Worker
GET SPUC OFF OUR BACKS!

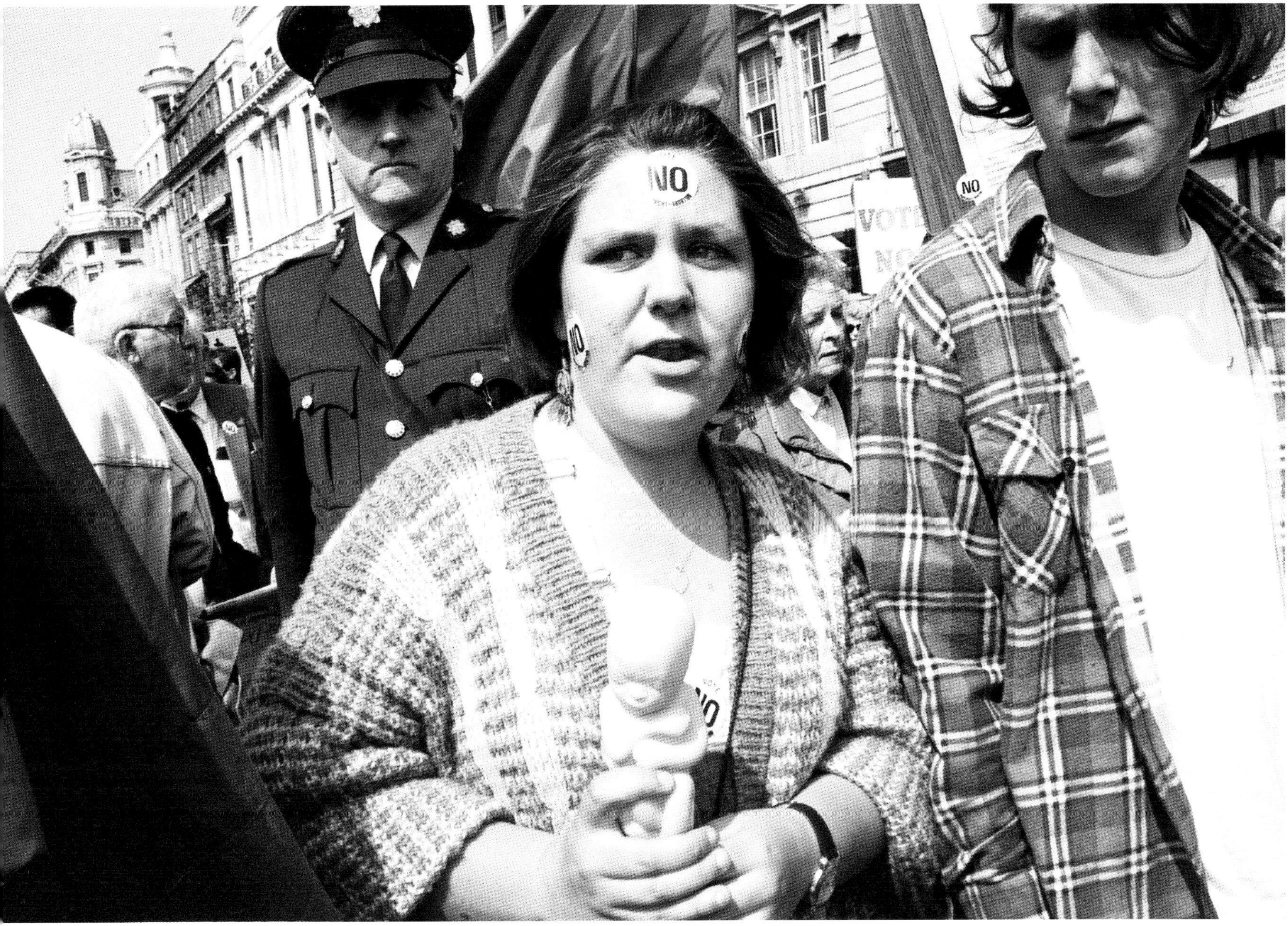
NO
VOTE

RED ACTION
ABORTION INFORMATION
01-6794700
For a Workers' Fightback against European Capitalism

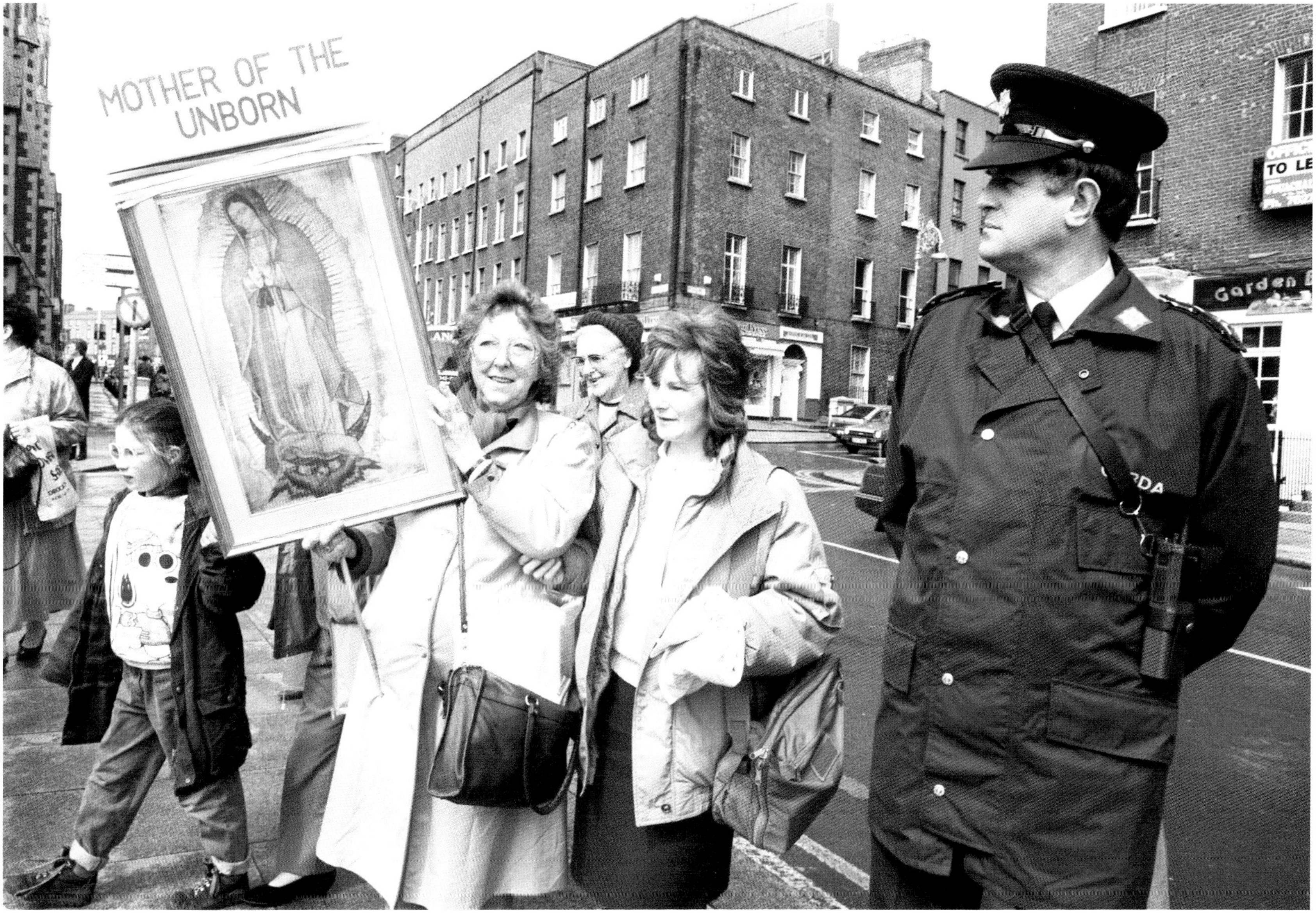
MOTHER OF THE
UNBORN

Week-Old Baby — Before & After
After torn and stretched body
ocialist
orker
Socialist W
SCRAP

WANTED
for Treachery &
Extradition of
Political prisoners
WANTED
for Treachery &
Extradition of
Political prisoners

NIST PARTY
RELAND
WANT
for Treachery &
Extradition of
Political prisoners
PEDESTRIANS
HAUGHEY'S

77

Socialist Worker
Student Society
SMASH
LE Pen's
Fascist's
BEARS
Power!

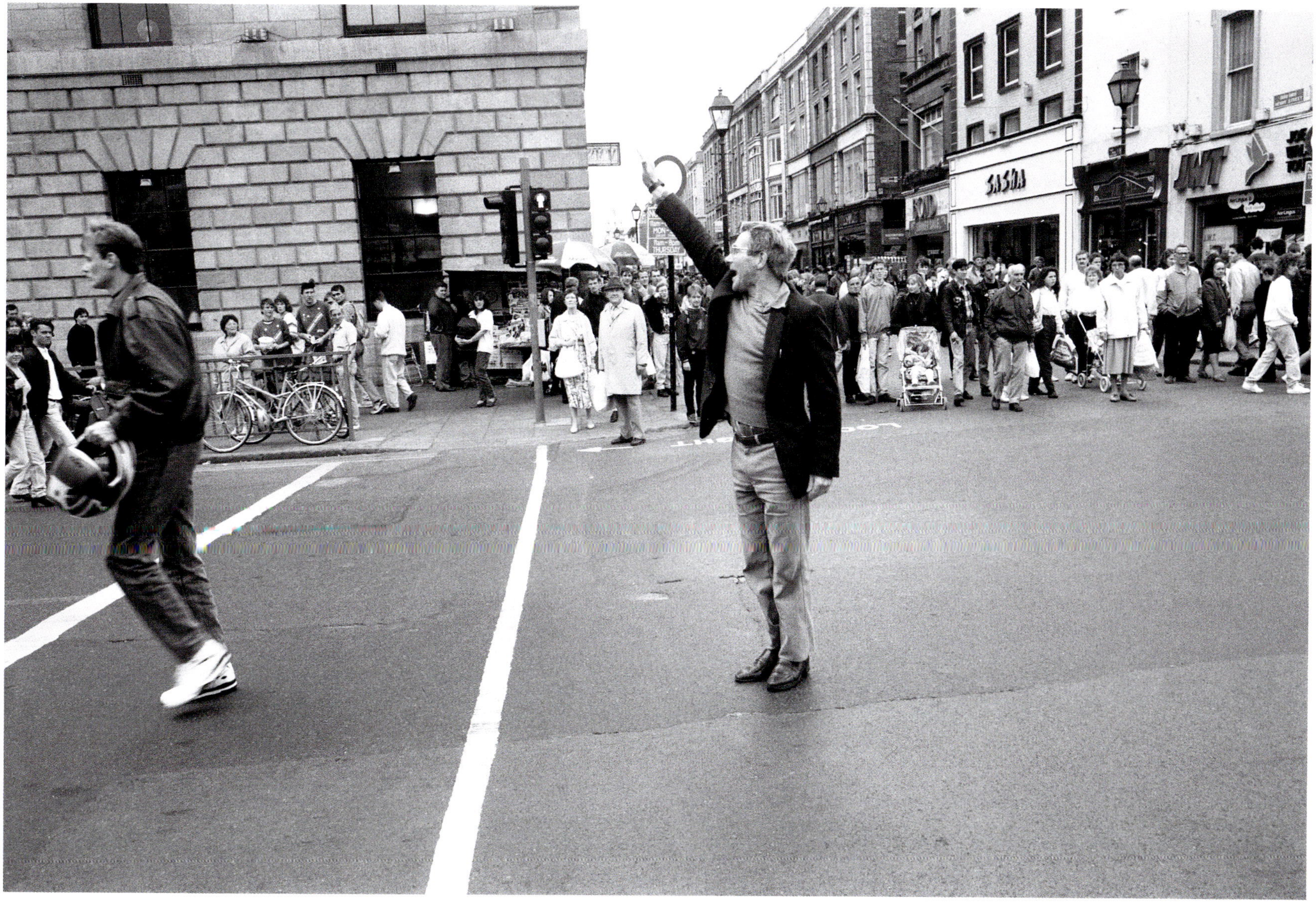
SASHA

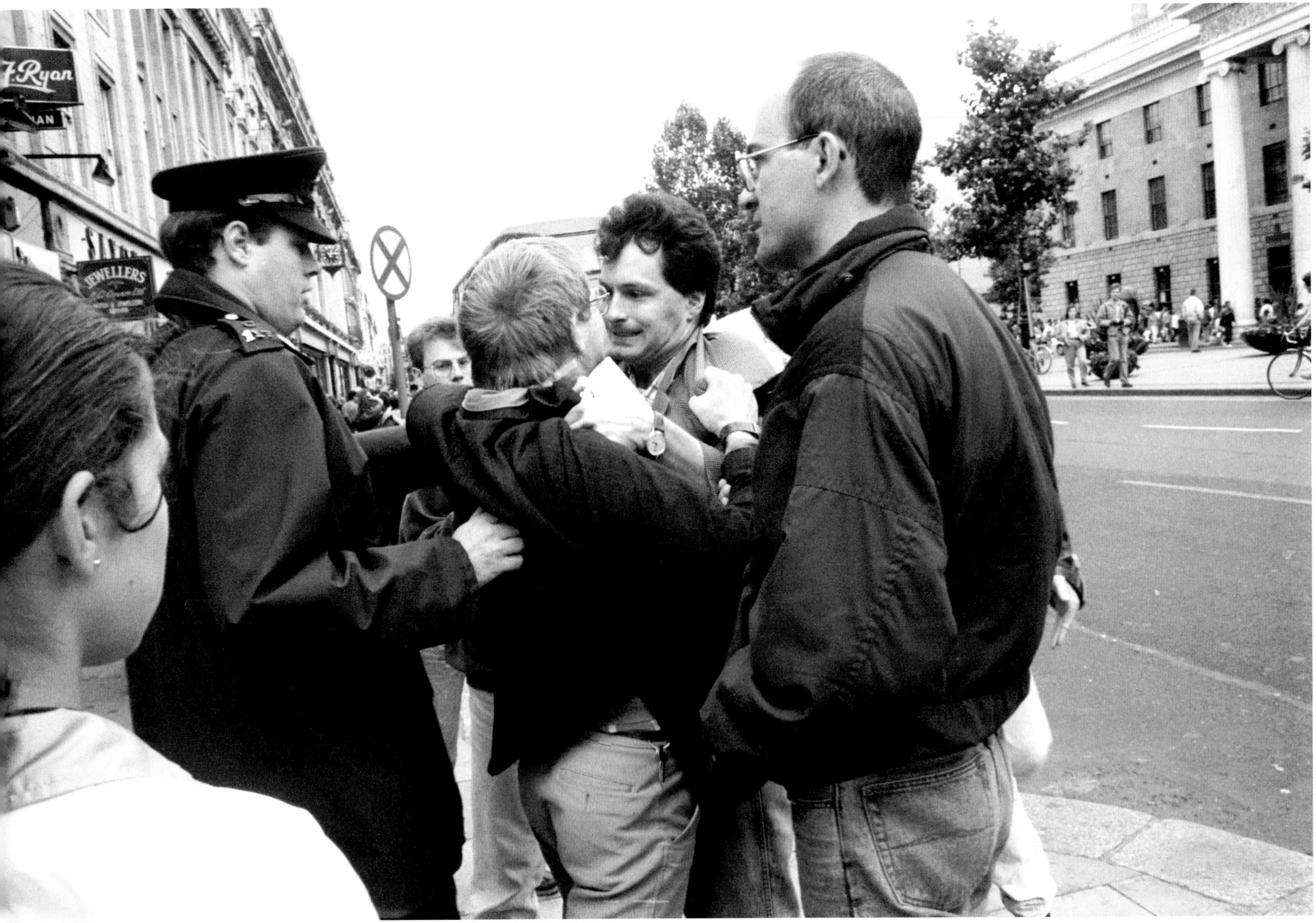
J.Ryan
JEWELLERS

81

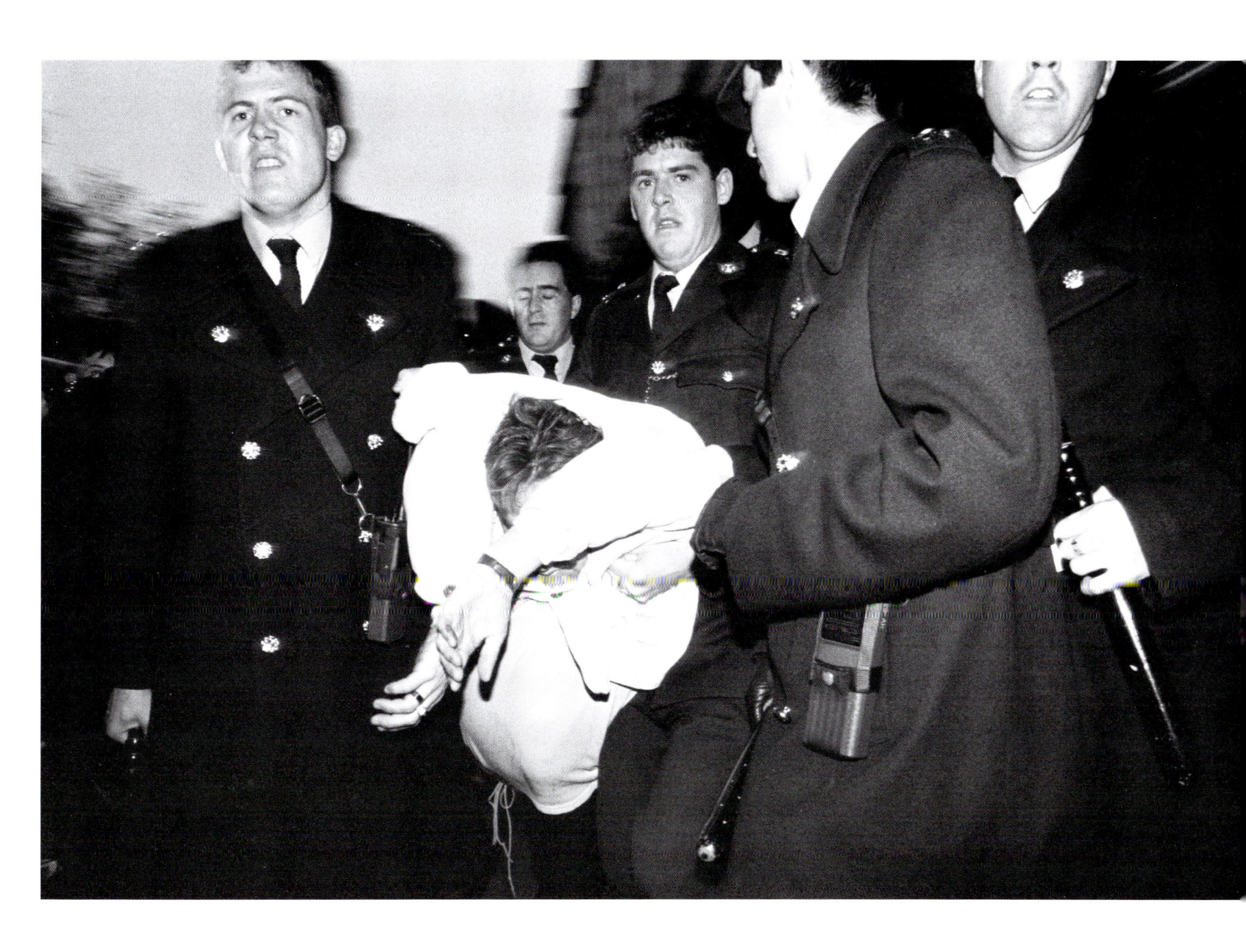

SMITHFIELD

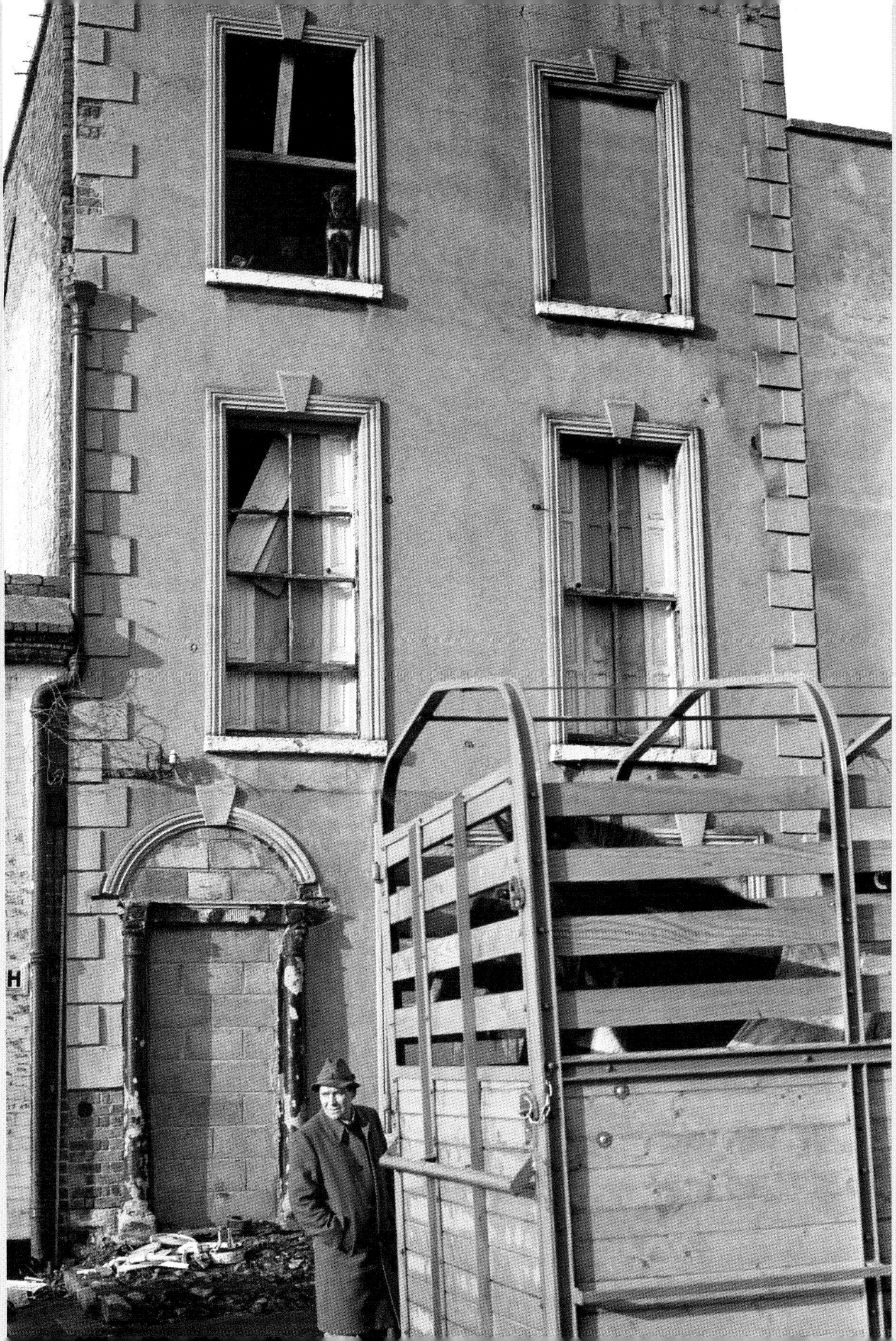
H

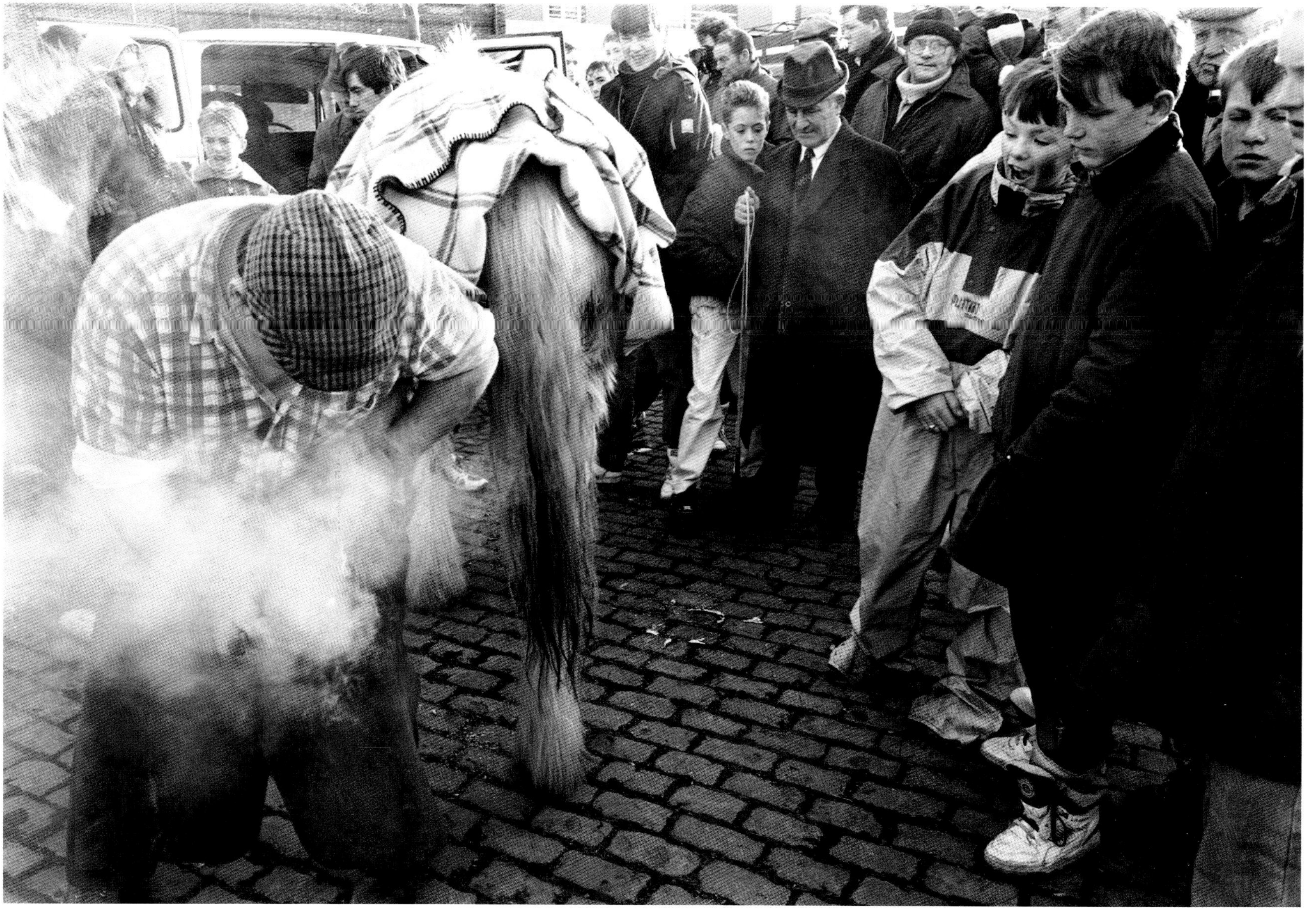

85

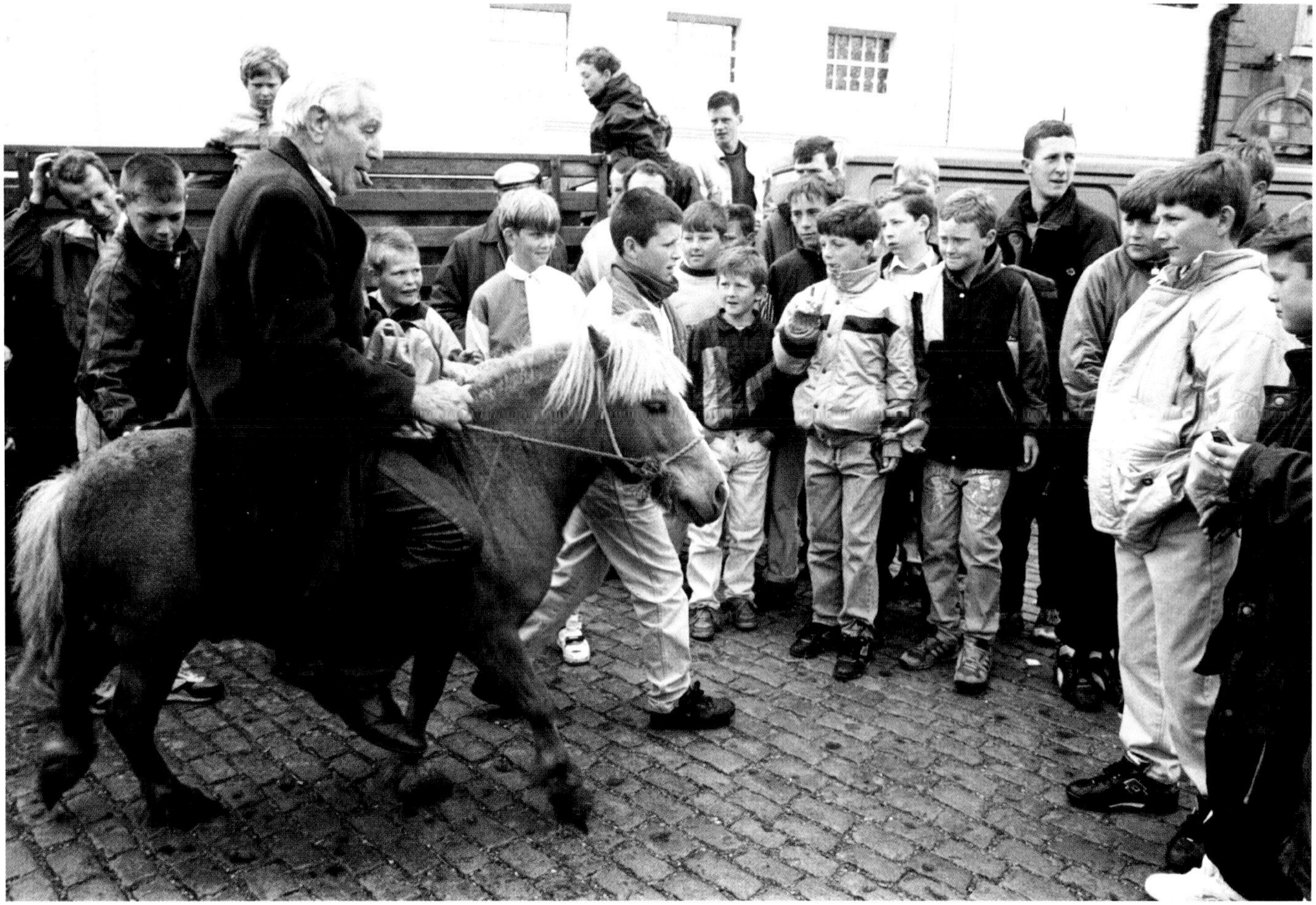

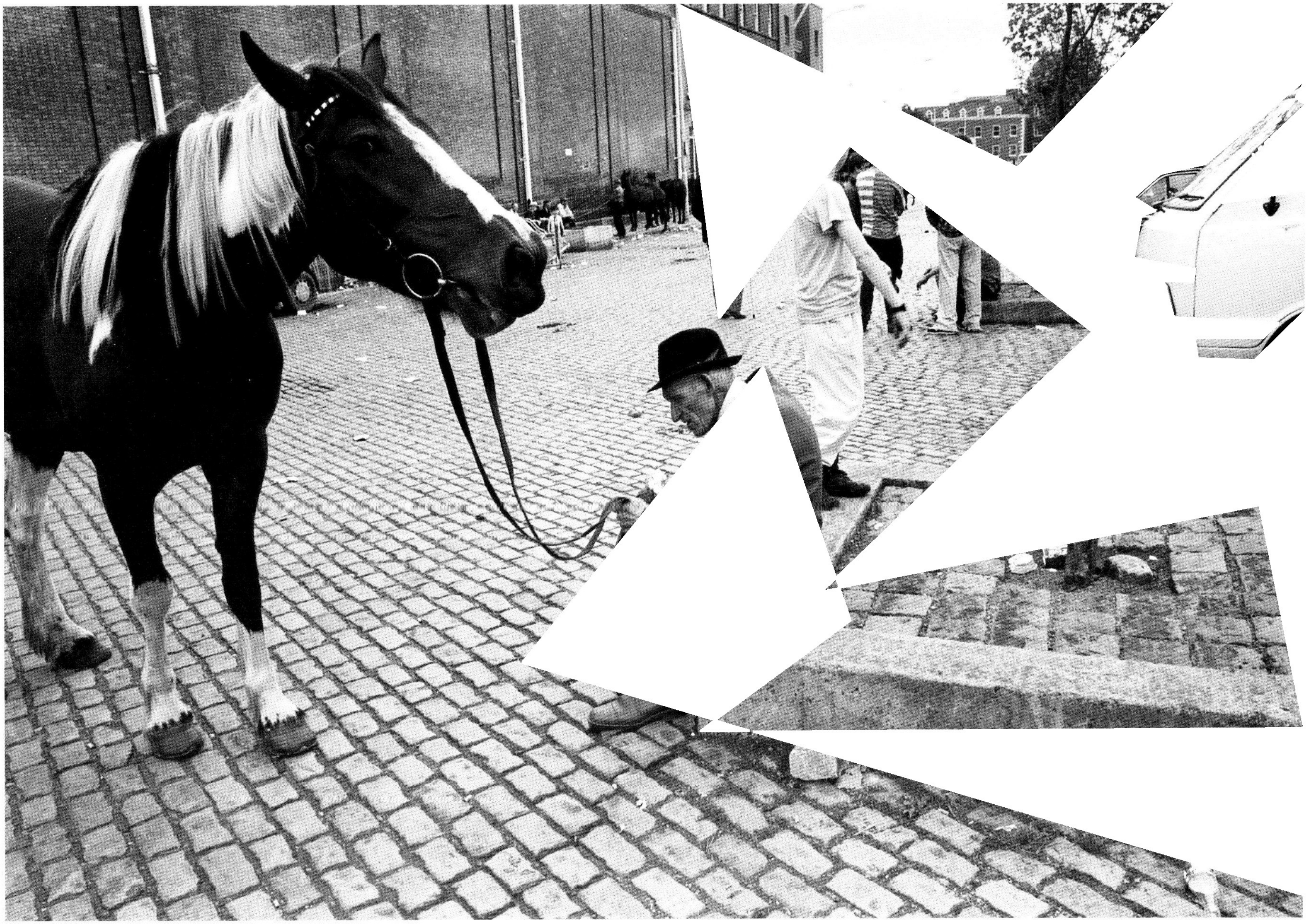

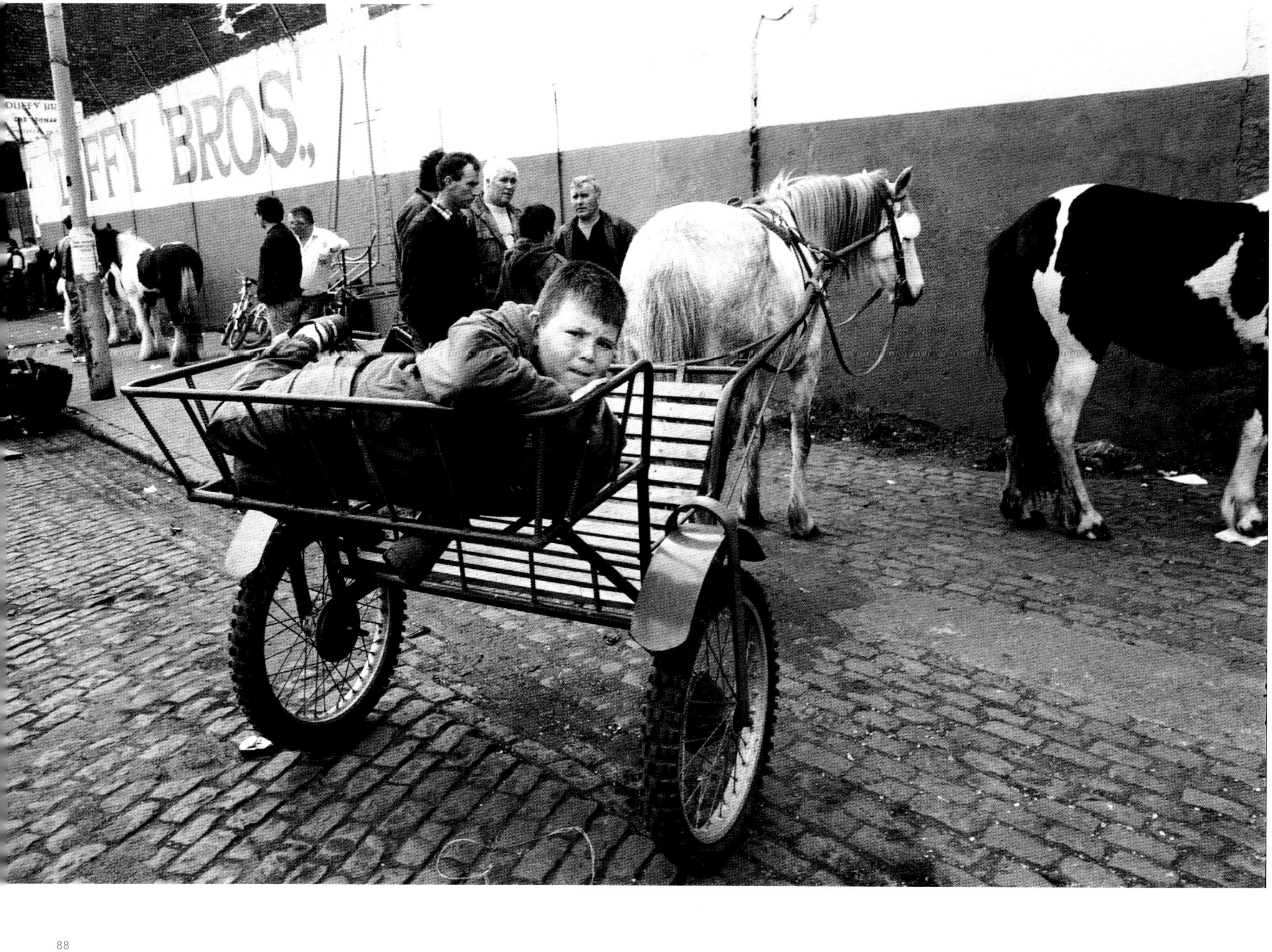
BROS.,

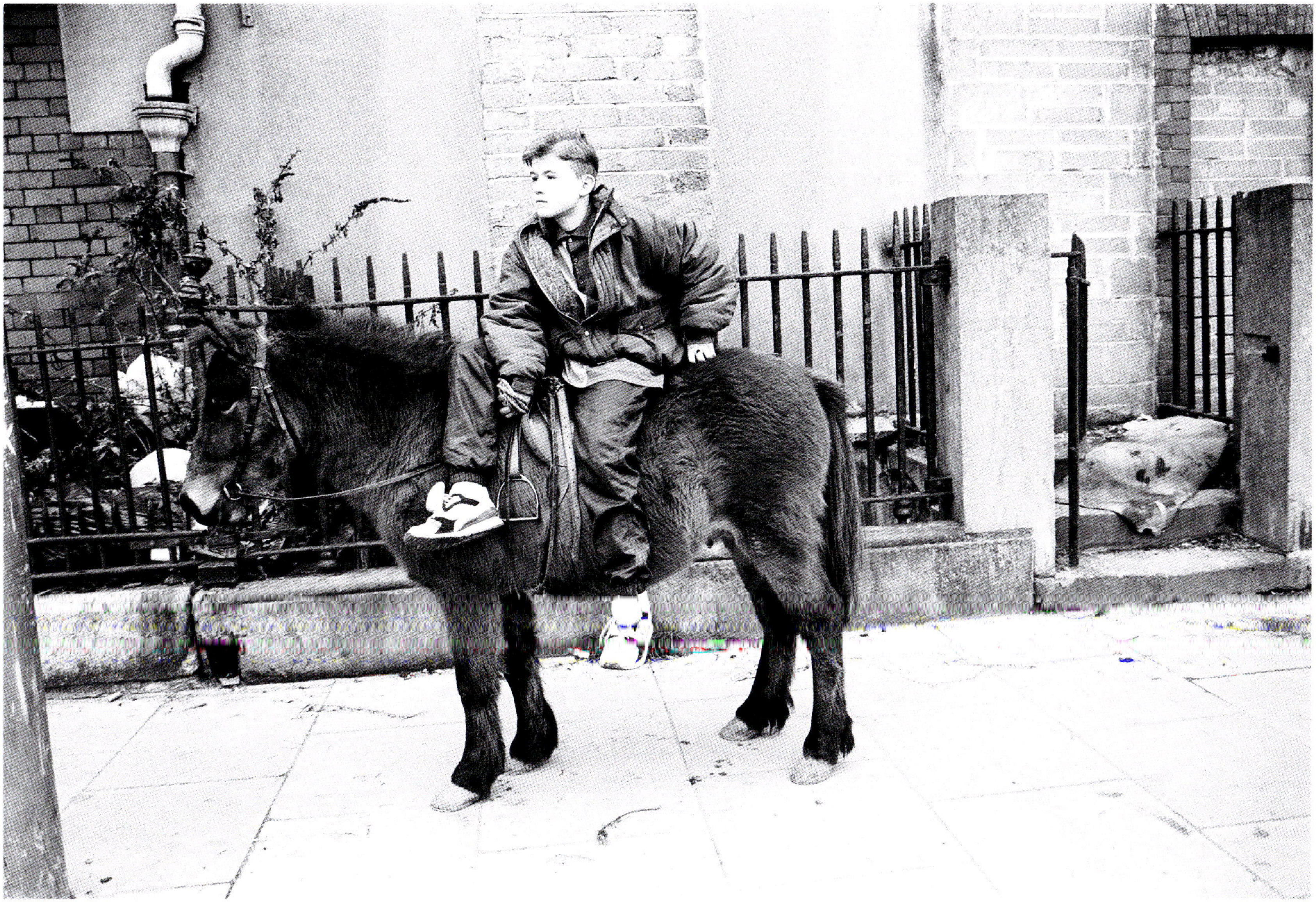

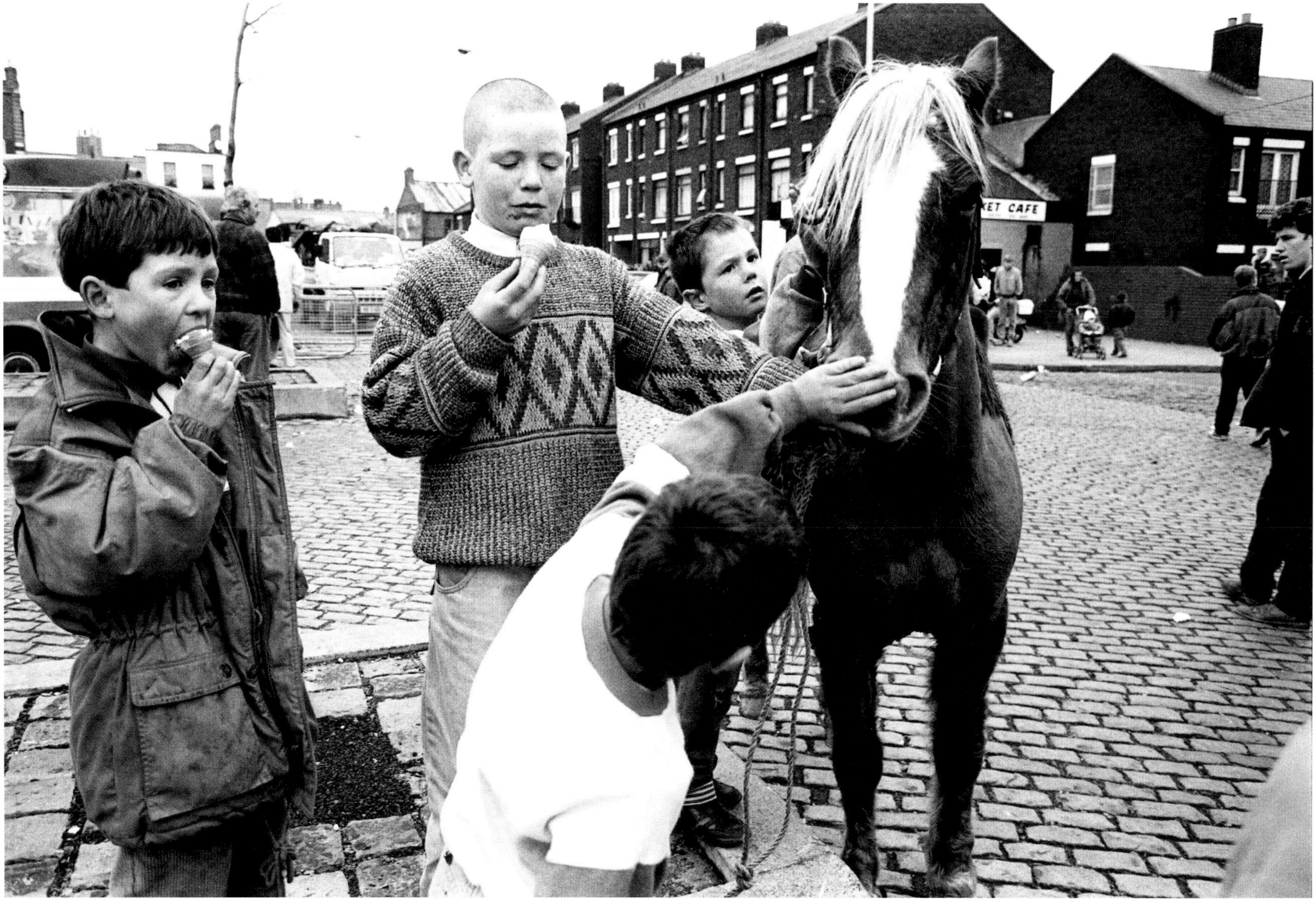
KET CAFE

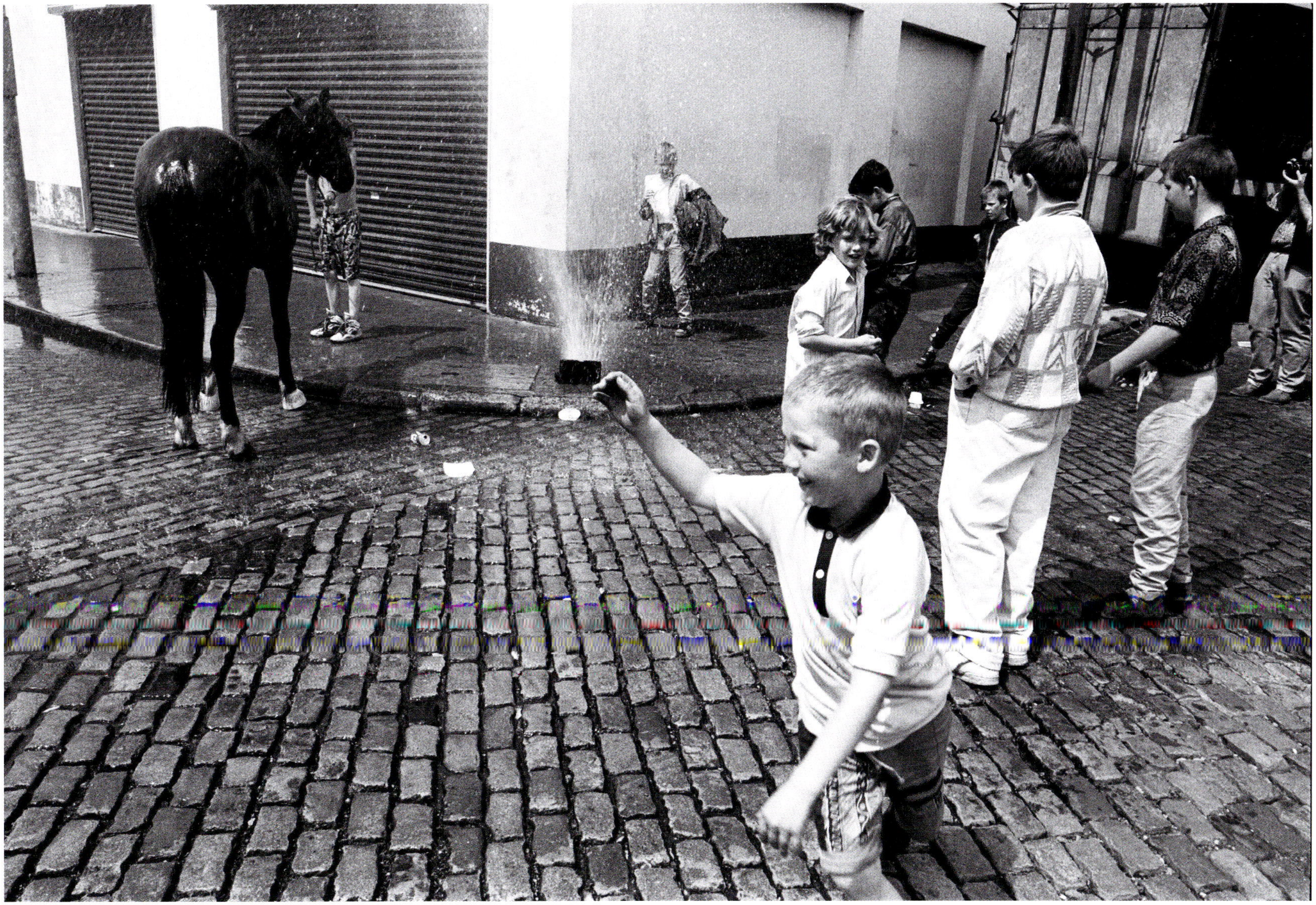

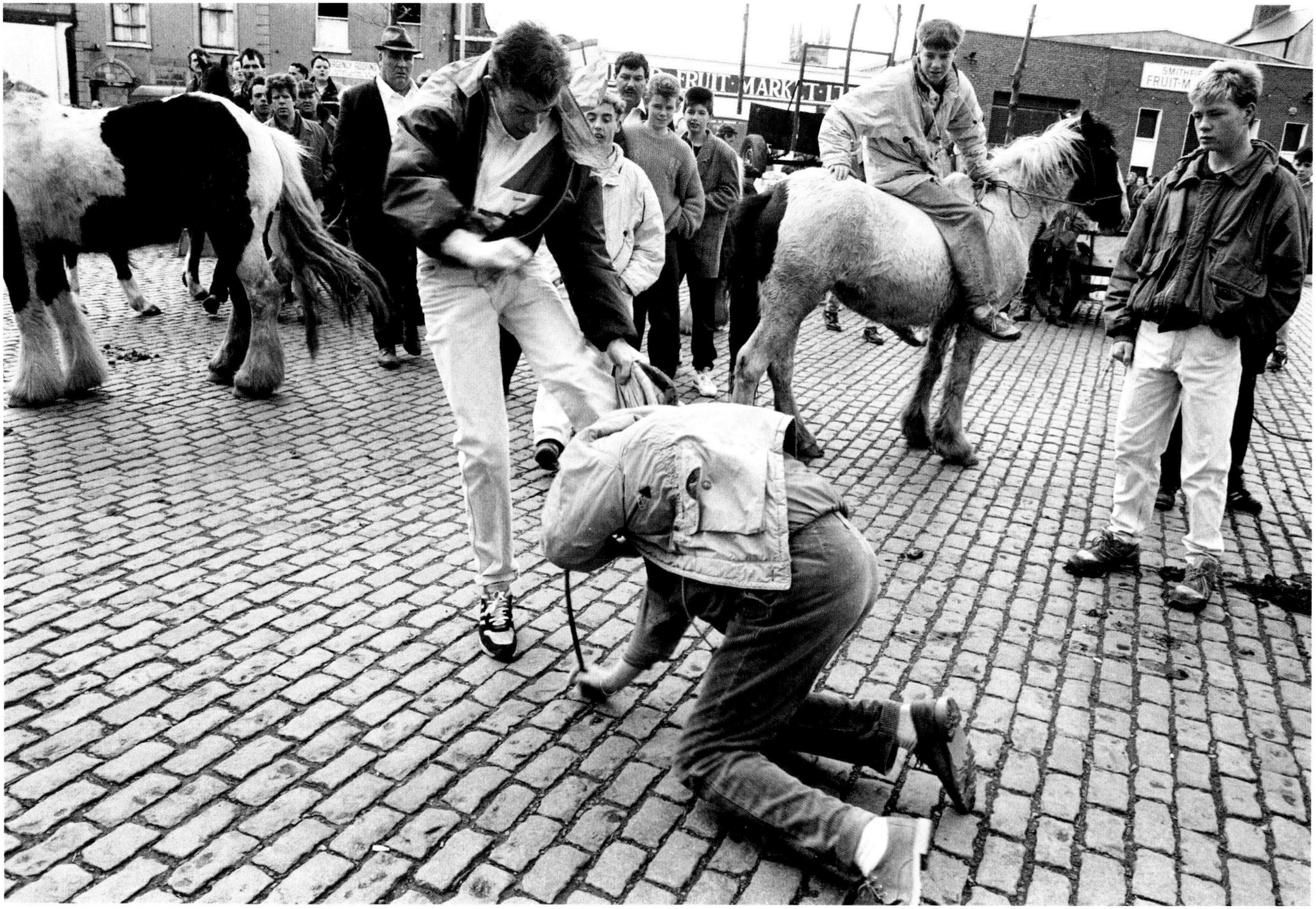

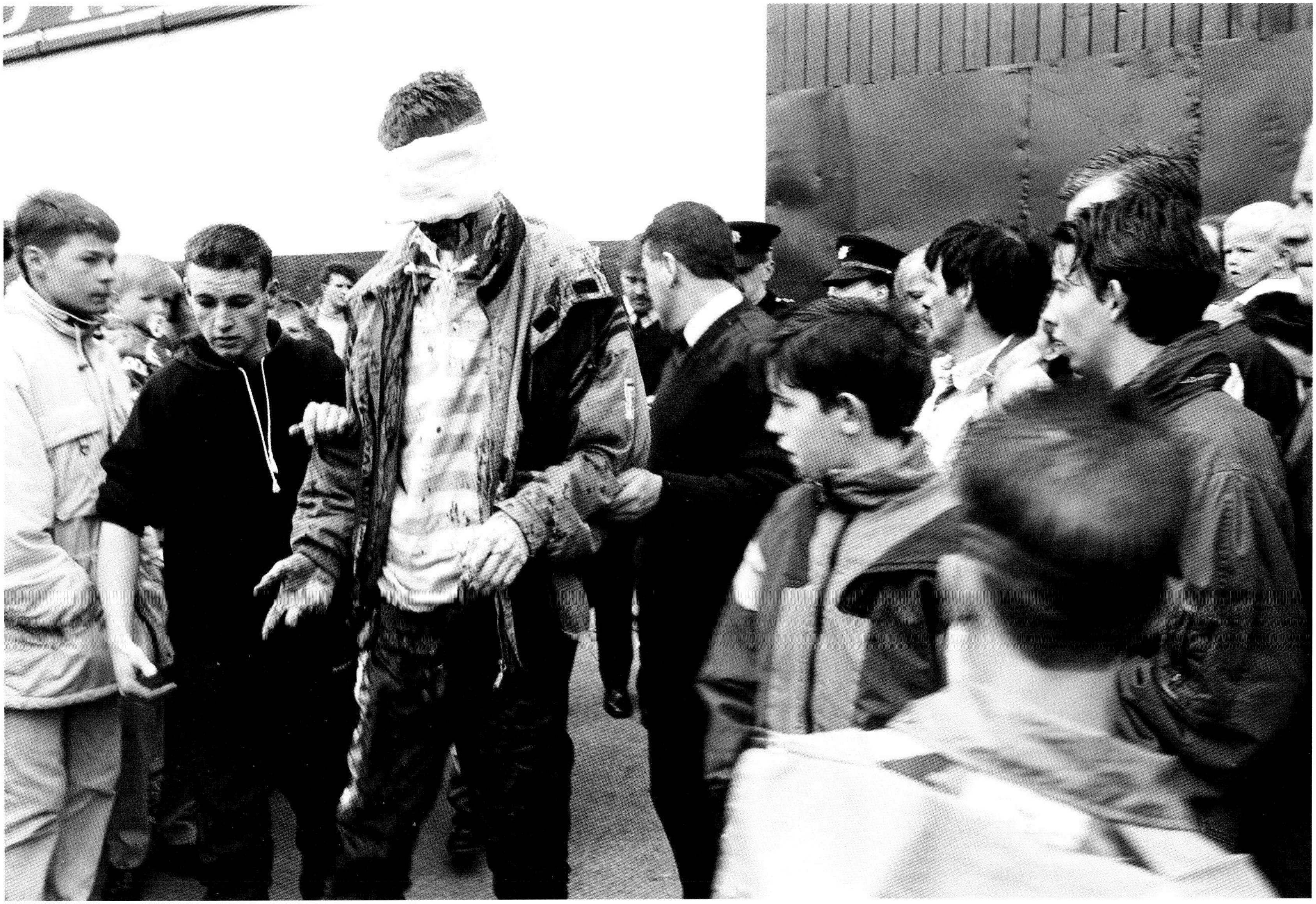

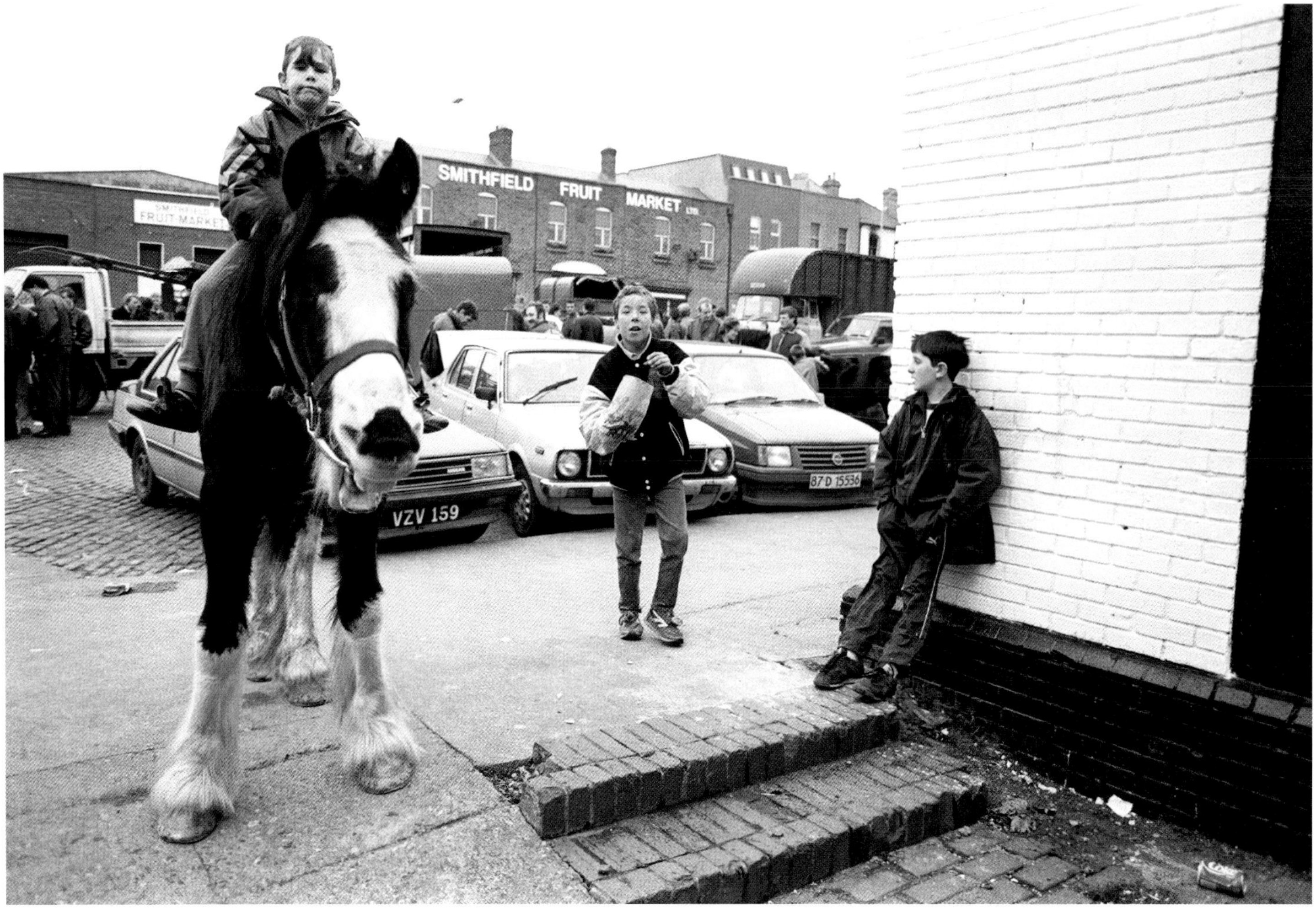
SMITHFIELD FRUIT MARKET
FRUIT MARKET
VZV 159
87 D 15536

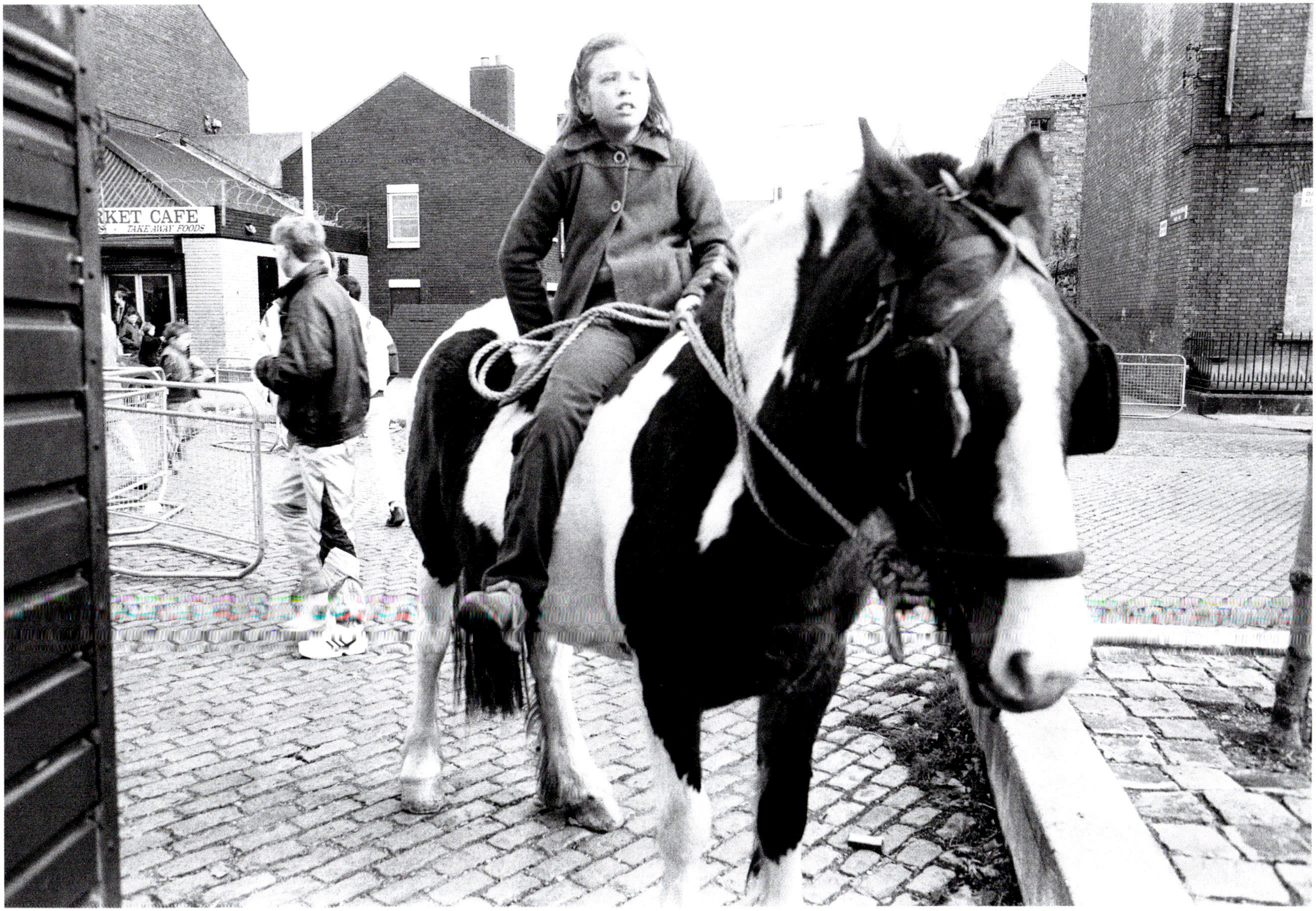
RKET CAFE
TAKE AWAY FOODS

96

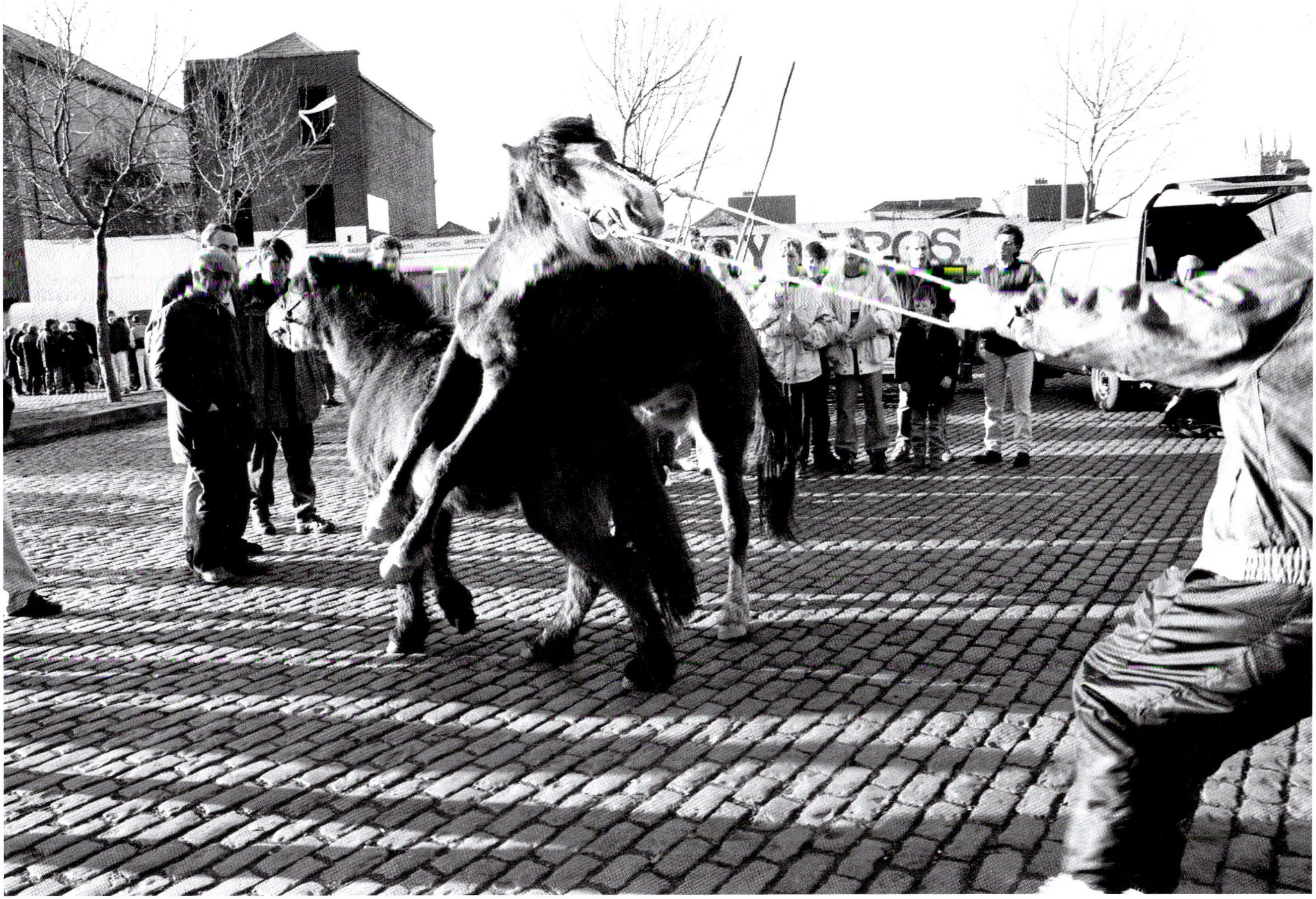

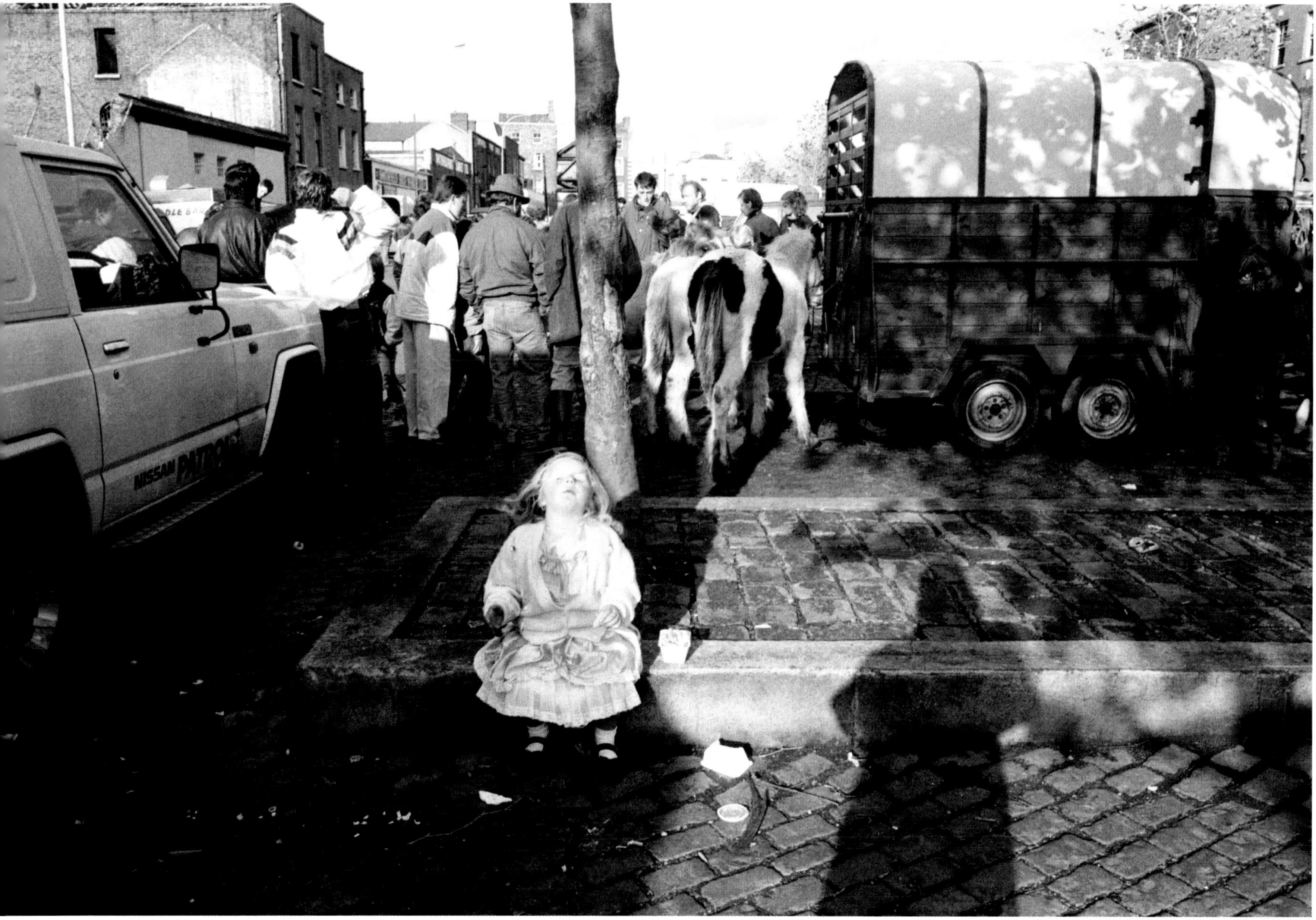
NISSAN

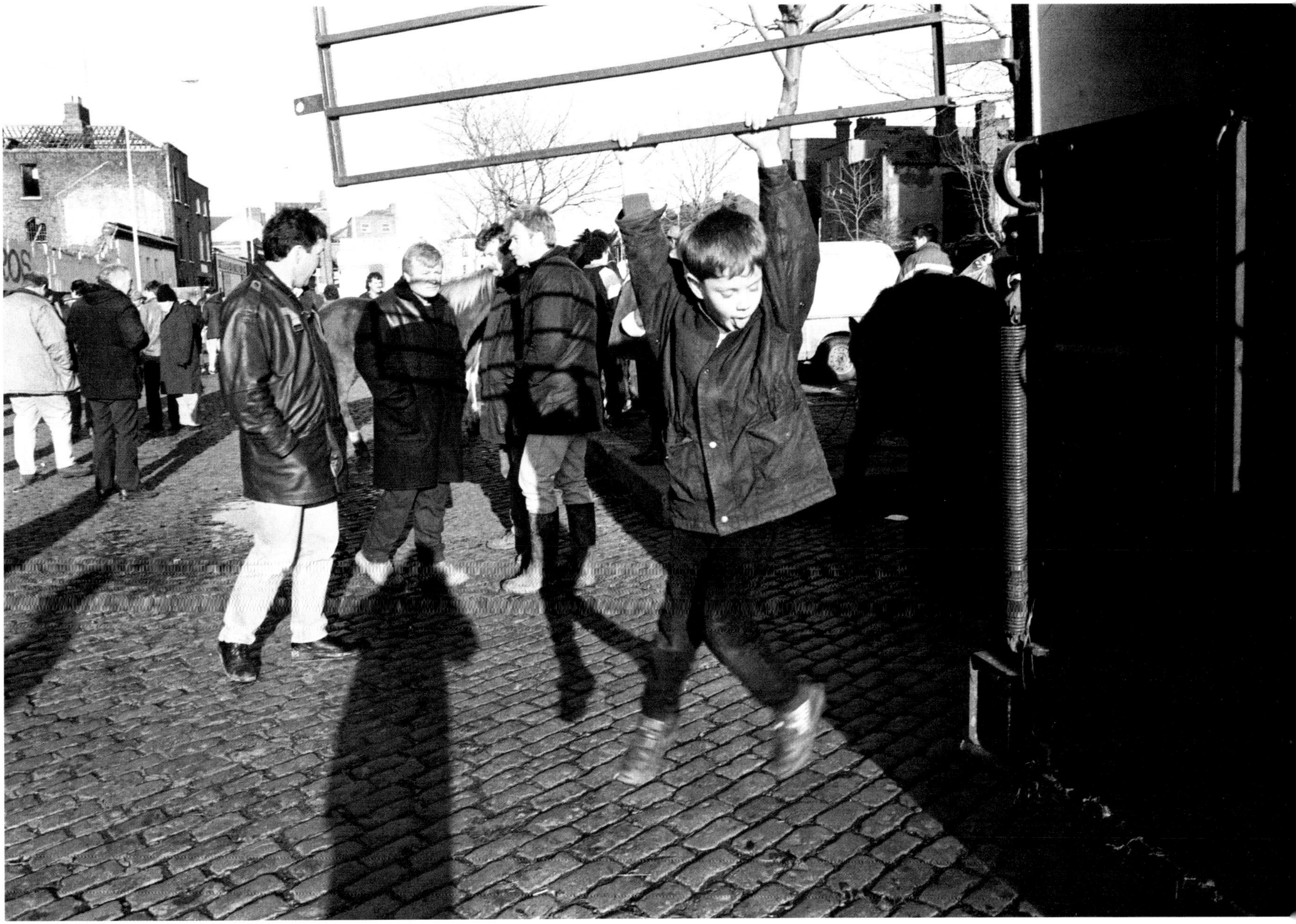

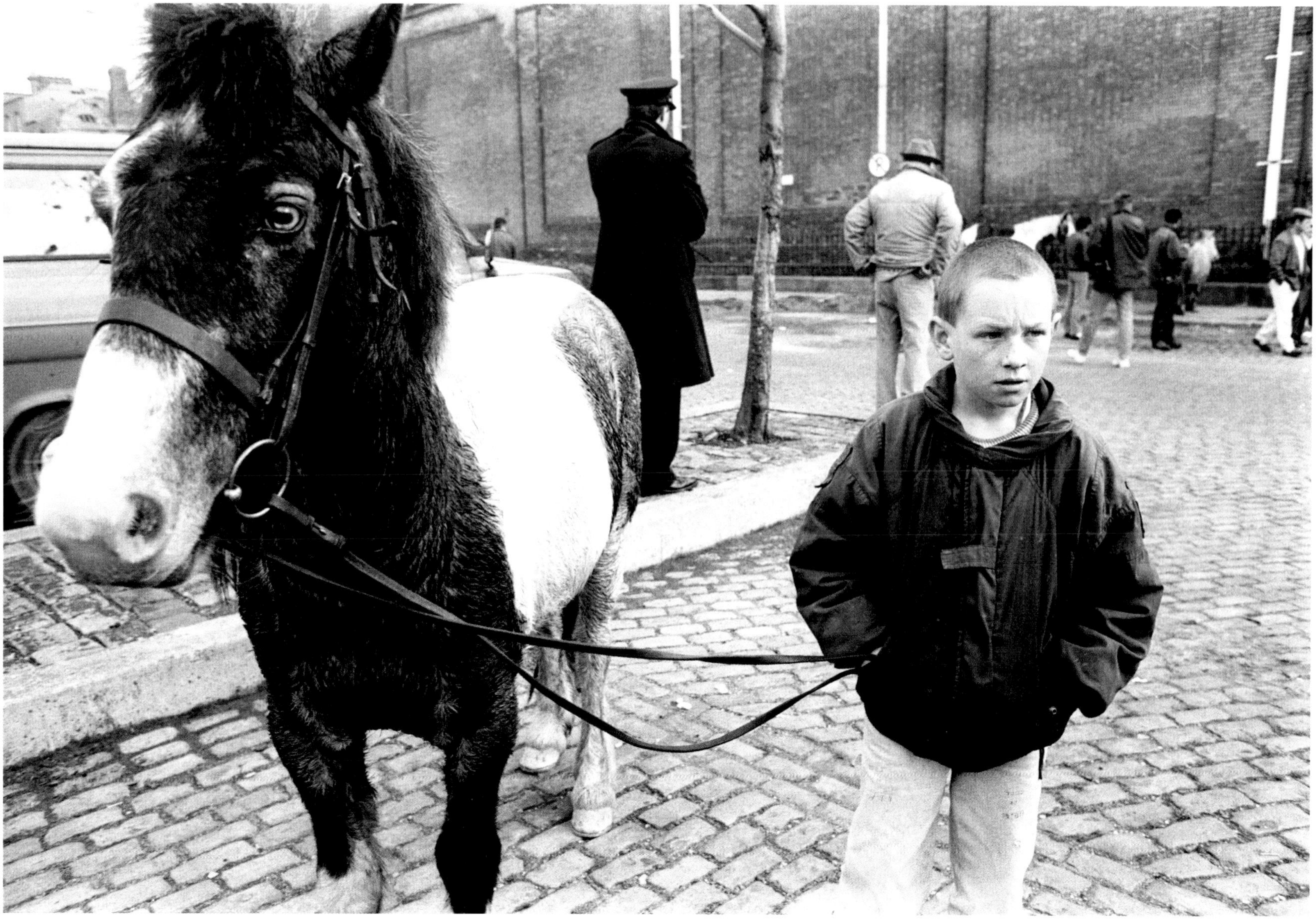

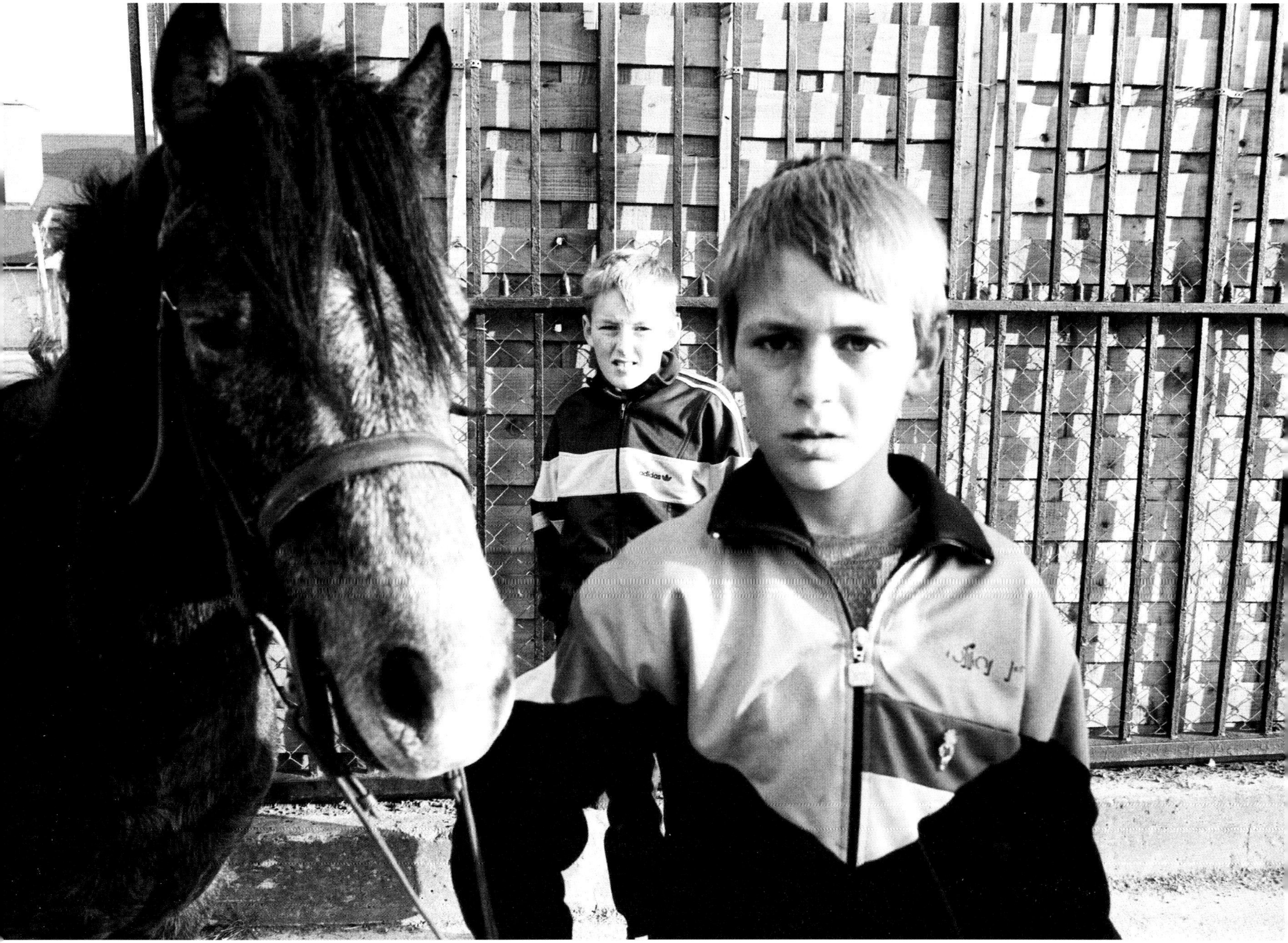
adidas

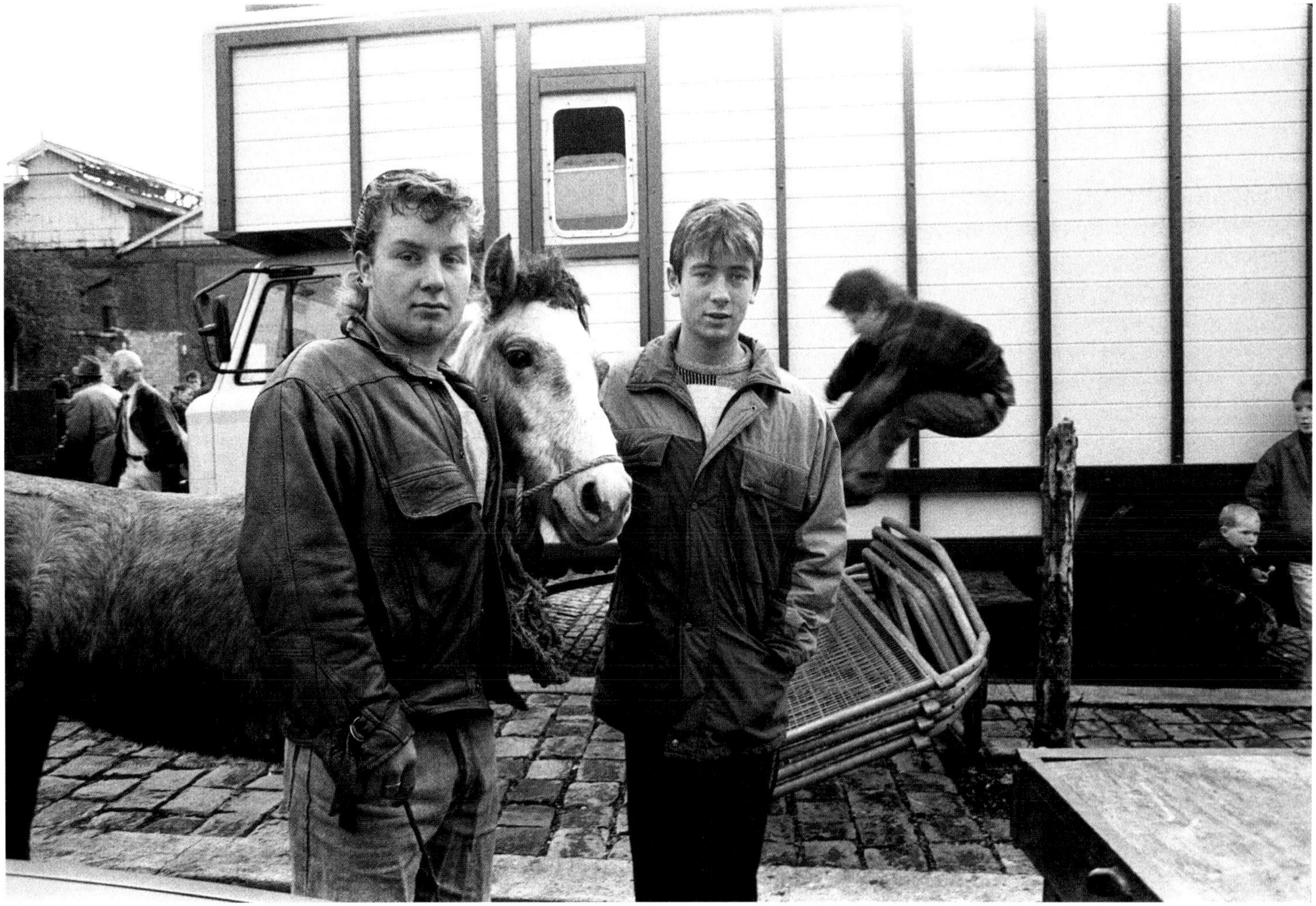

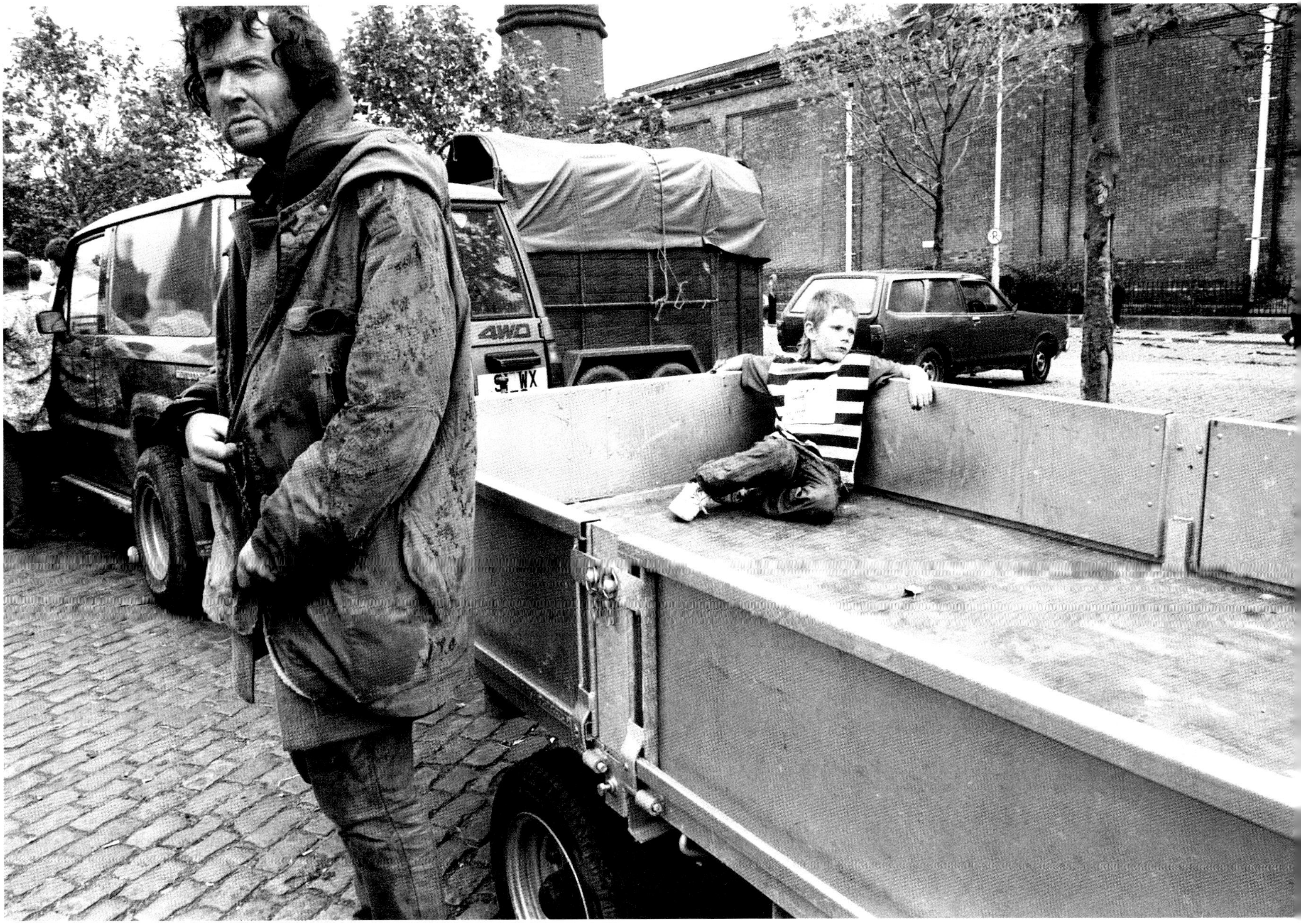
4WD

PUNKS

Theatre ROYAL
PRESENTS "PARANOID VISIONS"
JUDJEMENT BLUE BABYS
CONCERT SUN 17 FEB AT 8PM
Theatre ROYAL

VISIONS
PARANOID VISIONS
PARANOID VISIONS
SCRAWLS ON WALLS

SEX PISTOLS
CHARLIES
SAT 2ND MAR
PARANOID VISIONS
PARANOID VISIONS
SCRAWLS ON WALLS

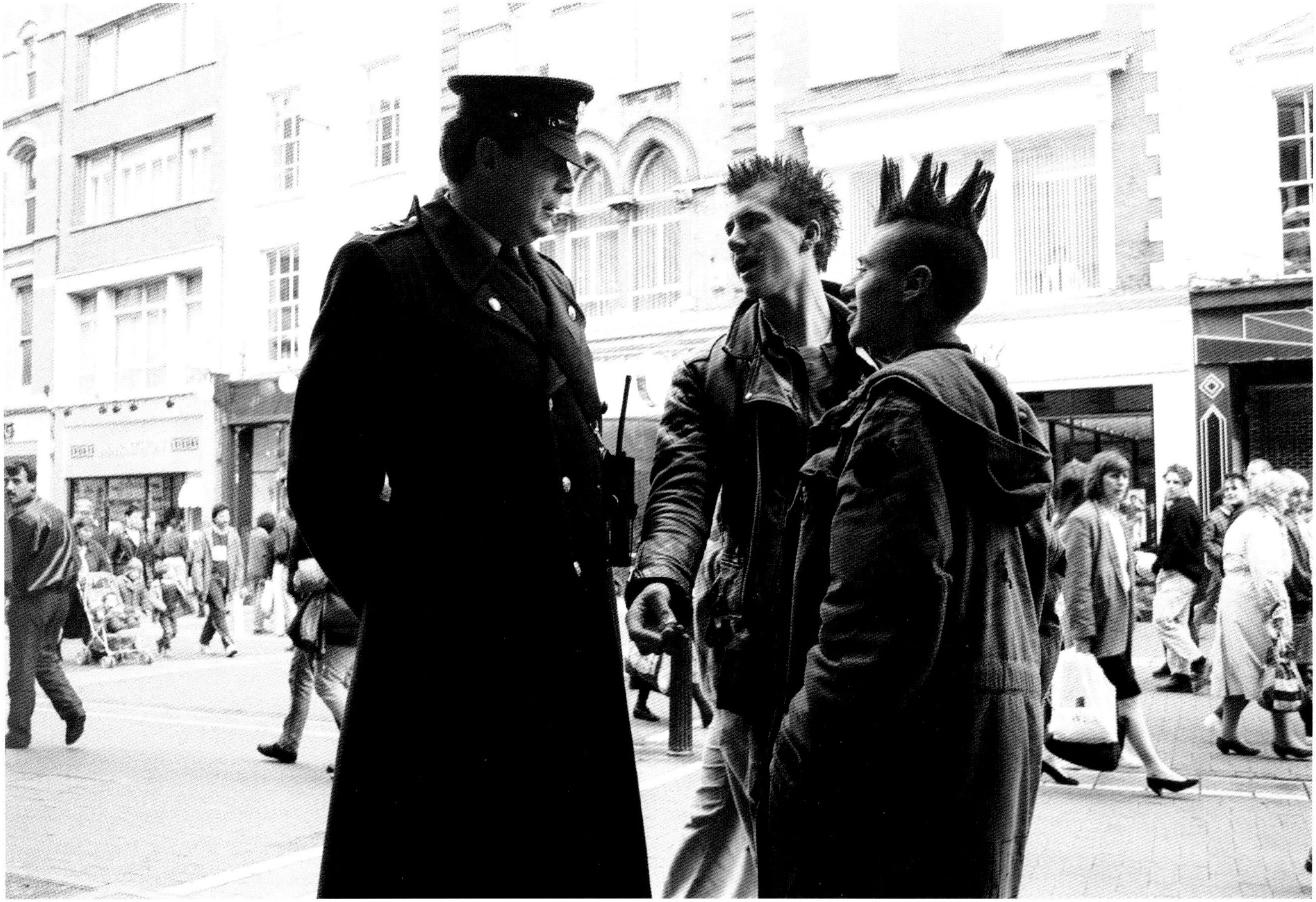

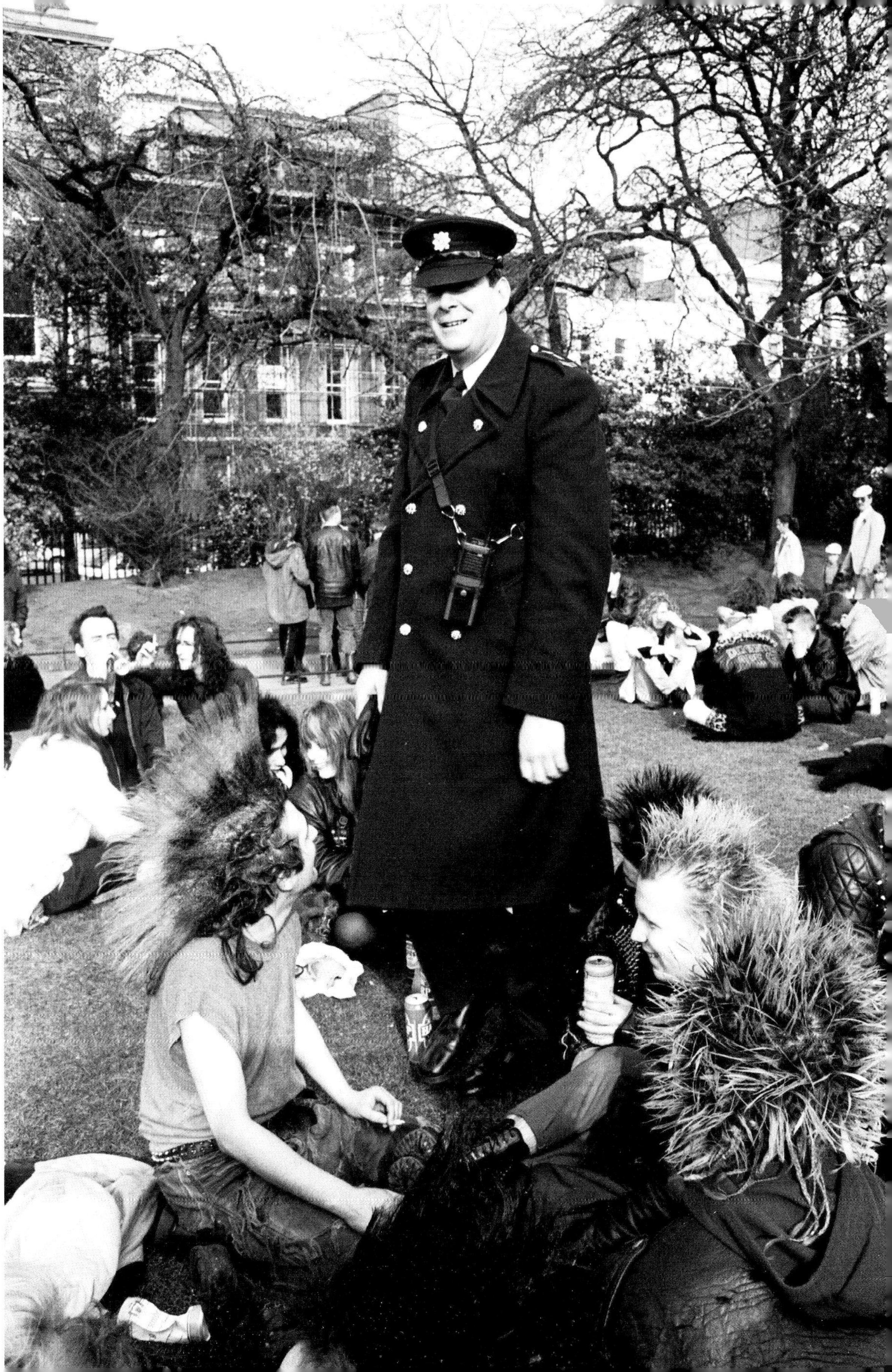

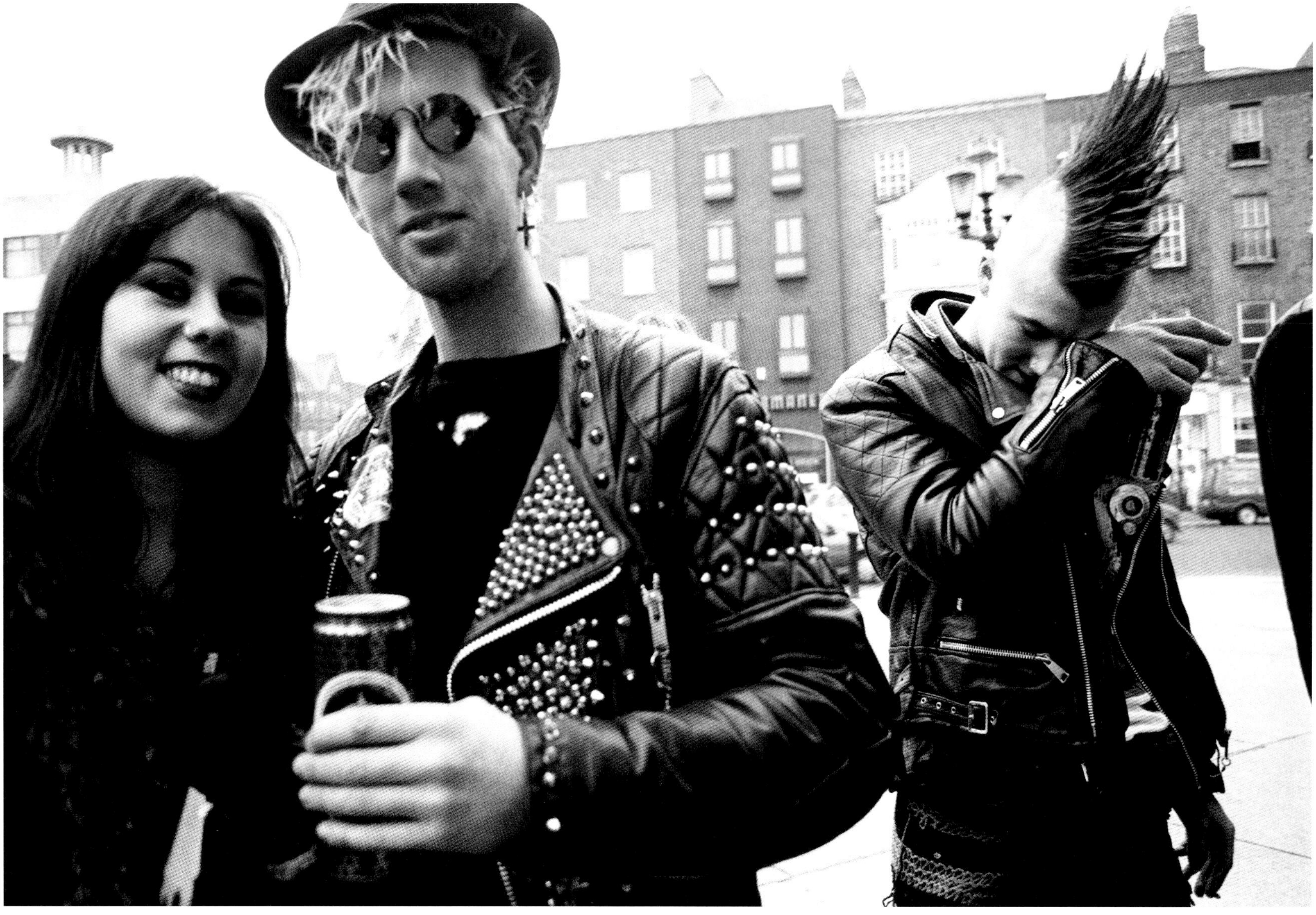

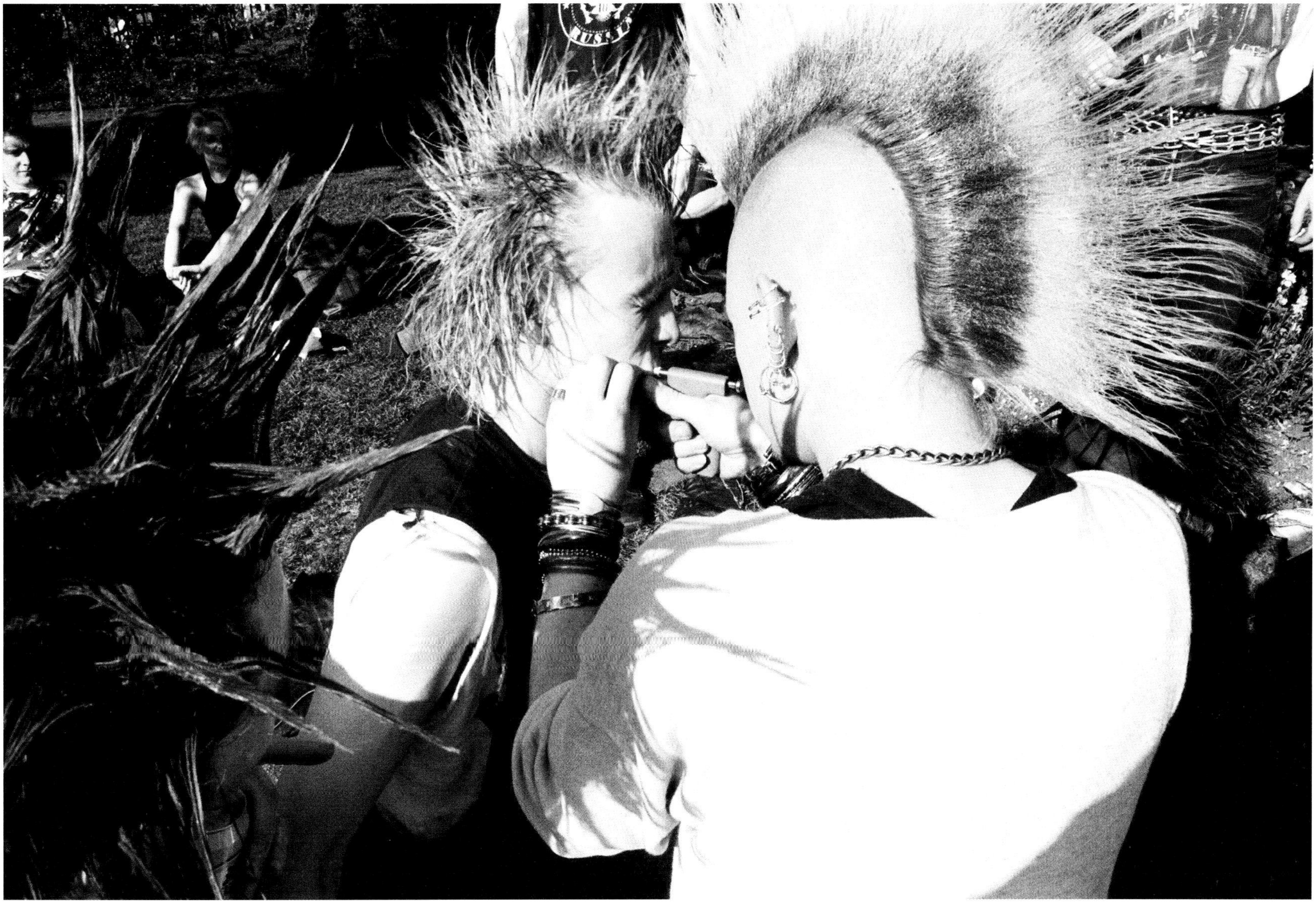

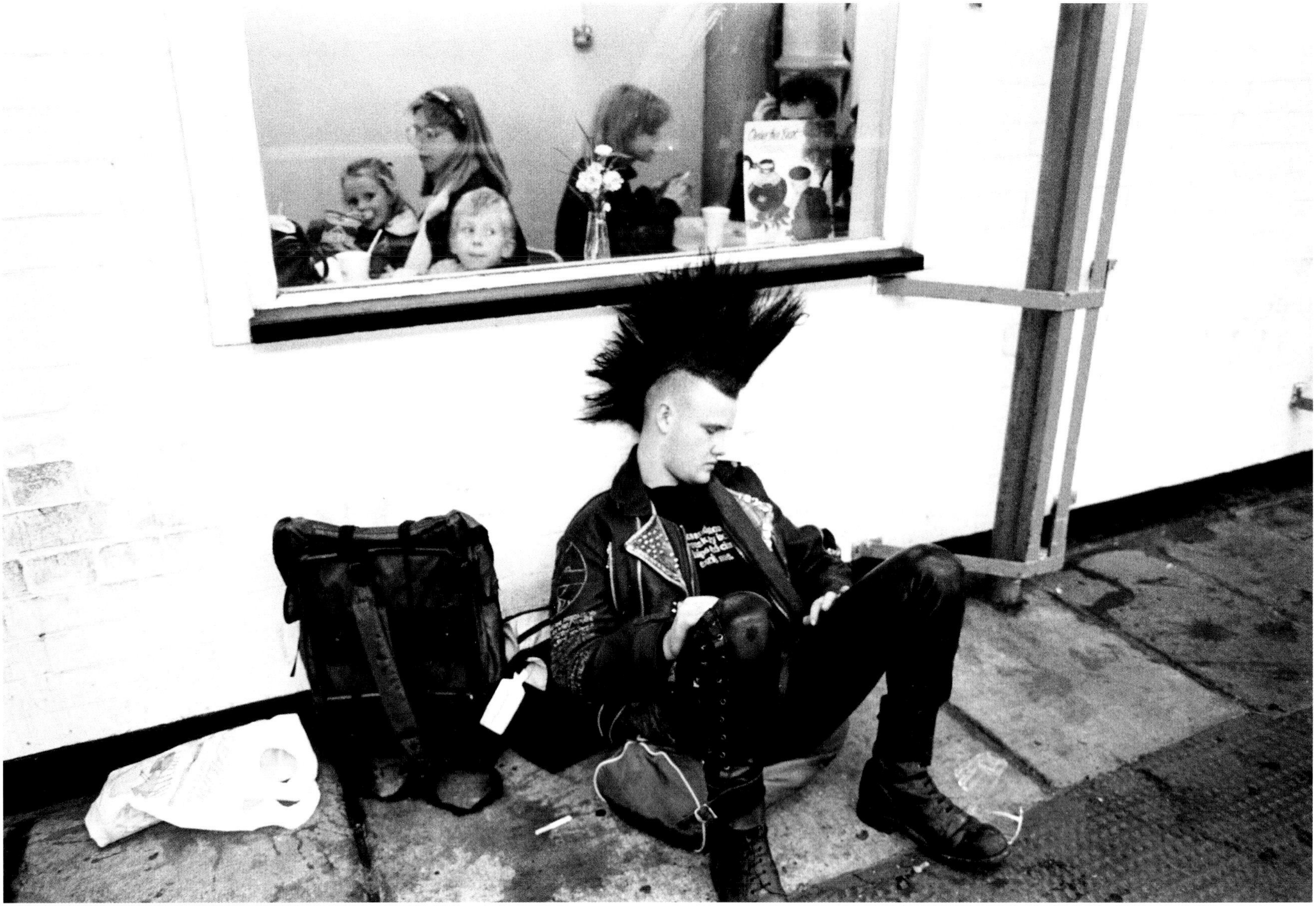

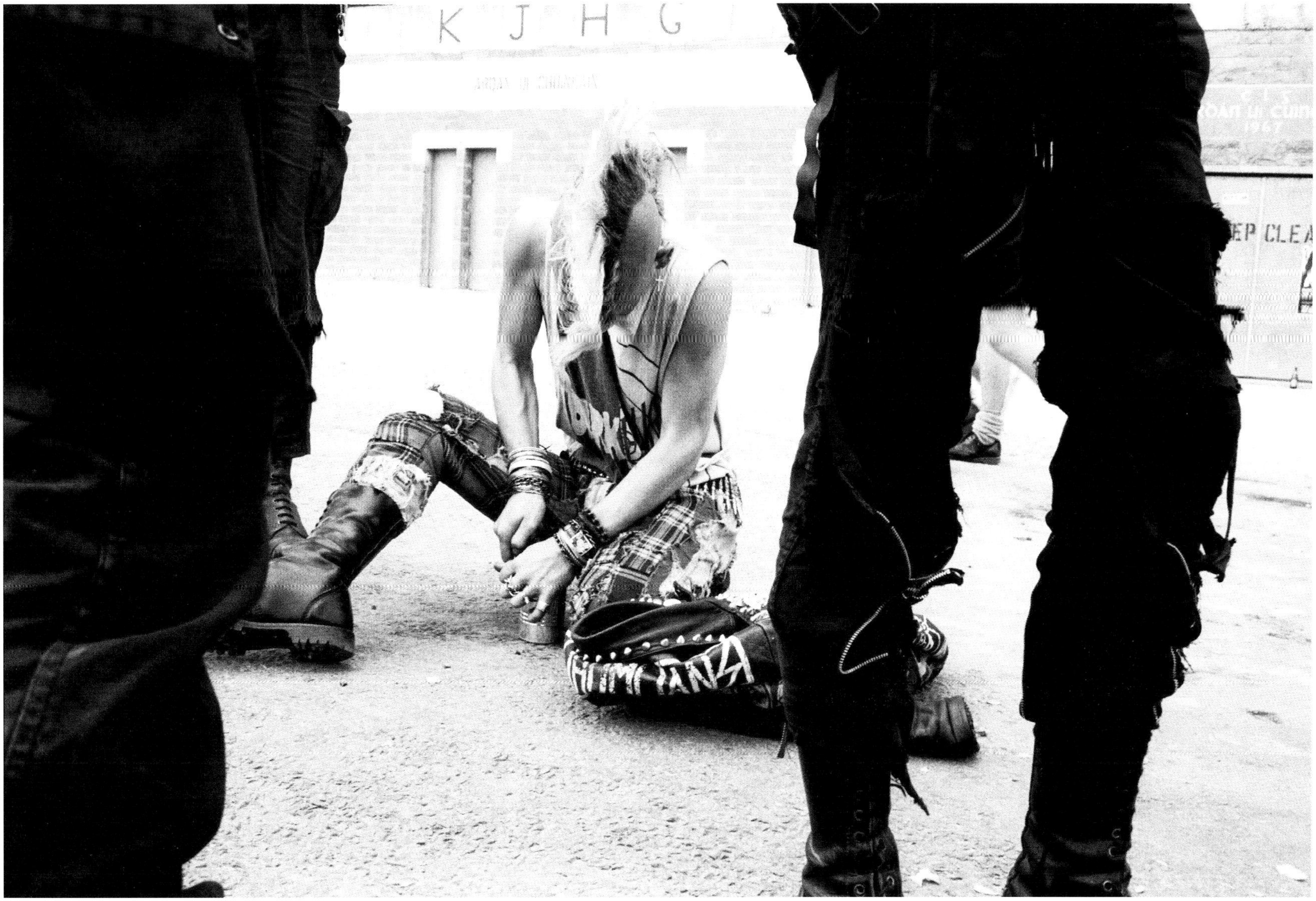
K J H G
EP CLEA

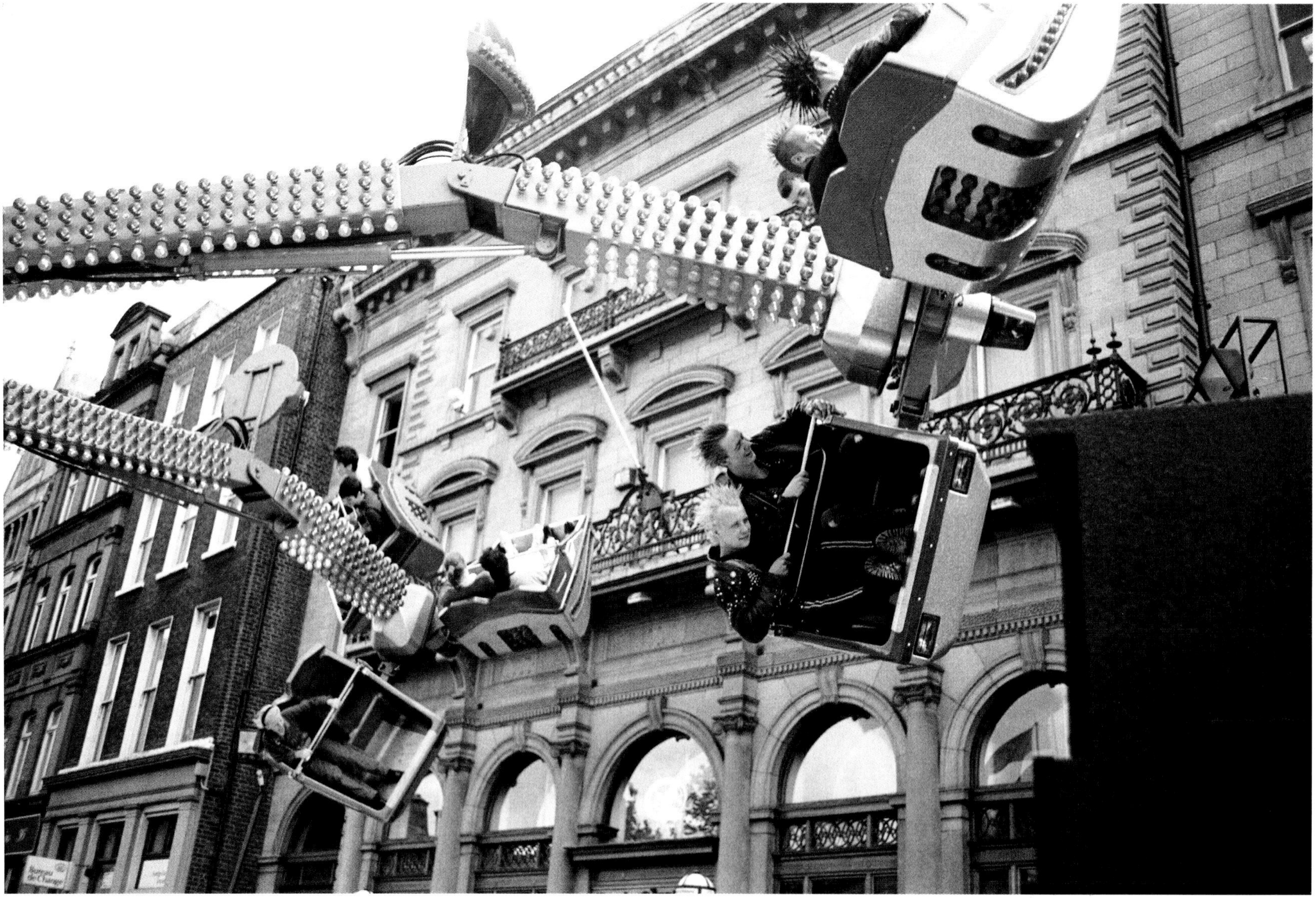

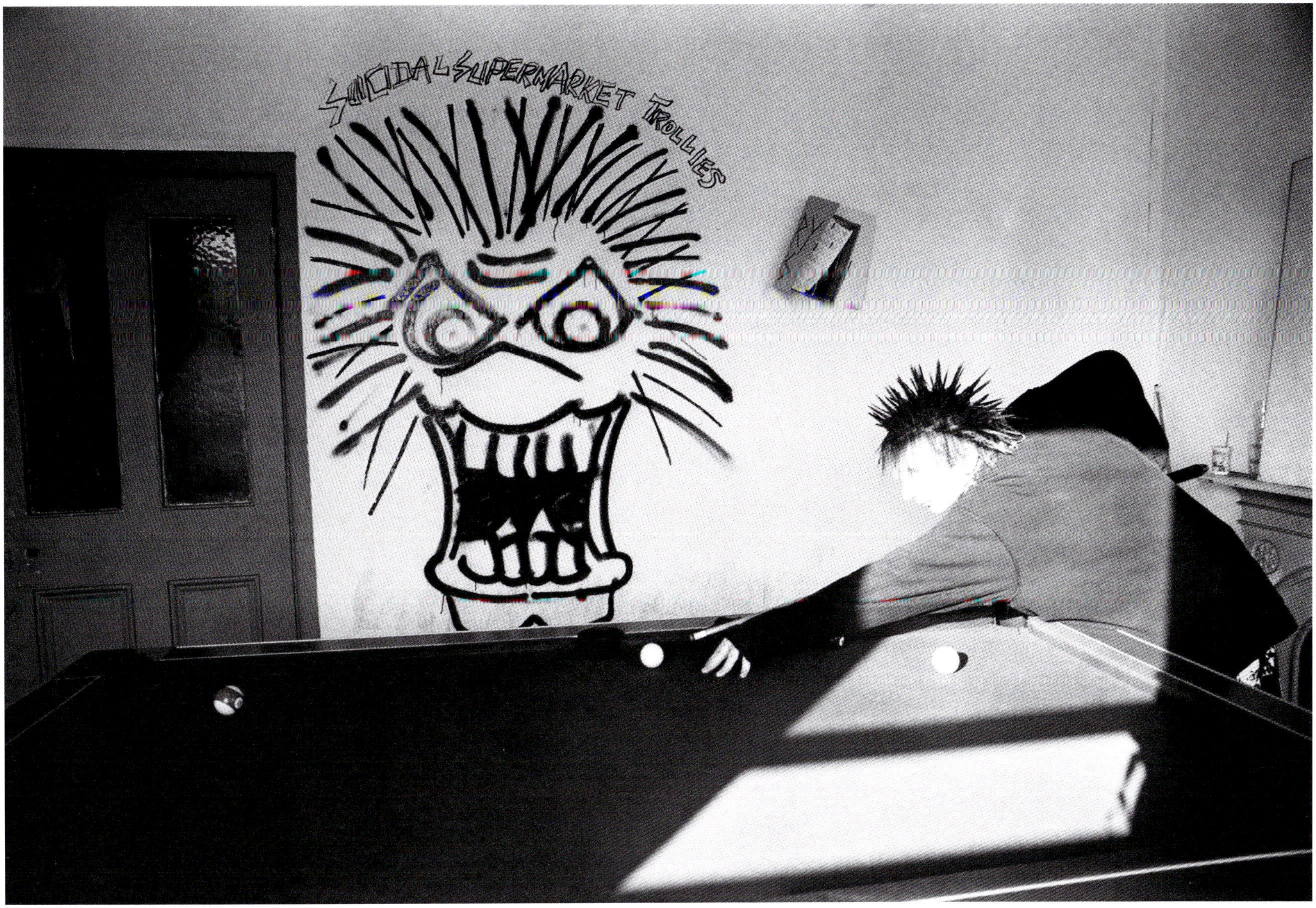
SUICIDAL SUPERMARKET TROLLIES

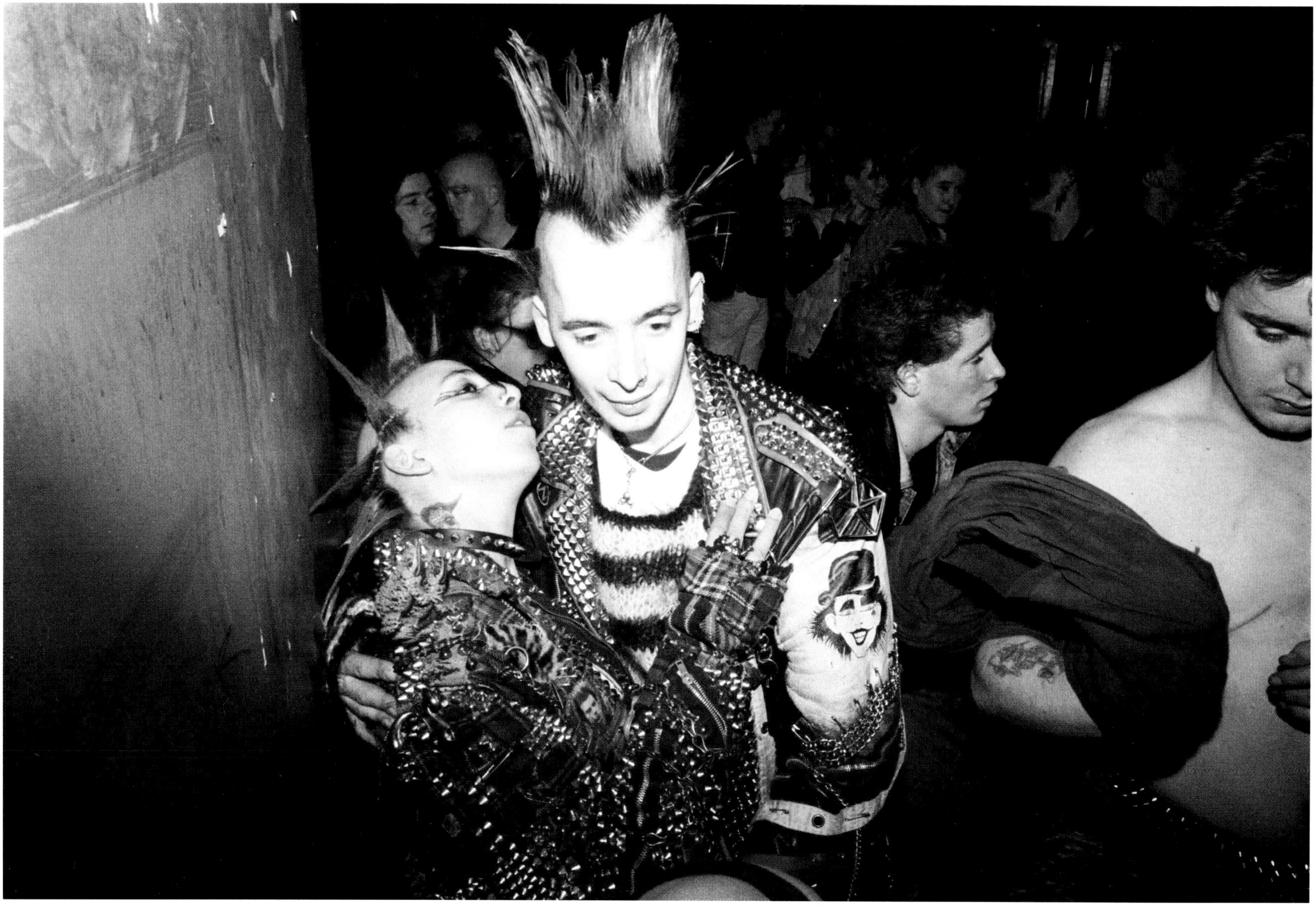

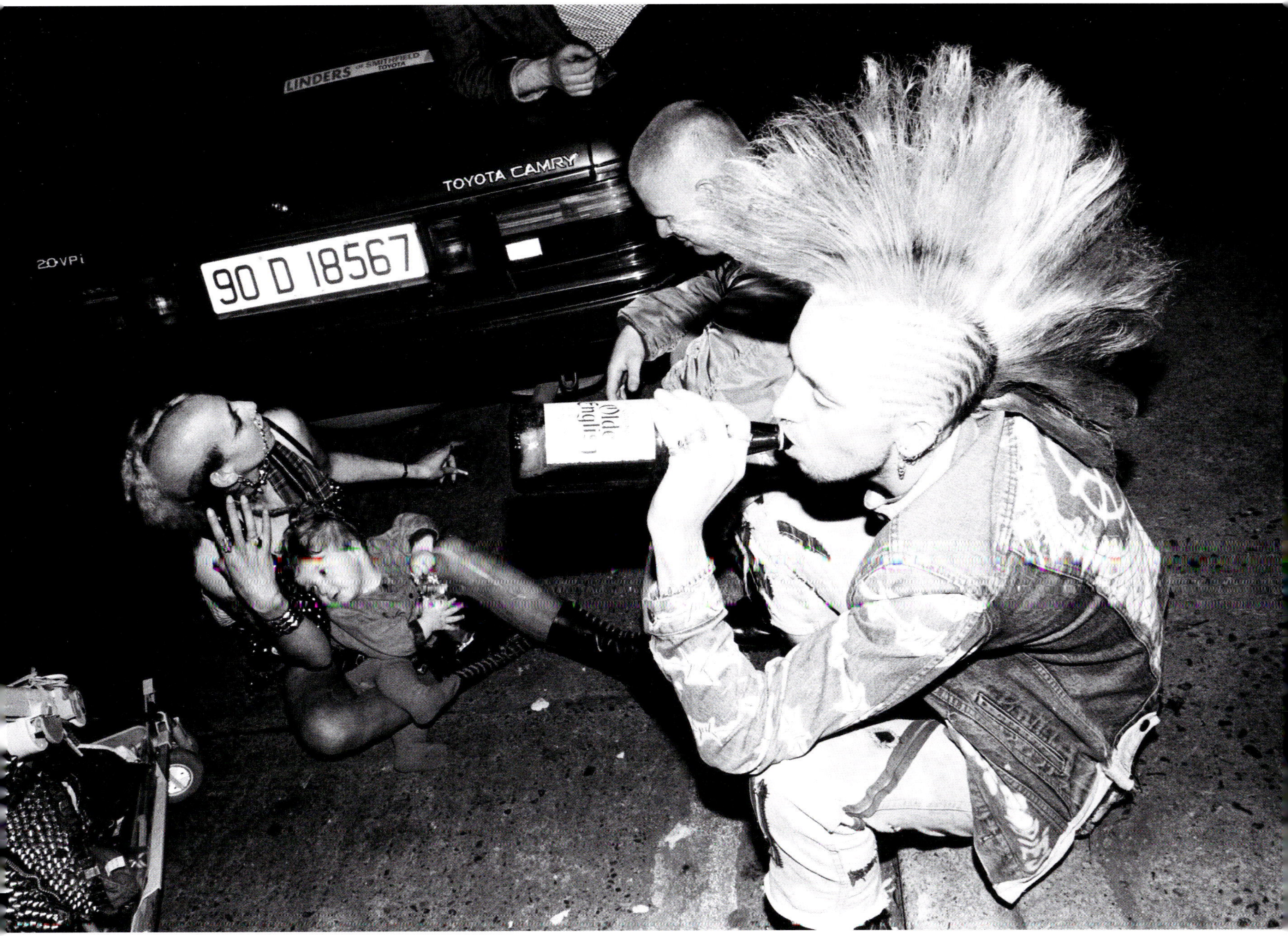
LINDERS
TOYOTA CAMRY
2.0VPi
90 D 18567

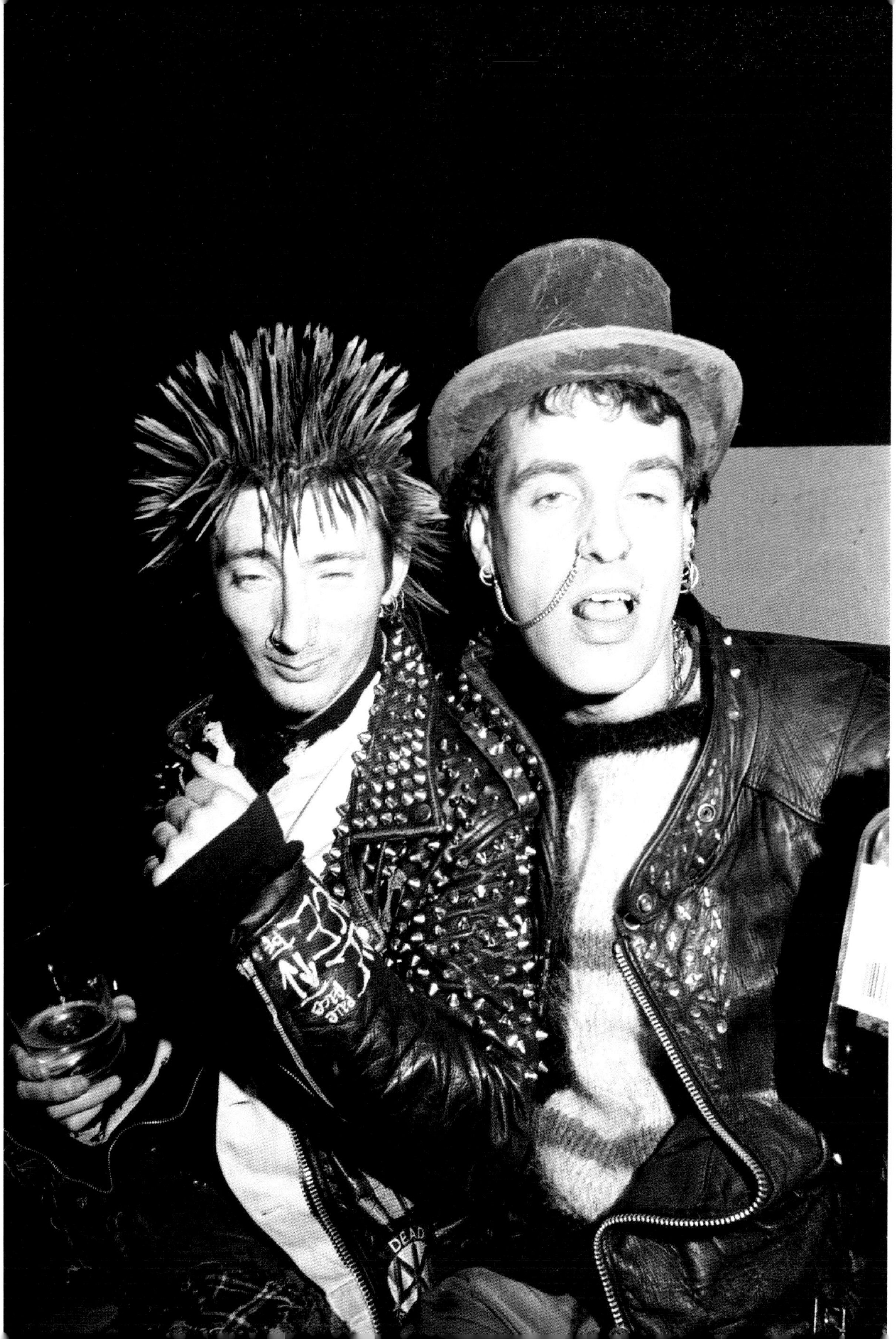
DEAD

119

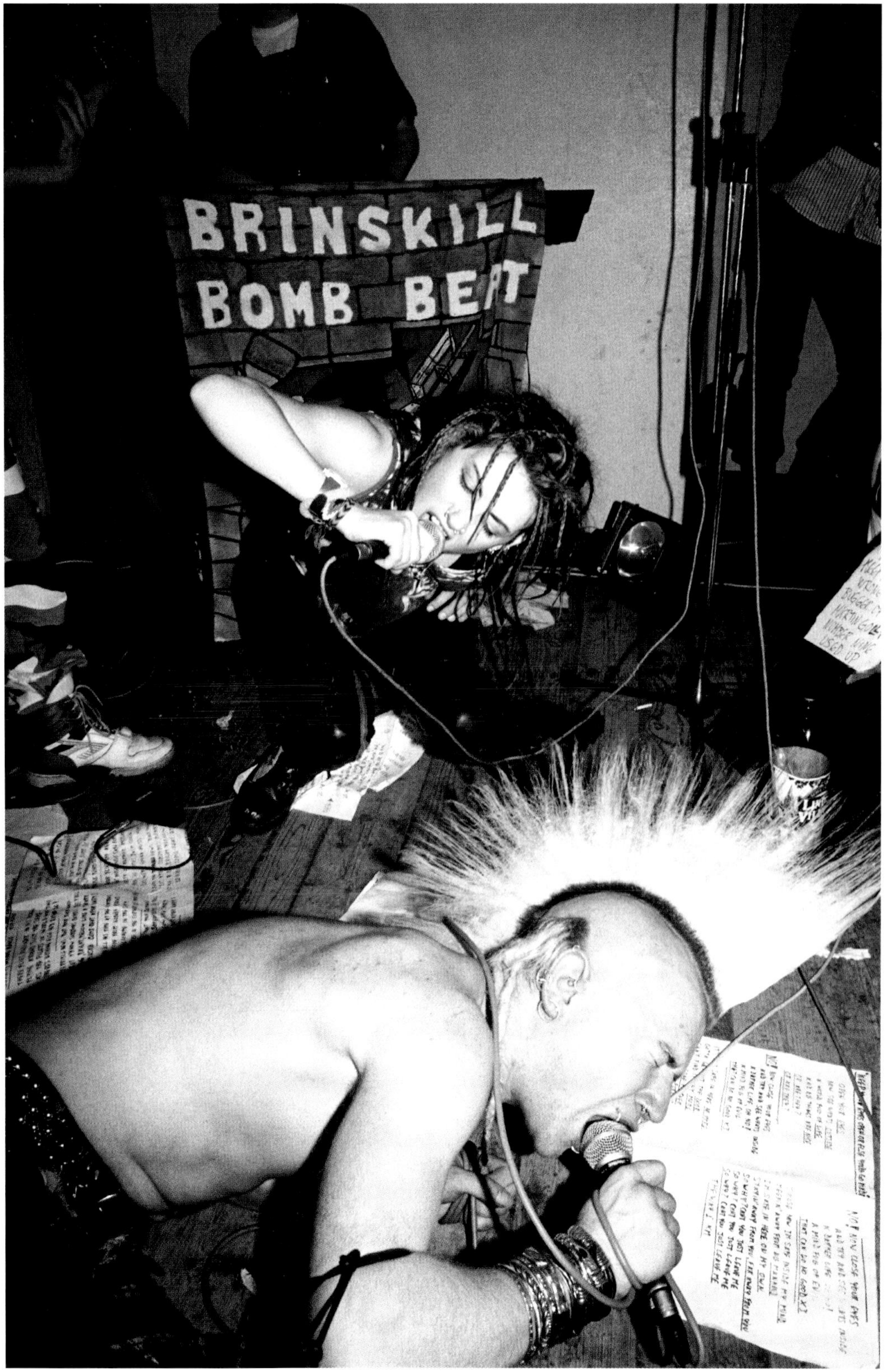
BRINSKILL
BOMB

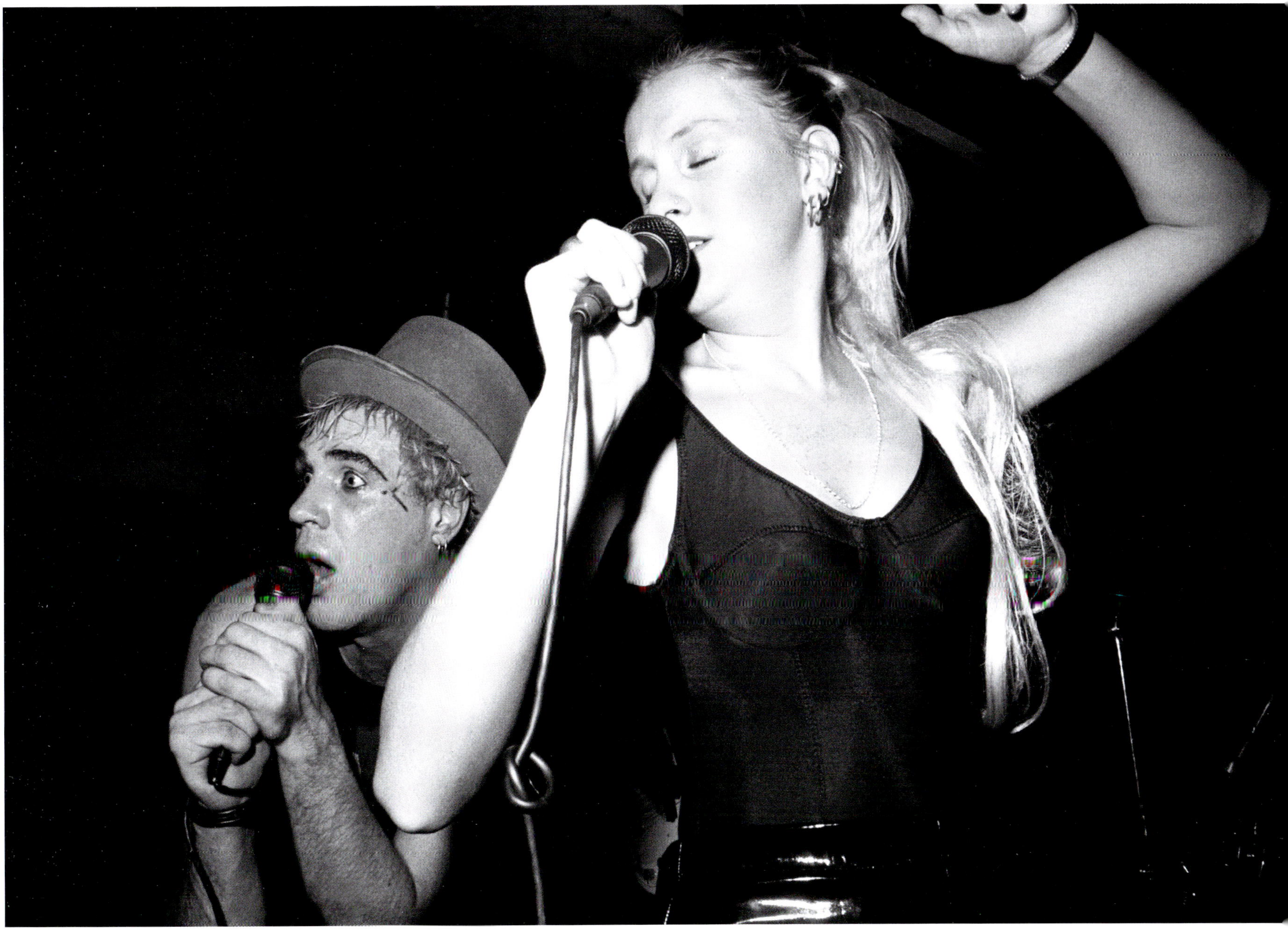

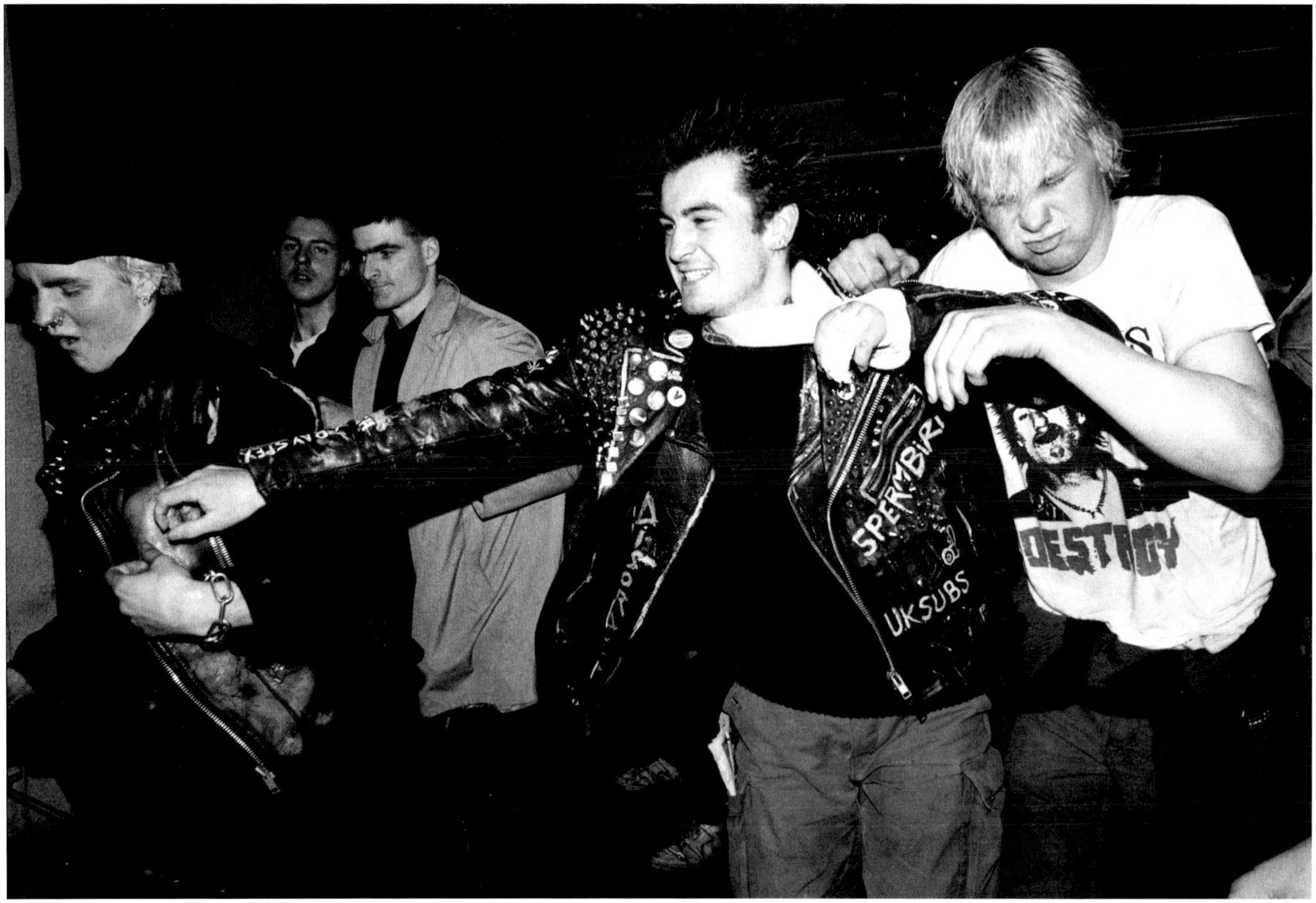
UKSUBS
DESTROY

123

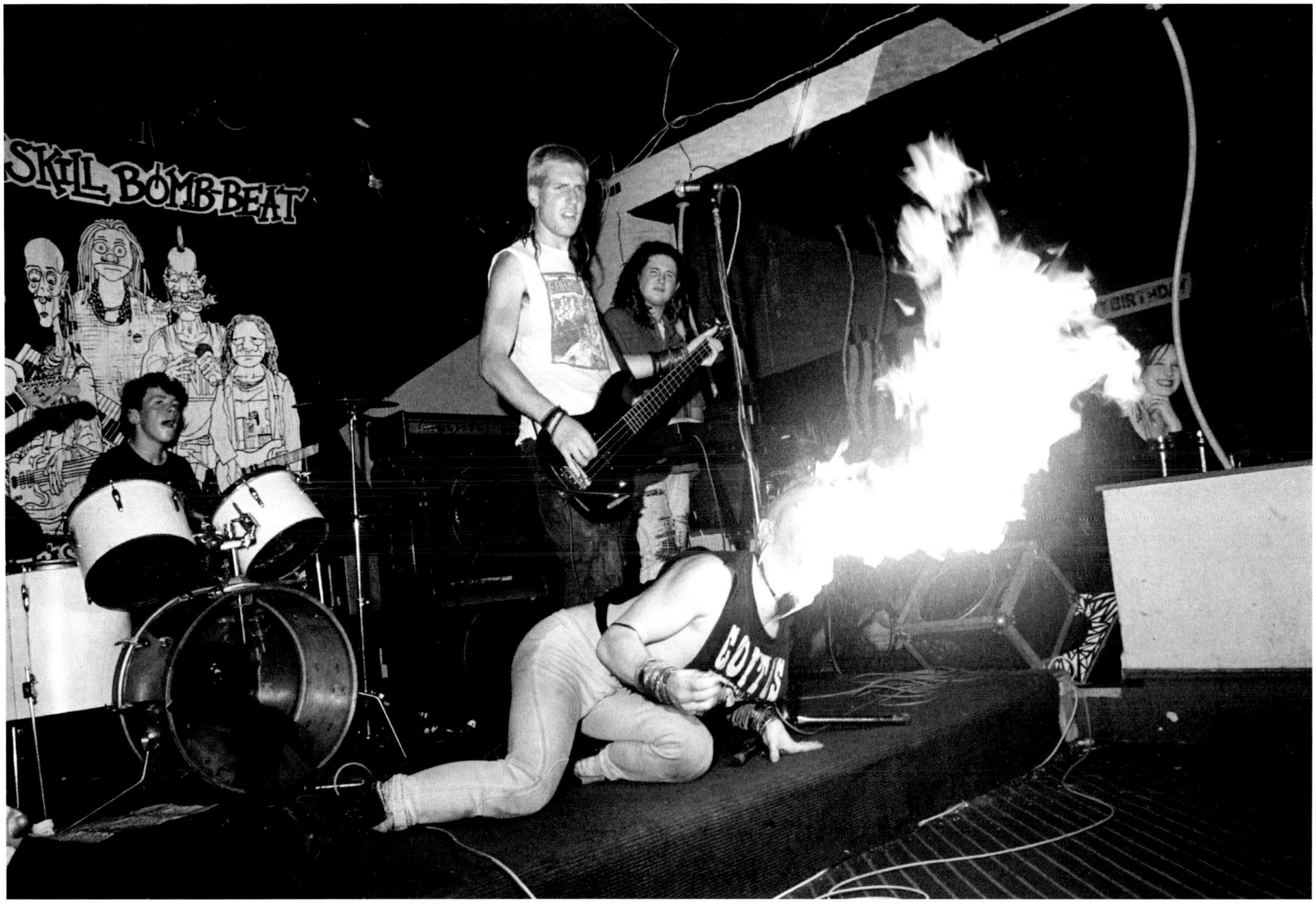
SKILL BOMB BEAT
BIRTHDAY
COITUS

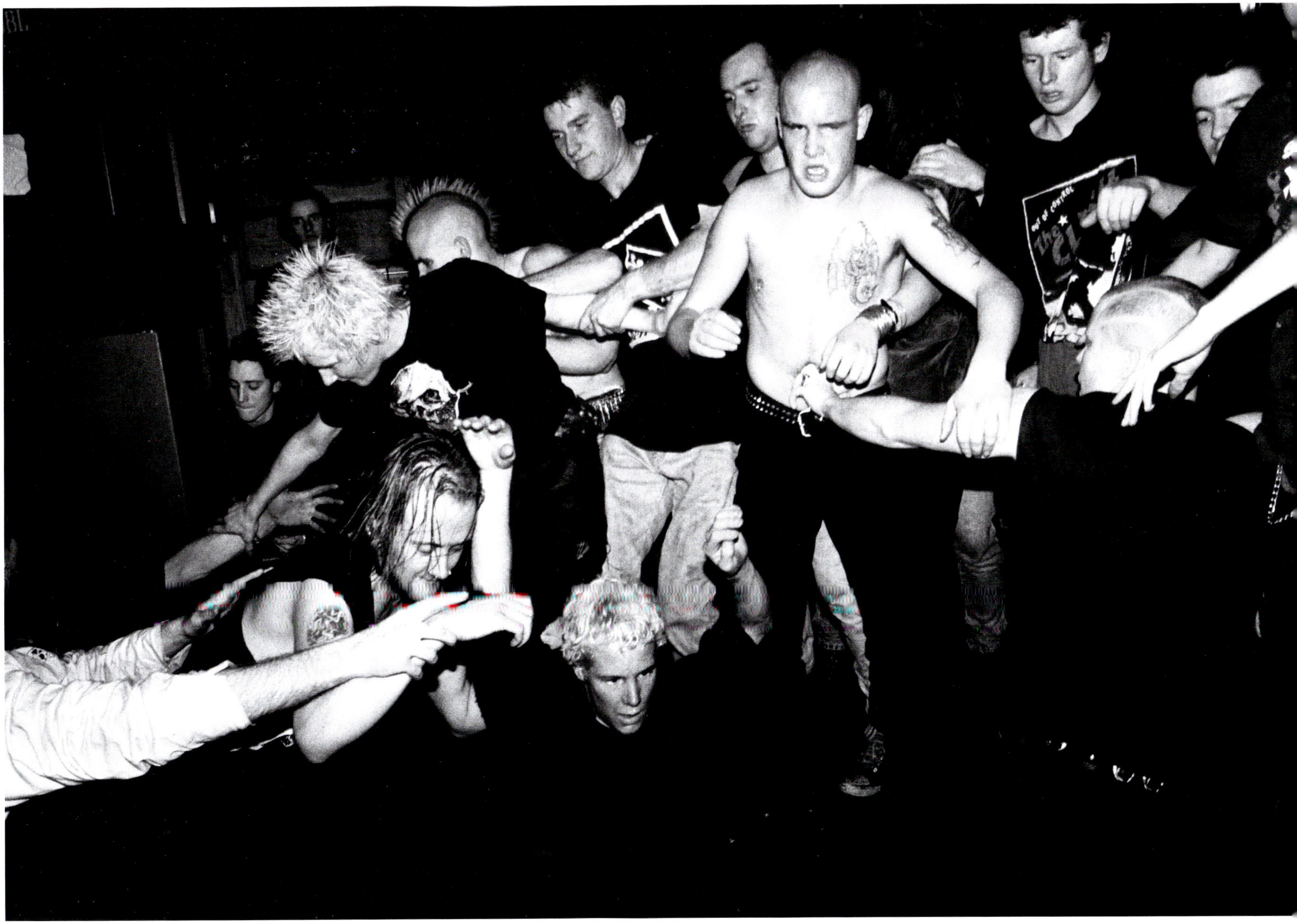

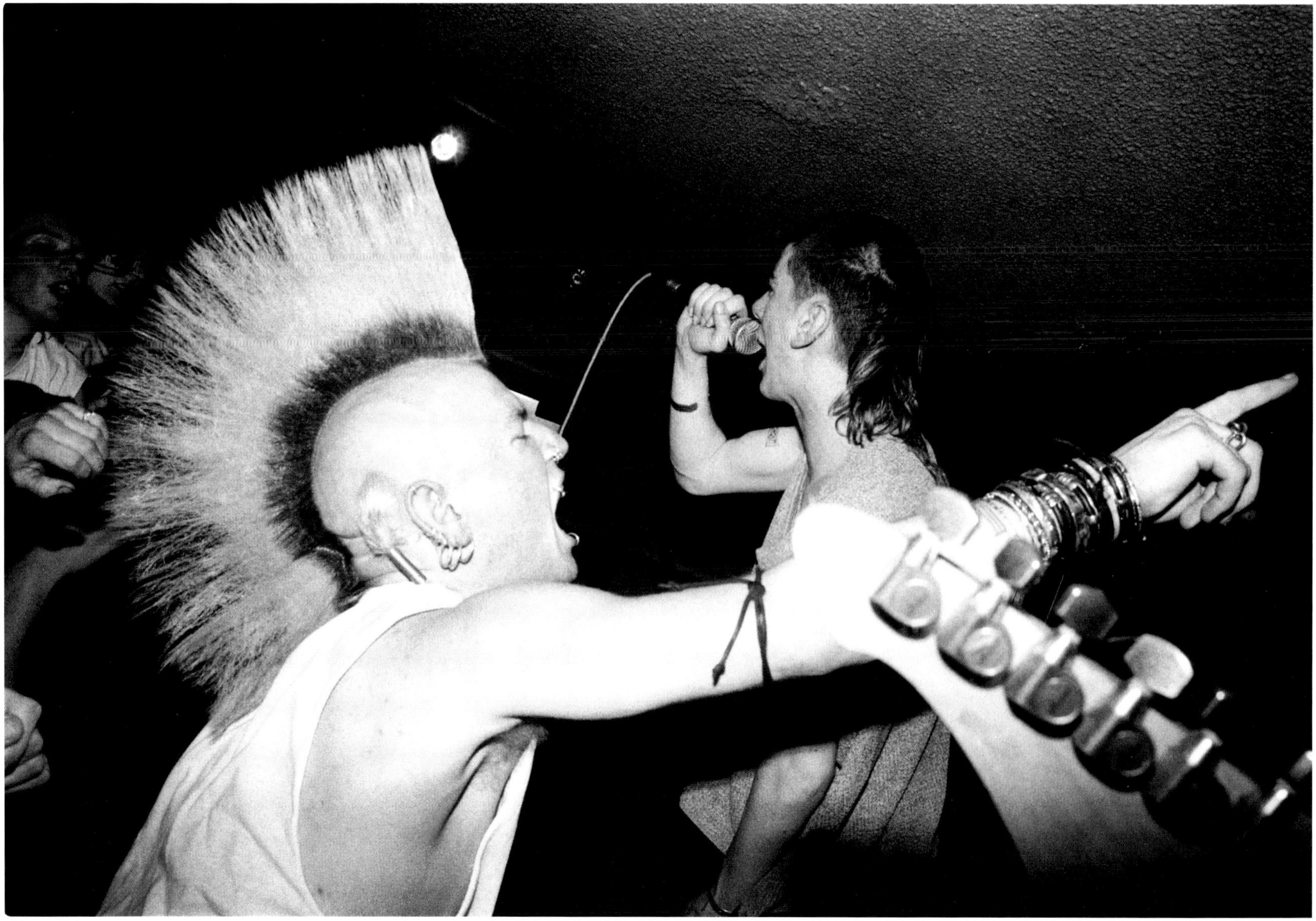

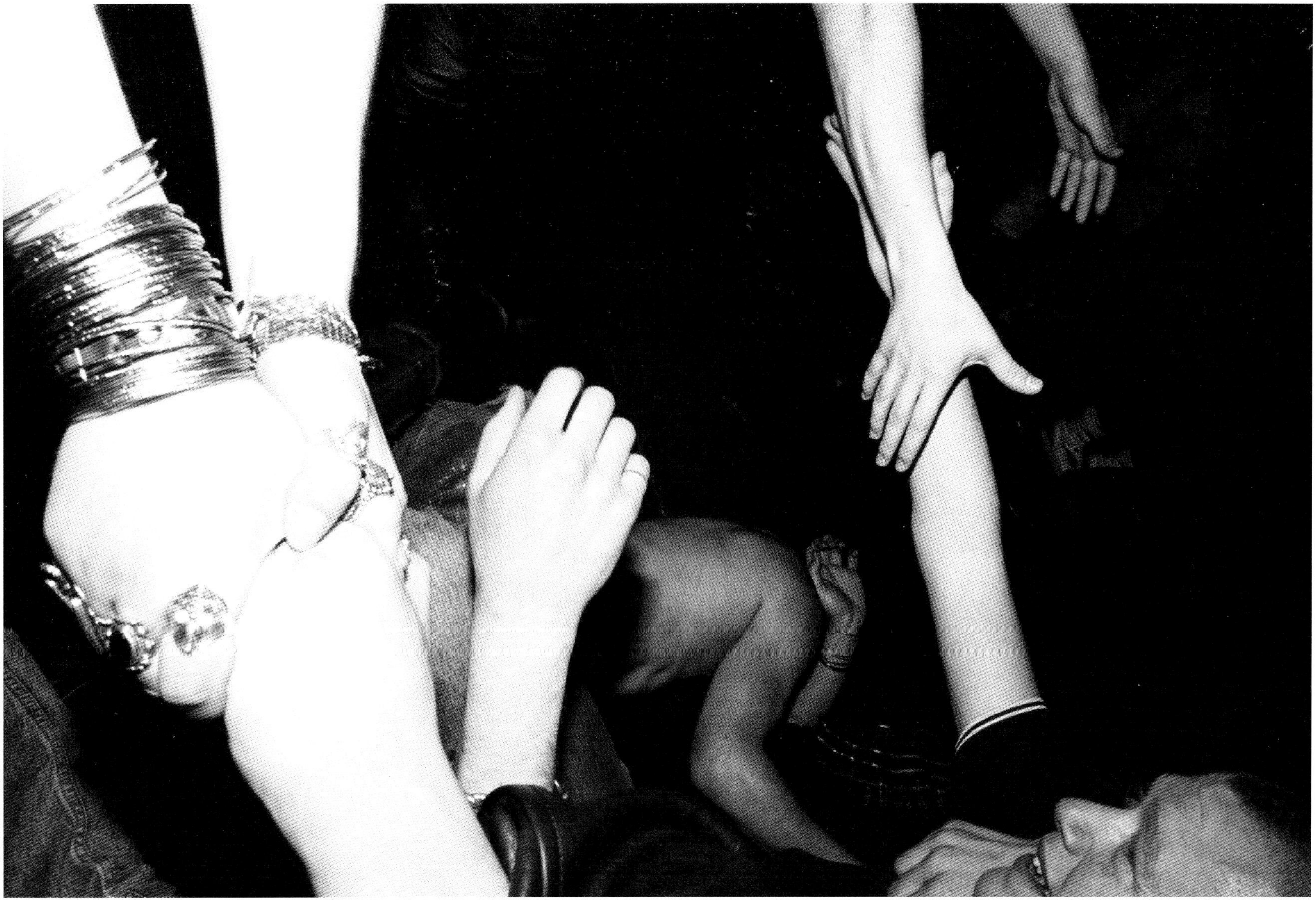

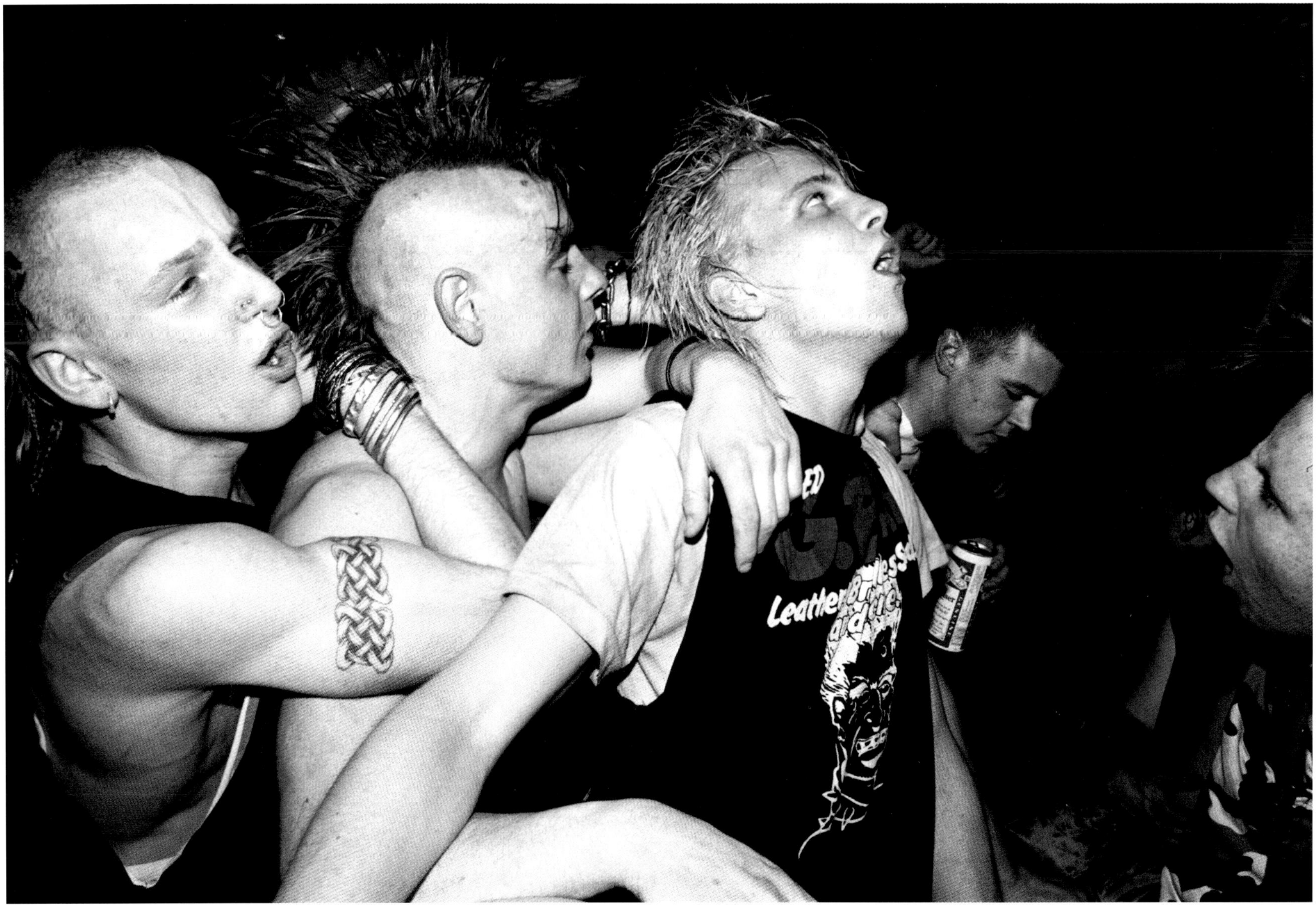

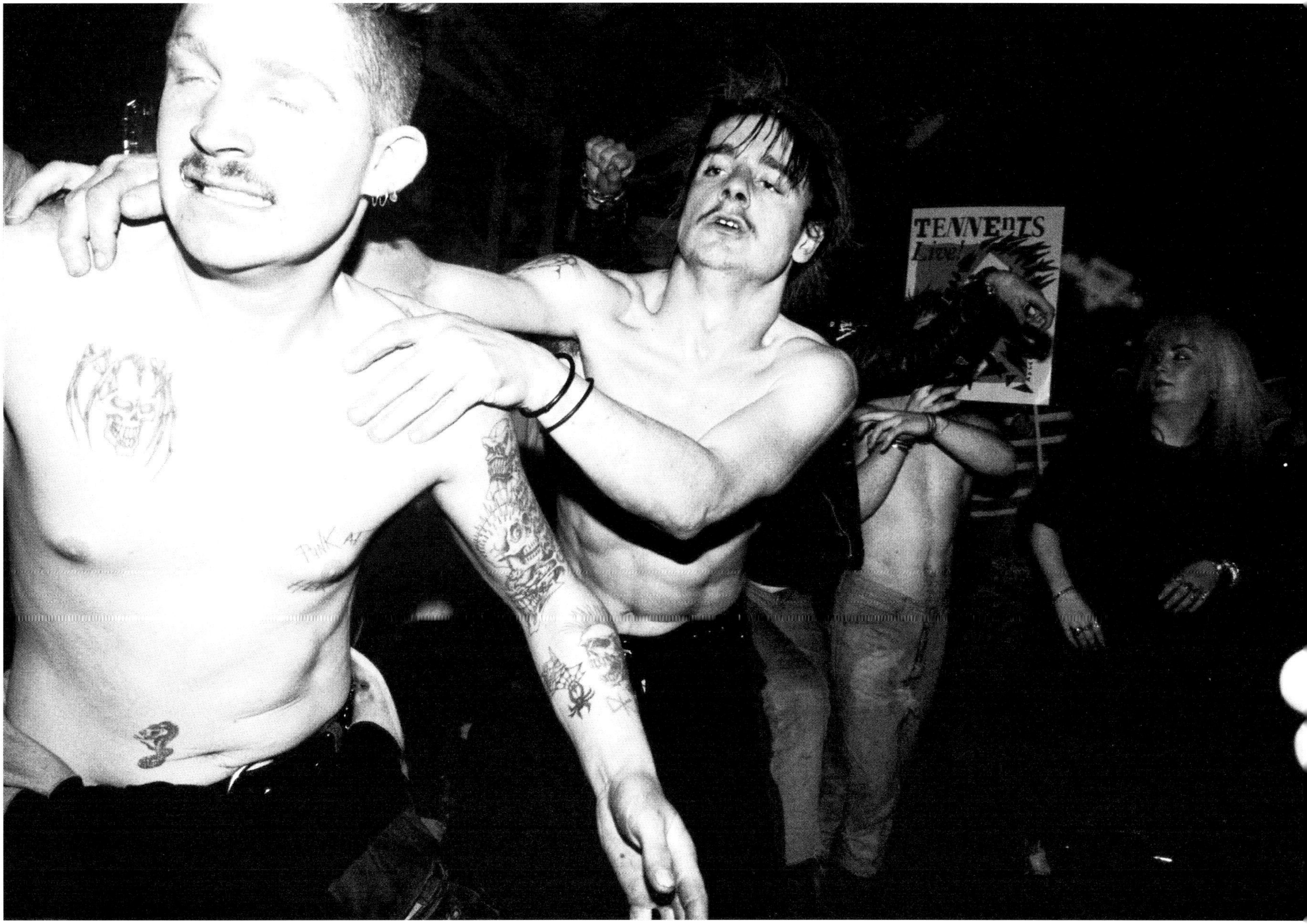
TENNENTS

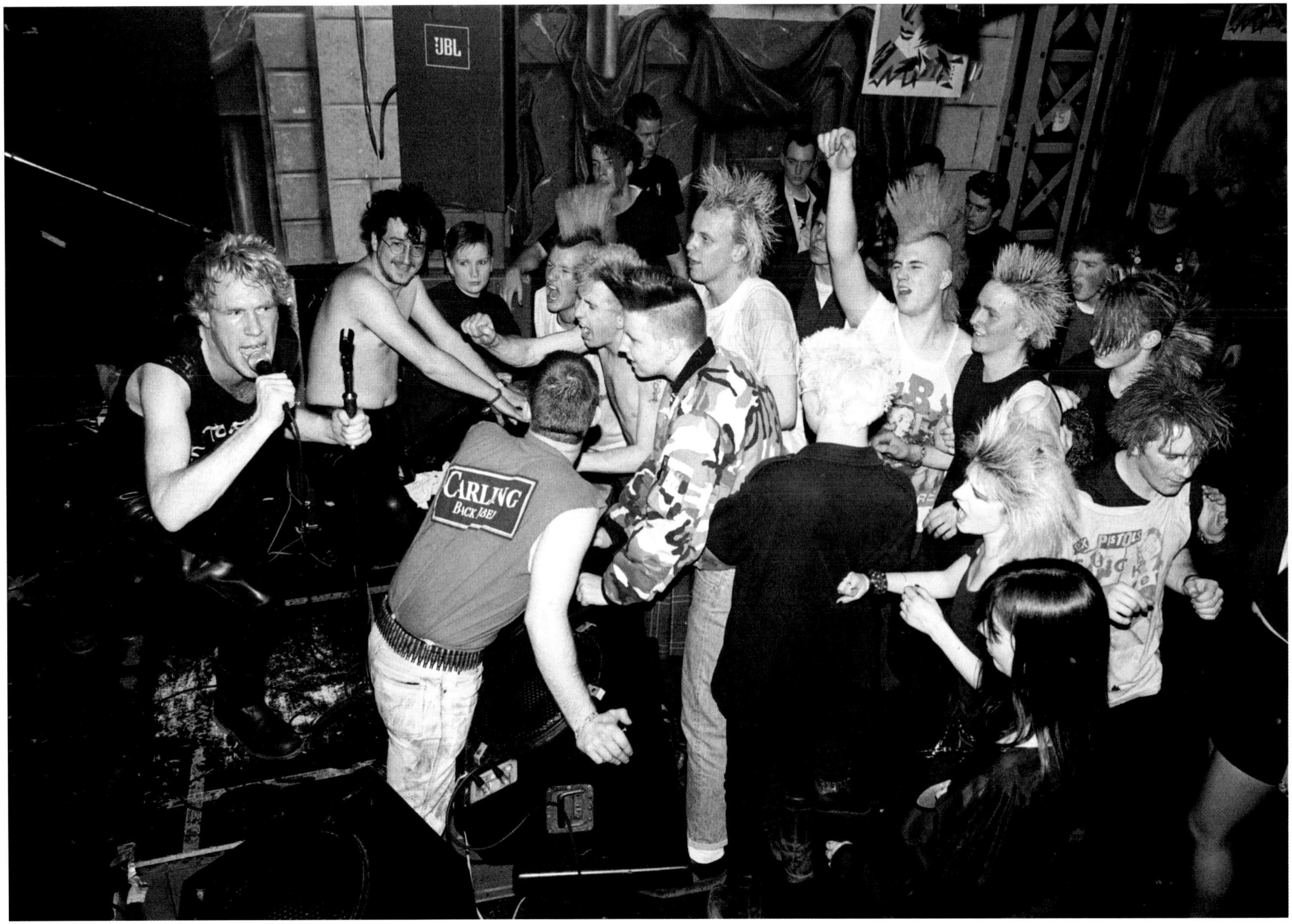
JBL
CARLING

131

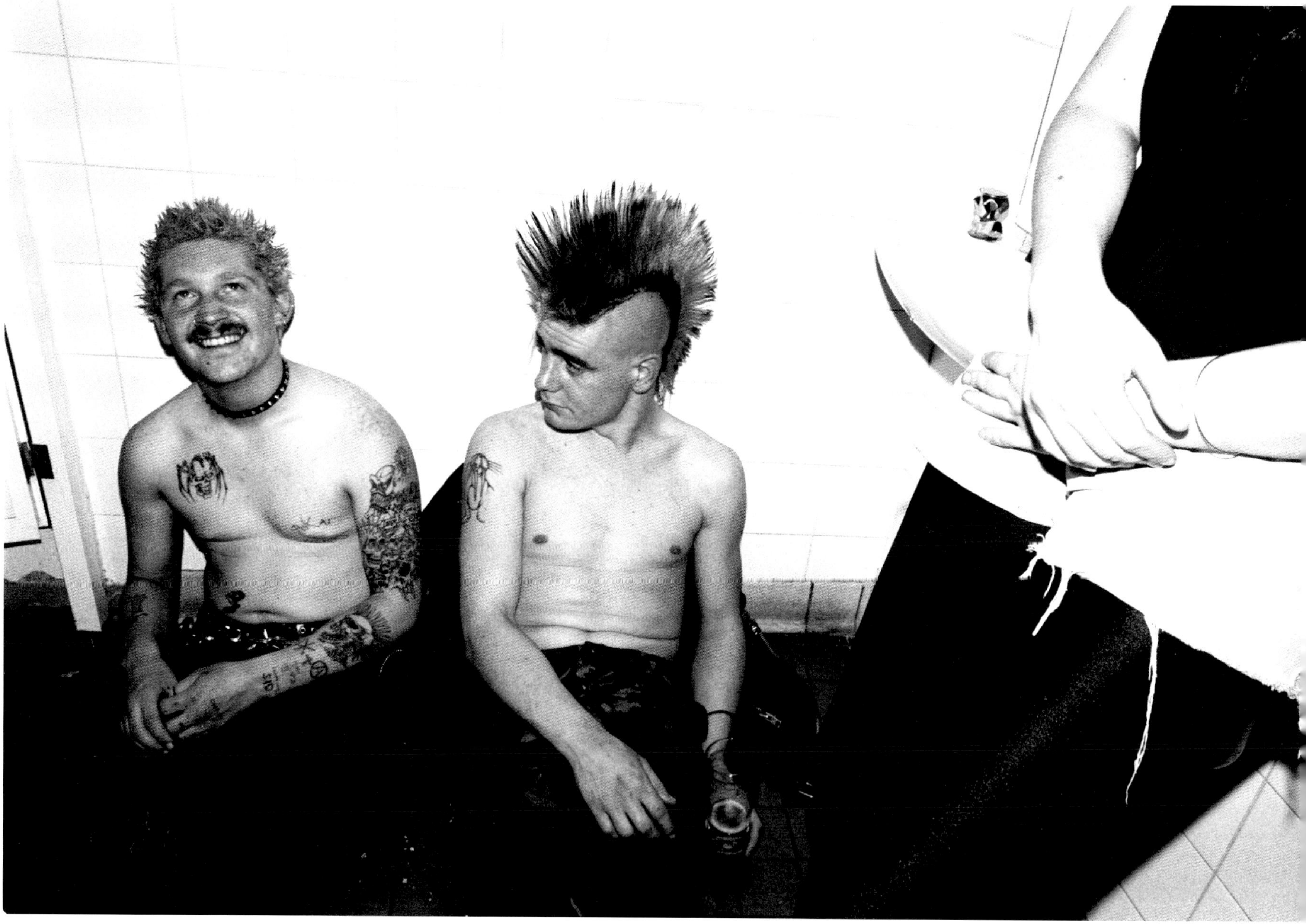

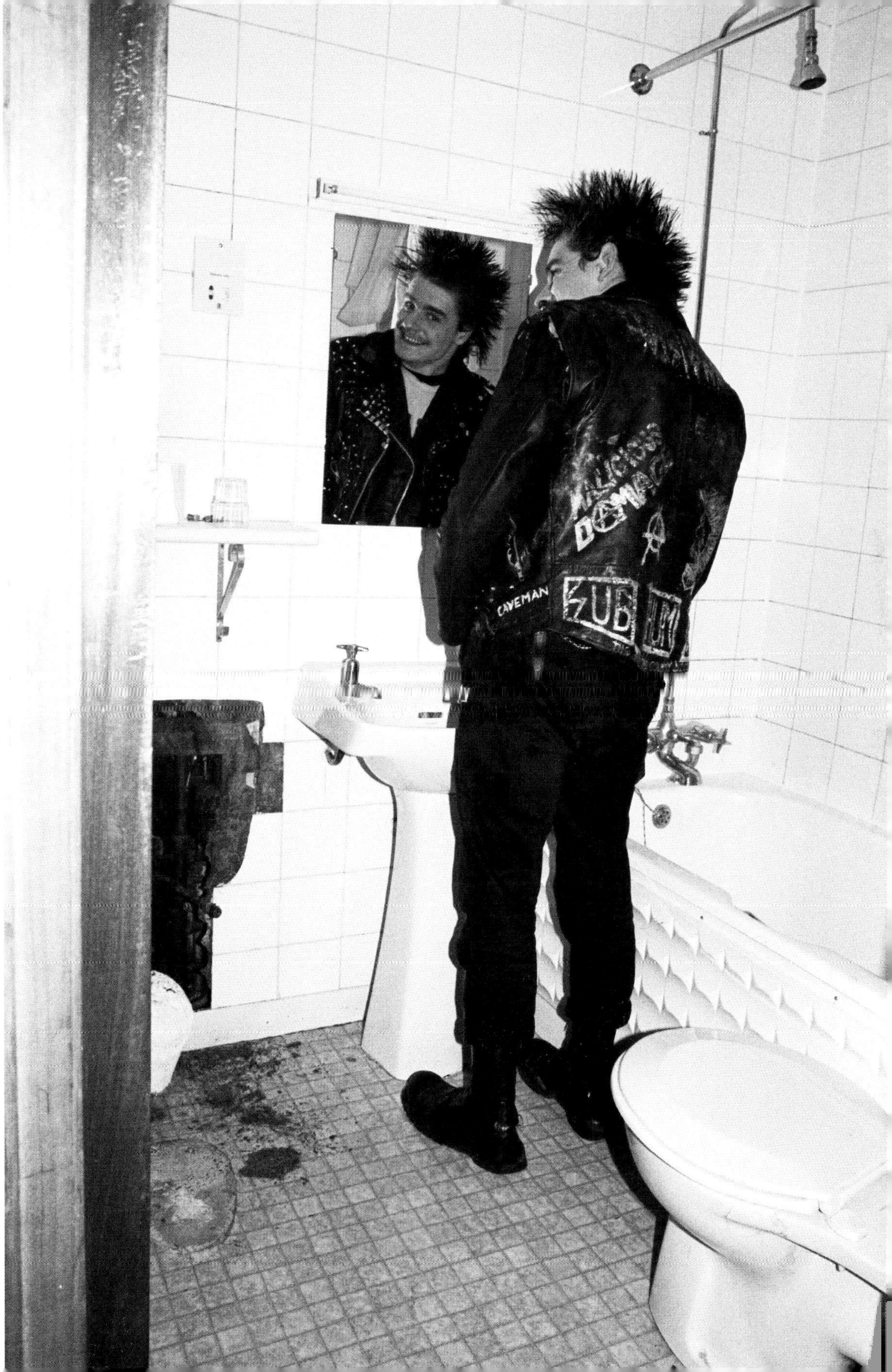
CAVEMAN

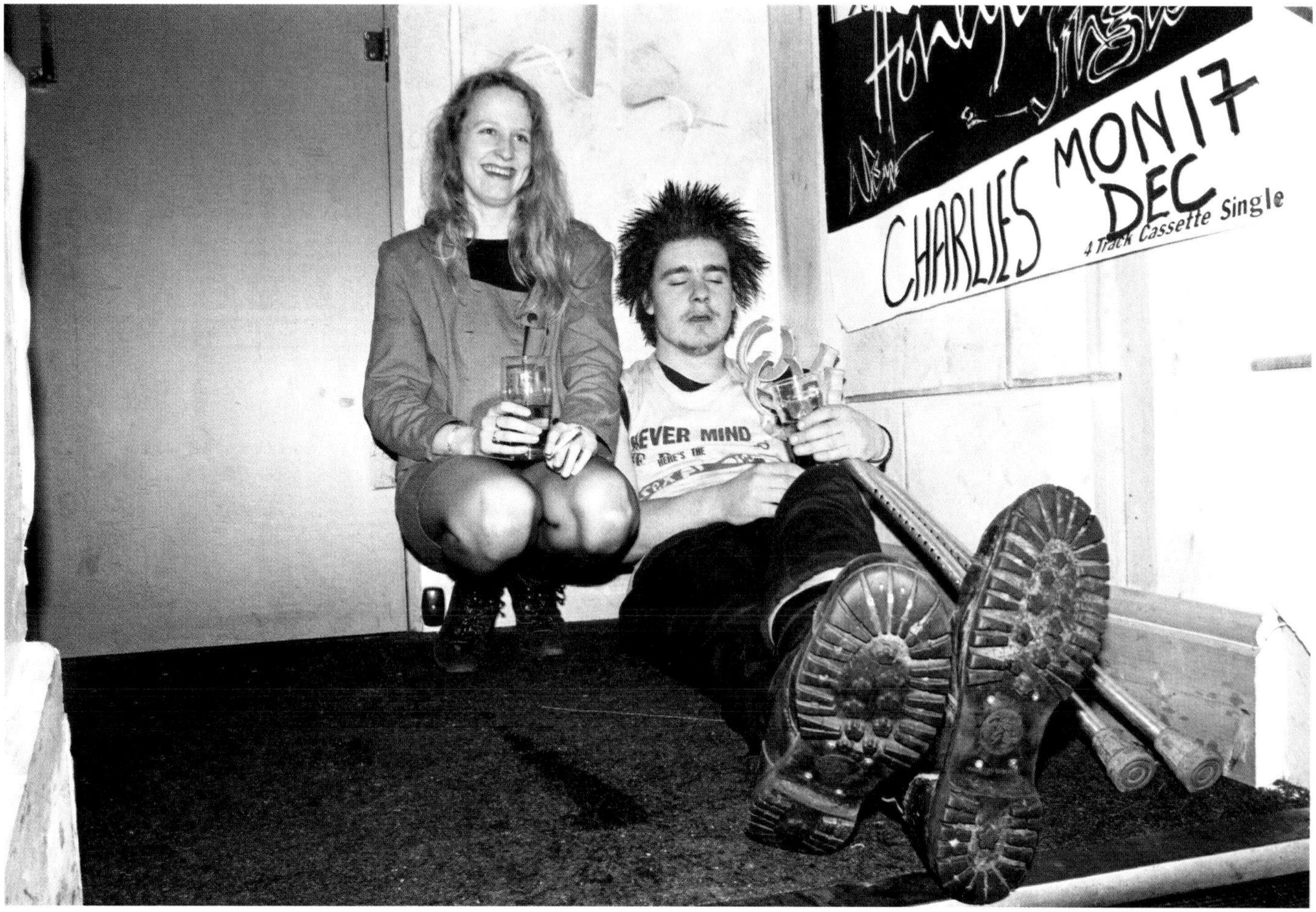
CHARLIES MON 17
DEC
4 Track Cassette Single

135

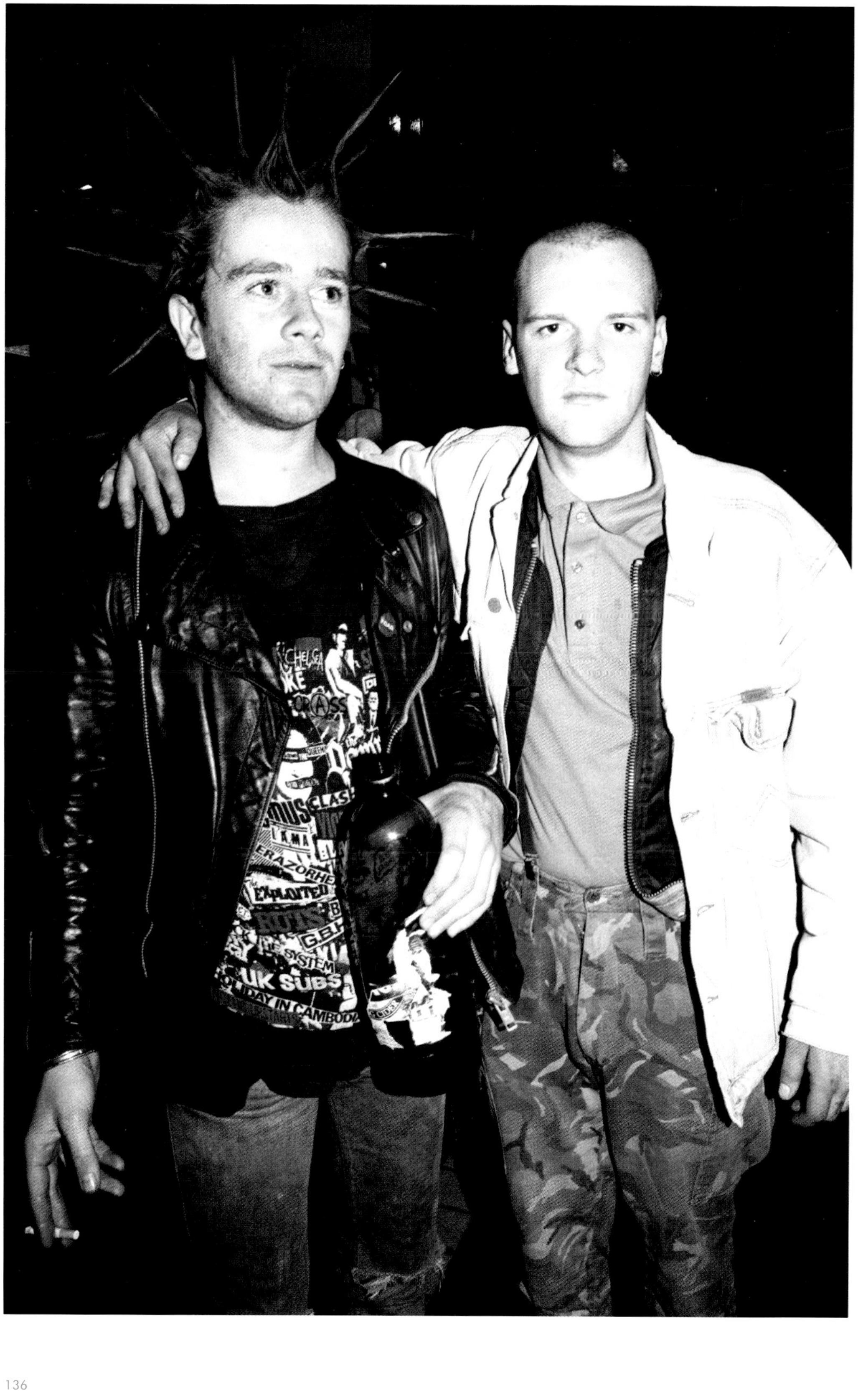

CLASH
EXPLOITED
G.B.H
UK SUBS

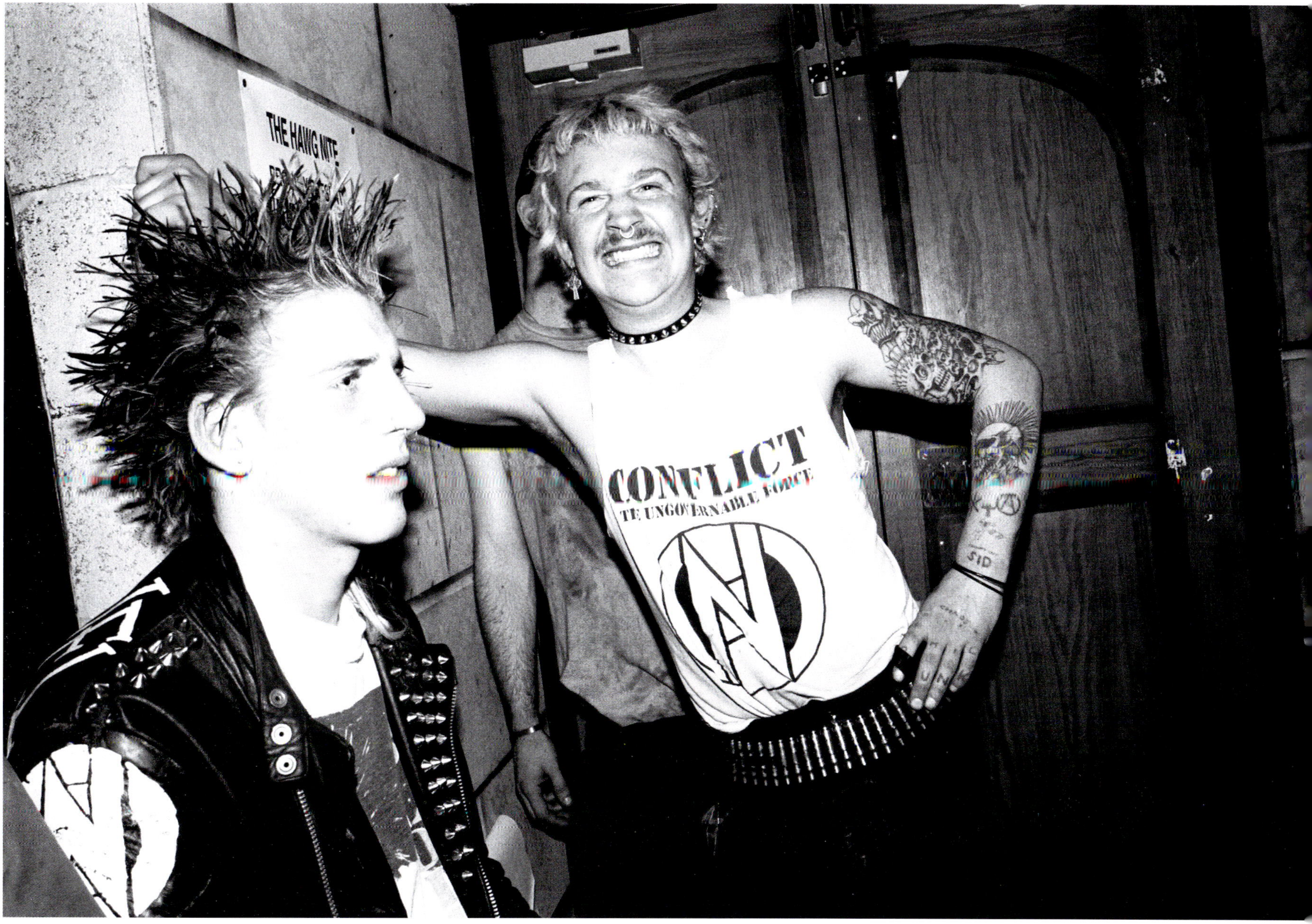
THE HAWG NITE
CONFLICT
SID

Crofton
2 HOUR
DRY CLEANERS
CONVENIENCE STORE
8 TO 10
THORN
Fire Protection & Security ... in depth

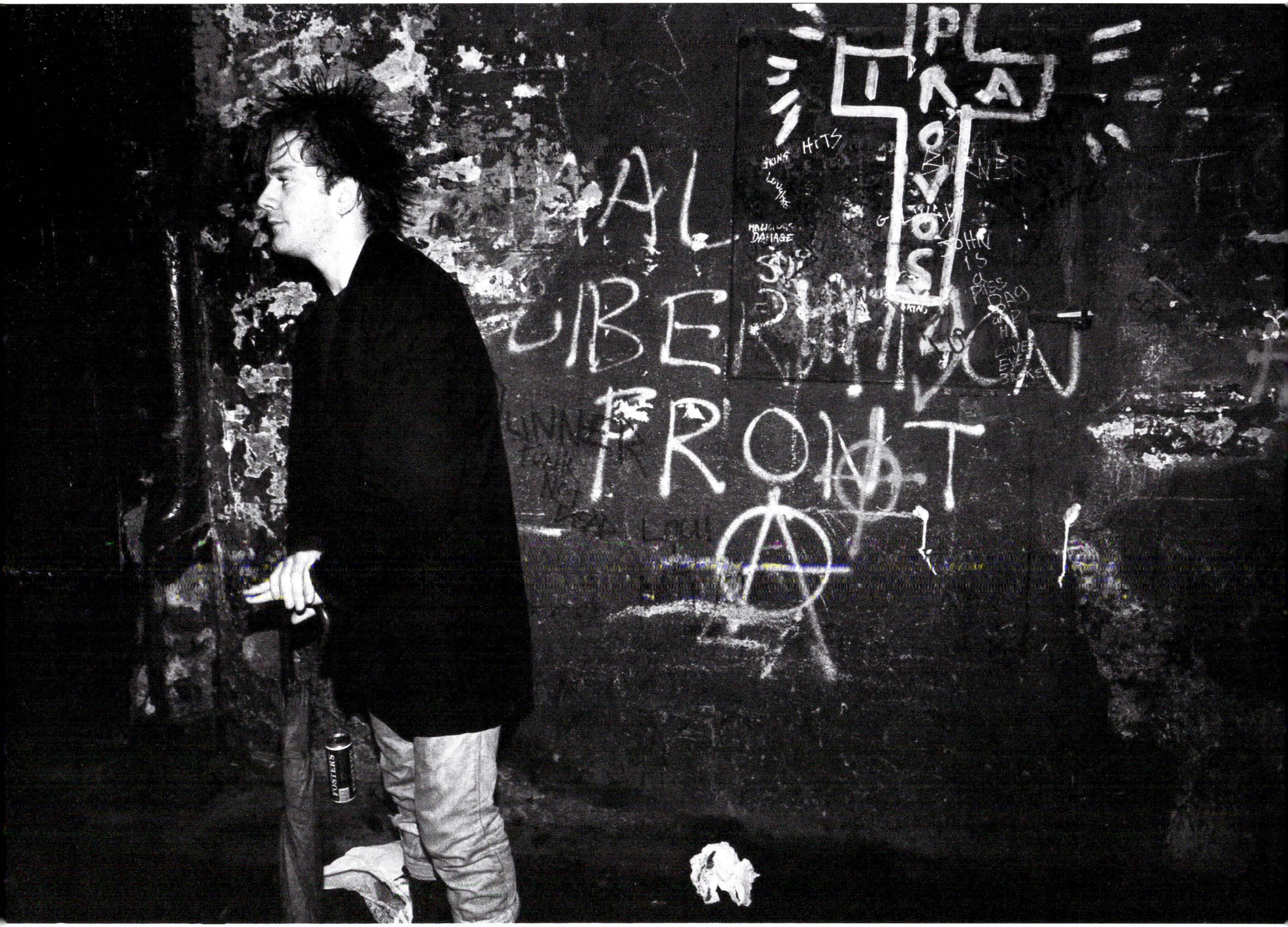
FRONT
HITS
JOHN IS
MALICIOUS DAMAGE
FOSTERS

SEASON'S GREETINGS
PARANOID VISIONS
PARANOID VISIONS
AerLingus
the BRITISH are coming
BIG VALUE CAN
THE SIMPSONS

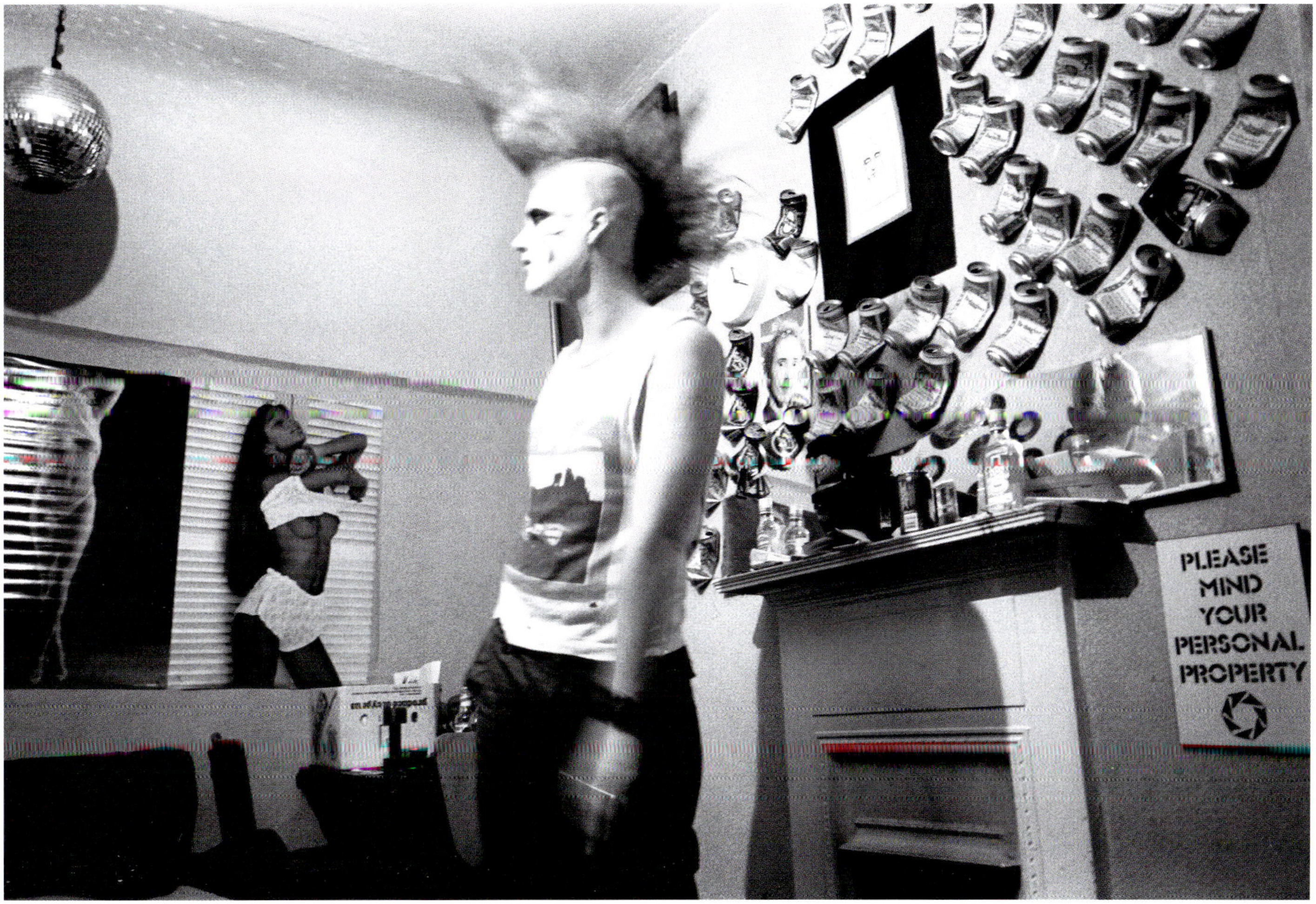
PLEASE
MIND
YOUR
PERSONAL
PROPERTY

NOTES ON PHOTOGRAPHS

FRONTISPIECE
Smithfield, Dublin, November 1990

PAGE 9
George's Quay, Dublin, March 1991

PAGE 11
Smithfield, Dublin, October 1992

PAGE 13
Russell Street, Dublin, September 1992

PAGE 14
St. Stephen's Green, Dublin, October 1991

PAGE 15
St. Stephen's Green, Dublin, January 1991

PAGE 16
O'Connell Street, Dublin, March 1991

PAGE 17
Dame Street, Dublin, October 1991

PAGE 18
Liffey Street Lower, Dublin, October 1990

PAGE 19
Dublin city centre, January 1991

PAGE 20
Adam's Court, Dublin, April 1990

PAGE 21
Smithfield, Dublin, July 1991

PAGE 22
Boat to Hollyhead, October 1991

PAGE 23
Dublin city centre, 1992

PAGE 24
O'Connell Street, Dublin, May 1992

PAGE 25
O'Connell Street, Dublin, June 1990

PAGE 26
Grafton Street, Dublin, March 1991

PAGE 27
O'Connell Street, Dublin, May 1989

PAGE 28
Grafton Street, Dublin, July 1991

PAGE 29
Nassau Street, Dublin, 1992

PAGE 30
South Great George's Street, Dublin, August 1991

PAGE 31
York Street, Dublin, 1990

PAGE 32
St. Stephen's Green, Dublin, March 1991

PAGE 33
Dublin city centre, March 1991

PAGE 34
St. Stephen's Green, Dublin, March 1991

PAGE 35
Westmoreland Street, Dublin, June 1991

PAGE 36
Duke Street, Dublin, Bloomsday, 1990

PAGE 37
Ladyswell, Mulhuddart, 1991

PAGE 38
Grafton Street, Dublin, June 1991

PAGE 39
Westmoreland Street, Dublin, November 1990

PAGE 40
Westmoreland Street, Dublin, June 1991

PAGE 41
Prince's Street North, Dublin, June 1990

PAGE 42
Féile, Thurles, Co. Tipperary, August 1991

PAGE 43
Féile, Thurles, Co. Tipperary, August 1991

PAGE 44
Phoenix Park, Dublin, June 1991

PAGE 45
Féile, Thurles, Co. Tipperary, August 1991

PAGE 46
Féile, Thurles, Co. Tipperary, August 1991

PAGE 47
Féile, Thurles, Co. Tipperary, August 1991

PAGE 48
27 Bus, January 1991

PAGE 49
O'Connell Street, Dublin, April 1991

PAGE 50
Coolock, Dublin, 1991

PAGE 51
Glasnevin Cemetery, Dublin, April 1991

PAGE 53
Westmoreland Street, Dublin, March 1991

PAGE 54
Pembroke Road, Dublin, January 1991

PAGE 55
Pembroke Road, Dublin, January 1991

PAGE 56
Pembroke Road, Dublin, January 1991

PAGE 57
St. Stephen's Green, Dublin, 1992

PAGE 58
Molesworth Street, Dublin, October 1990

PAGE 59
Molesworth Street, Dublin, October 1990

PAGE 60
Merrion Road, Ballsbridge, Dublin, August 1989

PAGE 61
College Green, Dublin, 1992

PAGE 62
Merrion Road, Ballsbridge, Dublin, August 1989

PAGE 63
O'Connell Street, Dublin, October 1989

PAGE 64
O'Connell Street, Dublin, March 1991

PAGE 65
College Green, Dublin, April 1991

PAGE 66
Dawson Street, Dublin, February 1991

PAGE 67
Central Bank, Dame Street, Dublin, 1991

PAGE 68
O'Connell Street, Dublin, June 1992

PAGE 69
Parnell Square, Dublin, April 1992

PAGE 70
O'Connell Street, Dublin, February 1992

PAGE 71
O'Connell Street, Dublin, June 1992

PAGE 72
O'Connell Street, Dublin, June 1992

PAGE 73
Parnell Square, Dublin, 1992

PAGE 74
O'Connell Street, Dublin, 1992

PAGE 75
St. Stephen's Green, Dublin, November 1991

PAGE 76
O'Connell Street, Dublin, November 1990

PAGE 77
Molesworth Street, Dublin, November 1990

PAGE 78
City Hall, Dublin, February 1991

PAGE 79
O'Connell Street, Dublin 1992

PAGE 80
O'Connell Street, Dublin 1992

PAGE 81
O'Connell Street, Dublin, November 1990

PAGE 83
Smithfield, Dublin, January 1991

PAGE 84
Smithfield, Dublin, January 1991

PAGE 85
Smithfield, Dublin, November 1990

PAGE 86
Smithfield, Dublin, May 1991

PAGE 87
Smithfield, Dublin, July 1991

PAGE 88
Smithfield, Dublin, May 1992

PAGE 89
Smithfield, Dublin, November 1990

PAGE 90
Smithfield, Dublin, December 1990

PAGE 91
Smithfield, Dublin, July 1991

PAGE 92
Smithfield, Dublin, April 1991

PAGE 93
Smithfield, Dublin, April 1991

PAGE 94
Smithfield, Dublin, December 1990

PAGE 95
Smithfield, Dublin, November 1990

PAGE 96
Smithfield, Dublin, May 1992

PAGE 97
Smithfield, Dublin, January 1991

PAGE 98
Smithfield, Dublin, October 1991

PAGE 99
Smithfield, Dublin, January 1991

PAGE 100
Smithfield, Dublin, November 1990

PAGE 101
Smithfield, Dublin, November 1990

PAGE 102
Smithfield, Dublin, December 1991

PAGE 103
Smithfield, Dublin, July 1991

PAGE 105
Cecil Street, Limerick, February 1991

PAGE 106
Stamer Street, Dublin, May 1991

PAGE 107
Stamer Street, Dublin, May 1991

PAGE 108
Grafton Street, Dublin, April 1990

PAGE 109
St. Stephen's Green, Dublin, March 1991

PAGE 110
St. Stephen's Green, Dublin, February 1991

PAGE 111
St. Stephen's Green, Dublin, May 1991

PAGE 112
UK, October 1991

PAGE 113
Féile, Thurles, Co. Tipperary, August 1991

PAGE 114
College Green, Dublin, June 1991

PAGE 115
Mulligans, Hill Street, Dublin, 1992

PAGE 116
Charlies Bar, Aungier Street, Dublin, December 1991

PAGE 117
Dublin city centre, 1991

PAGE 118
The Roxey, Green Street, Dublin, April 1993

PAGE 119
Aungier Street, Dublin, April 1991

PAGE 120
Arklow, circa 1992

PAGE 121
The Venue, Temple Bar, Dublin, October 1991

PAGE 122
Fox & Pheasant, Great Strand St., Dublin, February 1991

PAGE 123
Charlies Bar, Aungier Street, Dublin, February 1990

PAGE 124
Mulligans, Hill Street, Dublin, July 1993

PAGE 125
Barnstormers, Capel Street, Dublin, 1991

PAGE 126
The Roxey, Dublin, 1992

PAGE 127
Charlies Bar, Aungier Street, Dublin, May 1991

PAGE 128
Charlies Bar, Aungier Street, Dublin, April 1991

PAGE 129
Charlies Bar, Aungier Street, Dublin, March 1991

PAGE 130
Charlies Bar, Aungier Street, Dublin, March 1991

PAGE 131
Charlies Bar, Aungier Street, Dublin, 1991

PAGE 132
Charlies Bar, Aungier Street, Dublin, May 1991

PAGE 133
West County Hotel, Ennis, Co. Clare, February 1991

PAGE 134
Charlies Bar, Aungier Street, Dublin, December 1990

PAGE 135
The Roxey, Green Street, Dublin, 1991

PAGE 136
Grafton Street, Dublin, May 1991

PAGE 137
Charlies Bar, Aungier Street, Dublin, March 1991

PAGE 138
Kevin Street Lower, Dublin, May 1991

PAGE 139
Tangier Lane, Dublin, February 1991

PAGE 140
Harrington Street, Dublin, April 1991

PAGE 141
Seville Place, Dublin, October 1991